Questions

**Bible-based
answers to your
questions about life**

Answers

by Jimmy Swaggart

Jimmy Swaggart Ministries
P.O. Box 2550
Baton Rouge, LA 70821-2550

ii

TABLE OF CONTENTS

EVOLUTION

FAITH

FALL OF MAN

GOSPEL PREACHING

HEAVEN

HELL

HOLY COMMUNION

HOLY SPIRIT

HOLY TRINITY

HOMOSEXUALITY

INFANTICIDE

MARRIAGE

MONEY

POLITICS

PRAYER

SALVATION

SATAN

WINE

QUESTION:

ABORTION

■ If a young, unmarried girl is pregnant, would abortion, then, be wrong?

QUESTION:

IF A YOUNG, UNMARRIED GIRL IS PREGNANT, WOULD ABORTION, THEN, BE WRONG?

ANSWER:

This is a difficult question, but I will try to answer it as best I can.

ABORTION IS SIN

First of all, abortion is sin, absolutely and without question. It is the equivalent of murder, in this instance the murder of an unborn infant. For long centuries no decent person, and certainly no respected Christian, has advocated killing an unborn baby. Like any other act of killing, it is murder. This is the law of civilized nations, and more important, it is the law of God. Yet now, Godless people are saying, "Kill the baby. It will be good for the mother's mental health. She doesn't want the child. She has become pregnant [most of the time] because of the sin of fornication and adultery. She doesn't want to feed, clothe, or rear the child." She will then go to a doctor and pay him to kill the unwanted baby, and somehow greed will still the conscience.

ABORTION IS MURDER

All murder is wrong. In the Old Testament, even before the law, God said, *"Whoso sheddeth man's blood, by man shall his blood be shed: for in the image of God made he man"* (Genesis 9:6). Under the Mosaic law, God plainly commanded, *"He that smiteth a man, so that he die, shall be surely put to death"* (Exodus 21:12).

The death penalty for murder is also clearly implied in the New Testament: The ruler of a nation is *"the minister of God . . . for he beareth not the sword in vain"* (Romans 13:1-7). Murderers are kept outside the heavenly Jerusalem (Revelation 21:8; 22:15).

To God the killing an unborn child is murder. The person guilty of that murder is subject to the same conviction and deserving of the same punishment as the person who pulls the trigger of a gun to kill a person.

A HUMAN BEING

Second, the unborn child, the fetus, is a human being — a person —

3

from the time of conception. Some persons have foolishly said that the unborn child, up to the sixth or seventh month, is little more than a "blob" of flesh; but that is simply not true. The little unborn baby is not just a part of the mother's body. He is a separate life altogether. All of the child's particular traits have already been charted in his genes. The sex of the child, the color of his eyes and hair, his physical features, his special talents and gifts are all determined at the time of conception. Both the mother and the father of the child have already, at this point, passed down to their baby every genetic characteristic they will contribute.

A LIVING SOUL

The Bible also teaches that the fetus, from conception, is a person and, consequently, a living soul. David was inspired to say, *"Behold, I was shapen in iniquity, and in sin did my mother conceive me"* (Psalm 51:5). When David said, *"I was shapen,"* it was his honest inference that from the moment of conception, he was the person who would later be known as David, the great king of Israel.

Again, the Psalmist David was inspired to write, *"Thou hast covered me in my mother's womb. I will praise thee; for I am fearfully and wonderfully made"* (Psalm 139:13, 14). From the moment of conception, and as the Holy Spirit gave the intent, David was, indeed, a person. It was David's body, his very substance, in the womb of his mother.

We have the same kind of teaching concerning Jeremiah, who said, *"Then the word of the Lord came unto me, saying, Before I formed thee in the belly, I knew thee; and before thou camest forth out of the womb I sanctified thee, and I ordained thee a prophet unto the nations"* (Jeremiah 1:4, 5). God knew the Prophet Jeremiah before he was born. If, by abortion, the fetus had been murdered, it would have been Jeremiah who died. The mother would not have known his name, but God would have. The mother might not have known that this was to be a mighty prophet of God, but God would have known that too.

Yes, a fetus is a person, a living soul, from the time of conception.

A CHILD — BORN OR UNBORN

John the Baptist was *"filled with the Holy Ghost, even from his mother's womb"* (Luke 1:15). Mary, the mother of Jesus, came to greet

Elisabeth. *"And it came to pass, that, when Elisabeth heard the salutation of Mary, the babe leaped in her womb"* (Luke 1:41). The fetus of John the Baptist, in the womb of his mother, may not have understood clearly why he leaped at the sound of the voice of Mary (the mother of the Saviour), but God knew.

It is interesting to note the words of Jesus, *"Suffer the little children to come unto me, and forbid them not: for of such is the kingdom of God"* (Mark 10:14). He was speaking in reference to the infants brought to be blessed by Him. The term used for "infants" in the Greek is *brephos,* which *Young's Analytical Concordance* defines as "a child born or unborn." Does that mean, then, that all the little ones who died before had an immortal soul (*"of such is the kingdom of God"*) and that they will meet us there? Well, certainly it is implied if not stated in this passage of Scripture.

PSYCHOLOGICAL PAIN AND GUILT

Third, the psychological pain of abortion is never quite erased from the mother's heart and mind. The psychic trauma and the sense of loss regarding personal morality will persist throughout life. So many times the mother becomes troubled and consumed with guilt so that she develops significant psychiatric problems following, and as a direct result of, abortion. I believe it can be stated with certainty that abortion causes more deep-seated guilt, depression, and mental illness than it could ever cure. The mother will always wonder: What would the baby have looked like? Would he have had curly hair? What color would his hair have been? Would he have been a boy or a girl?

1 SIN + 1 SIN = 2 SINS

Fourth, some persons have said that if the baby is illegitimate, then he should be aborted. Of course, the answer to that is you do not erase, correct, or even justify one sin by committing another. The only real answer to sin is repentance and trusting the Saviour for forgiveness and for rearranging the soiled life. To compound sin upon sin is not the way to peace or mental health. Some persons say the end justifies the means, but it never does.

Of course, some persons may question, "Would it not be proper to undergo an abortion to save the life or preserve the health of the mother?" I suppose that in a few rare cases, probably not more than one in hundreds of thousands of cases, the doctor would have to choose between saving the life of the baby and saving the life of the mother. Actually, I have never known of such a case personally, although I am confident they have existed. This so rarely happens, however, that it is not worth the sake of argument.

A MORAL QUESTION

The fact is, abortion is a sin. The killing of an unborn child is a terrible sin; actually, it is murder. It is also a moral question. It is essentially the same thing as murdering the incompetent, the retarded, the handicapped, and the aged or senile. If we are going to kill the unwanted, possibly there are many one-, two-, five-, 10-, even 50-year-olds who are unwanted. Why not just kill them, too? You see how horrendous this terrible crime becomes when carried to its ultimate conclusion. To slay the innocent because he cannot protest or swear out a warrant is a sin. The Scripture says, *"Be sure your sin will find you out"* (Numbers 32:23). There is a God who cares for the weak, the unloved, and the unprotected. He will bring judgment. "God's mills grind slow but sure" (Greek Proverb).

If the abortionists win their cause in the United States, where do we go from there? If you remember, Nazi Germany enacted a law permitting the elimination of "useless" members of society. Consequently, 18 million people were slaughtered (among them, 6 million Jews) because they represented a category that was considered useless.

We have the same pattern before us in America today, in which a whole category of human beings — unborn babies who cannot yet speak for themselves — are to be slaughtered at the whim of a mother or a doctor who decides that the mother is somehow unable or unwilling to have a baby.

Where do we go from here? What is the next class of humanity to be destroyed?

No, abortion is *not* of God. It is totally ungodly, a terrible case of man's inhumanity to man, and one day man will answer to God for this terrible sin.

CAPITAL
PUNISHMENT

■ Do you believe in capital punishment?

QUESTION:

DO YOU BELIEVE IN CAPITAL PUNISHMENT?

ANSWER:

In the past few years, our nation has changed its course in respect to capital punishment. Years ago when Frances and I were traveling from meeting to meeting, I would turn on the car radio. Many times I would hear forums on capital punishment. Although the subject was discussed both pro and con, most of the feeling was negative. "We must abolish capital punishment," was the cry. "No civilized nation can afford such a travesty of justice." Many modern religious leaders took up the cry in opposition to the death penalty. Educators said we could not afford it. Psychologists cried out against it. Consequently, most states struck these laws from their books. For all practical purposes capital punishment was abolished.

At that point the nation entered an era in which crime and the criminal were treated differently than in the past. Psychologists said that the criminal acted the way he did because of his environment. The advice was: Change the environment and you change the man; throw out punishment; try a different method; the psychological approach would work. The criminal was not responsible for his actions. All of society was responsible, the innocent as well as the guilty. All kinds of suppositions and proposals were put forth, most of which completely ignored God and His Word.

WHAT HAPPENED?

After this change in attitude toward crime, the nation entered into the most lawless era it had possibly ever known. Cities became animal-crawling jungles. Murder became commonplace; human life was held cheap. With no fear of reprisal, of the law, or of punishment, lawbreakers were released with a slap on the wrist to commit other crimes. Cold-blooded murder became, and is, the order of the day. With overworked and crowded court dockets, judges allowed the plea bargain to become a legal escape. Criminals with extensive records walked the streets, allowed to go free while awaiting trials that possibly would never be scheduled.

In spite of what the educators and the philosophers say, it is obvious that the problem is neither environmental nor social. It is a problem of the heart. Changing a man's environment changes only his surroundings. Changing his heart changes his very nature and character. Only God can do this.

WHAT DOES THE BIBLE SAY
ABOUT CAPITAL PUNISHMENT?

"Whoso sheddeth man's blood, by man shall his blood be shed: for in the image of God made he man" (Genesis 9:6). Of course, some persons may read this particular Scripture and say, "Oh, but that was in the old law." Actually, it was not *in* the law at all; it was *before* the law. In the New Testament — I will not quote all of it for lack of space, but please read the entire seven verses — the Bible tells us, *"For he is the minister of God to thee for good. But if thou do that which is evil, be afraid; for he beareth not the sword in vain: for he is the minister of God, a revenger to execute wrath upon him that doeth evil"* (Romans 13:1-7). Here God plainly upholds capital punishment for capital crimes.

Human government was instituted by God Himself. Christians are commanded in the New Testament to pay taxes and to support government (Romans 13:1-7; I Peter 2:13-17). Law, as a part of government, will continue as the rule of right in all eternal societies. If the right to govern is based upon the best public interest, then the right and duty to use any necessary means to attain this end must be recognized by all. It is somewhat absurd to believe that rulers have a right to govern, yet have no right to use the necessary means to enforce that government. Making the same error, many Christians object to the right of capital punishment, the right to deal with mobs, the right to suppress rebellions, and the right to make war. Erroneously they think that under all circumstances government can be carried on without resorting to any means that would take life. Others go so far as to maintain that government can be carried on without force to sustain the authority of the law. But these positions cannot be maintained with any degree of logic, and they are not backed by God and Scripture.

It is absurd to hold that rulers have a right to rule as long as their subjects voluntarily obey, but then when they refuse to obey, government should cease to exist. It is impossible for the right to govern to exist when the right to enforce obedience does not exist.

THOU SHALT NOT KILL

This particular commandment is taken to mean that no human life should be taken for any crime. Taken literally, *"Thou shalt not kill"* (Exodus 20:13) forbids the killing of animals, plant life, or any living creature. The question is, What kind of killing does it forbid? Certainly not all killing of human beings, for the next chapter commands that human life be taken for certain crimes. Six times in this one chapter, and scores of times in other chapters, God commanded the death penalty. Whenever a person sells himself to destroy the public good, and it becomes necessary to take his life as the necessary means of securing that good, his life is forfeited, and it is the duty of government to take it.

MURDER IS MORE TERRIBLE
THAN SOME PERSONS REALIZE

Murder is a crime against God who created man in His own image. It manifests hatred of God's image. It is a crime against society, of which each man is an important member. It is a crime against the family unit and against the individual whose life was ruthlessly taken away. Murder cuts him off from his duties to both God and man. Regarding eternal life in heaven, it seals the victim's doom if he is unconverted. It also forfeits the right of life for the unborn children that particular man or woman might have brought into this world.

WHAT DO THE RECORDS SHOW?

A study was made a short time ago in respect to capital punishment. Even though it cannot be proved, the study concluded that for every individual executed for a capital crime, eight lives would be saved. In other words, fear of punishment would deter the would-be murderers from carrying out their violent acts.

It is a terrible thing to have to take a human life, even under the circumstances of capital punishment for capital crime. Thank God it will be abolished. But until that day when Jesus comes back and former things pass away, the laws of God must be upheld.

GOD IS ALWAYS RIGHT

God was not wrong or beastly when He commanded the death penalty for capital crimes. His Word cannot be circumvented with success. When man tampers with it and thinks he knows more than God, he must reap the bitter consequences. The Scripture plainly tells us, *"Because sentence against an evil work is not executed speedily, therefore the heart of the sons of men is fully set in them to do evil"* (Ecclesiastes 8:11).

CHRISTIAN LIVING

■ According to Deuteronomy 22:5, do you think it is proper for a lady to wear pantsuits, et cetera, and what do you think about mixed swimming?

■ Is dancing sinful?

■ I have two questions actually: First, what does the Bible say about cigarettes (nicotine, smoking)? Second, is aerobic dancing proper for Christians?

■ Is it biblically wrong to join the Masons or other such secret orders?

■ Is it wrong for a Christian to attend movies, and is it wrong for a Christian to view a Christian movie in a movie theater?

QUESTION:

ACCORDING TO DEUTERONOMY 22:5, DO YOU THINK IT IS PROPER FOR A LADY TO WEAR PANTSUITS, ET CETERA, AND WHAT DO YOU THINK ABOUT MIXED SWIMMING?

ANSWER:

No, I do not feel it is improper for a Christian lady to wear pantsuits, et cetera, if they fit properly and are modest in appearance.

You must remember one thing about Deuteronomy 22:5 (*"the woman shall not wear that which pertaineth unto a man, neither shall a man put on a woman's garment"*). Of course, God said what He meant and meant what He said; however, *both men and women* wore robes in those days. Admittedly, the women's robes were cut a little differently, but men's wear and ladies' wear were both robes. Likewise, a lady's pantsuit is made for a woman; it is not made for a man. It is women's clothing. So, if its design, cut, style, fit, et cetera, are modest, I see no harm in it whatsoever.

I do feel that all women's clothing, be it dress, pantsuit, or other piece of clothing, should be exactly according to what Paul wrote to Timothy. The word he used was *"modest"* (I Timothy 2:9). Some dresses are not in character with a Christian lady, and you could say the same thing for some pantsuits. No problem exists, either scripturally or spiritually, if whatever is worn, by men or women, is in keeping with the Word of God.

AN EXAMPLE OF CHRIST

Now to answer the second part of your question about mixed swimming: I do not feel it is wrong for close friends or close kin to swim together. However, I do feel it is improper for a Christian girl or lady to wear skimpy bathing attire. There are bathing suits that are fashionable and yet in keeping with Christian character. Both men and women must never forget their body is a temple of the Holy Spirit (I Corinthians 6:19, 20).

Whenever my wife and I go swimming or to a beach, we always find a secluded spot where there are few, if any, people. Otherwise, I will not go. I will not swim in a public swimming pool. I do not feel the atmosphere is in keeping with good Christian character.

A person must always remember, in everything he does, that he is an example of Christ. He is an ambassador. Everything we do must be done to His glory (I Corinthians 10:31). There are times when we have to make judgments on the spot; and if we will listen to the voice of the Holy Spirit, He will guide us and direct us.

QUESTION:

IS DANCING SINFUL?

ANSWER:

Yes, I believe all dancing, by whatever name it may be called, is sinful and harmful. For example, all television dance programs show performances designed basically to incite and arouse lust in people's mind and heart. I imagine the contortions must be similar to the perversions of the heathen nations so long ago when God ordered that they be eliminated from the face of the earth.

Even ballroom dancing — where men hold women in their arms with their bodies touching (even lightly) and they glide along cheek to cheek — is definitely harmful. Jesus addressed Himself to this when He said, *"Ye have heard that it was said by them of old time, Thou shalt not commit adultery: But I say unto you, That whosoever looketh on a woman to lust after her hath committed adultery with her already in his heart"* (Matthew 5:27, 28).

AROUSES FEELINGS

There is no doubt that dancing has been proved, again and again, to arouse lust and sexual passion. This is always totally improper. Certainly, it is not wrong for a husband and wife to hold each other in this way, but to allow the same sexual desire to be stirred toward outsiders is definitely a sin.

When mixed couples dance, the tendency is always toward more bodily contact. Not only is this a continual temptation to dance partners, but also even when dancing is not mixed, the bodily contortions are such as to arouse sexual passions in those who observe. This kind of thing ought always to be avoided by all Christians. Paul put it this way: *"Abstain from all appearance of evil"* (I Thessalonians 5:22).

DANCING IN BIBLE TIMES

The Bible mentions *"a time to weep, and a time to laugh; a time to mourn, and a time to dance"* (Ecclesiastes 3:4). Now some persons take that to mean that dancing is permitted; it is satisfactory. They even refer to Miriam and Moses on the banks of the Red Sea leading the people in a holy dance (Exodus 15:20, 21). Of course, that is your answer — it was a *holy* dance — and people were worshiping God in the spirit. You will have to admit the vast, vast difference between these biblical examples and the modern dance of today.

The idea of a man and woman dancing closely with arms around each other is a modern thing. It was never even heard of in Bible times; hence, there is no definite or particular command in the Bible against dancing. Many other commands, however, leave no doubt but that the modern dance is wrong and hurtful. You can read Matthew 5:27, 28 and I Thessalonians 5:22 (both quoted above).

Actually, *"dance"* in Ecclesiastes 3:4 meant to leap for joy. Basically, that is what dancing always meant in Bible times unless it was specifically stated differently, such as the heathen dances that were incorporated in idol worship. God commanded that those be destroyed.

I can see where it would be a temptation for a girl to learn tap dancing or ballet dancing, but I would not advise it for Christian girls. Gymnastic dancing probably should be classed in the same category; of course, exercise is good; but we should never align ourselves with bad company or allow ourselves to be influenced by indecent habits of dress. Neither should we resort to bodily contortions that are of such nature that they set a bad example.

THE BOTTOM LINE

We must ever remember (and this is the bottom line!) that our body is a temple of the Holy Spirit (I Corinthians 6:19, 20). We are lights in the midst of darkness. We are not our own but are bought with a price — the shed blood of our Lord Jesus Christ at Calvary. We must exemplify righteousness and purity; anything else leads toward sin. Consequently, I feel all of today's modern dances are not proper for the child of God and can only encourage what is sinful, wicked, and wrong.

QUESTION:

I HAVE TWO QUESTIONS ACTUALLY: FIRST, WHAT DOES THE BIBLE SAY ABOUT CIGARETTES (NICOTINE, SMOKING)? SECOND, IS AEROBIC DANCING PROPER FOR CHRISTIANS?

ANSWER:

Your questions are quite diverse; however, I will do my best to approach them frankly and scripturally, praying that the answers will be of help to you.

SMOKING

In Bible times there was no such thing as cigarettes or tobacco — at least not as we know them today. Tobacco is native to the Western Hemisphere where aborigines cultivated and used it from remote times. Its generic name is derived from that of Jean Nicote who introduced tobacco in France in 1559 from Spain, where it had been introduced from Santo Domingo in the same year. In 1585 it was taken to England to Sir Francis Drake, and the practice of pipe-smoking was introduced among the Elizabethan courtiers by Sir Walter Raleigh.

The use of tobacco rapidly extended throughout Europe and soon became extensively prevalent among Oriental nations. Oddly enough, tobacco was at first recommended for its medicinal value and even as a strengthener for the voice and throat. This, of course, has been proved in the last few years to be utterly ridiculous, as it actually produces just the opposite effect.

Upon the advent of the cigarette, tobacco became one of the principal crops in certain southeastern states such as Virginia, the Carolinas, Tennessee, Kentucky, and perhaps others.

NICOTINE AND DEATH

Nicotine is the (poisonous) substance in tobacco that makes it desirous and addictive to its users. Being a poison, it was even used in times past by agriculture as an insecticide. Nicotine's greatest effect on man lies in its physiological stimulus. In small doses (as the user inhales the smoke) nicotine serves as a nerve stimulant — especially on the autonomic nervous system. It then promotes the flow of adrenaline and other internal secretions. In larger doses, nicotine can paralyze the nervous system. In still larger doses, nicotine can cause convulsions and death.

Medical science in the last few years has proved beyond doubt that nicotine is the greatest cause of lung cancer (among other physical difficulties such as heart trouble) of any type of stimulant. The cigarette habit has been said to be more difficult to break than some particular types of hard drugs. It is a terrible problem that plagues tens of millions of Americans as well as the majority of the world.

SINFUL HABIT

Paul wrote, *"Know ye not that ye are the temple of God, and that the Spirit of God dwelleth in you? If any man defile the temple of God, him shall God destroy; for the temple of God is holy, which temple ye are"* (I Corinthians 3:16, 17). It is fairly clear what the Apostle Paul was saying, but an enlarging upon the subject to give a complete explanation of the tobacco habit is called for in your question.

First of all, it should be understood that to fill one's system with such poison on a habitual basis is to defile this temple that God has made and is a direct disobedience to I Corinthians 3:16 (plus many other Scriptures). However, there are numerous ways that people defile the body, obesity being one of the most common. Obesity is probably killing as many people in the United States as the use of nicotine. Do not misunderstand. One wrongdoing does not cancel another, and we have to conclude that the use of tobacco is a definite sin against the body, which is the temple of the Holy Spirit.

THE CHRISTIAN AND TOBACCO

This is a problem in the heart and life of many Christians, and so I must qualify my answer in this manner. The moment an individual gives his heart to the Lord, he should allow the power and presence of the Lord immediately to take control of his life, laying down every evil habit (such as nicotine) causing difficulty. This is the will of God. However, we know that through weakness or whatever reason, some Christians simply do not do that. They continue to use tobacco.

Does this mean that a person ceases to be saved the moment he lights up a cigarette? No, it does not. God is a merciful and patient God, or else where would any of us be? He is a long-suffering God. *"The Lord is not slack concerning his promise, as some men count slackness; but is longsuffering to us-ward, not willing that any should perish, but that all should come to repentance"* (II Peter 3:9).

I have witnessed some Christians who continued to use tobacco after they gave their heart and life to Jesus Christ, but then the moment they received the baptism in the Holy Spirit (Acts 2:4) they immediately quit smoking. There have been a few exceptions, but most, once they receive the baptism, have the necessary power (Acts 1:8) to overcome this sinful habit.

PERSONAL EXPERIENCE

Years ago in a meeting in Illinois in a particular Friday night service, I was to pray for the sick. It was a rainy night and the crowd was sparse. After I had preached, I called the people up to be prayed for, and then the Spirit of God spoke to me. He told me that most of the people in the prayer line did not have any physical problems, but that many of them needed deliverance from cigarettes. I found that to be the case. There were people wanting spiritual help for this problem that they might be able to "kick the habit." Some had been using tobacco for as long as 30 years.

God gave us great victory that night. If I remember correctly, most were delivered. God spoke to my heart that night saying that He would grant me special faith to pray for those who needed deliverance from nicotine and we would see thousands delivered. We have seen this over the years since that night.

I learned something from this. I have never had a cigarette in my mouth so I have never known how the user feels. But I did learn that just about every single Christian who is still using tobacco wants desperately to quit the vile habit, but for whatever reason, it seems, he has not been able to do so. I also learned that it is an easy and natural thing for those Christians who have never been bothered by nicotine to criticize those who continue to use it after they are saved. These individuals even go so far as to say the people are not Christians, when other problems of other Christians — perhaps they themselves — are overlooked and are just as severe. I am speaking of such things as obesity, jealousy, envy, uncontrollable temper, and on and on we could go. I have learned we must be consistent in our thinking on spirituality.

HOLLYWOOD ROLE MODELS

Many Christians tend to be overcritical of tobacco users because of the environment from which most Christians are saved. For example, nightclubs, honky-tonks, and most other kinds of worldly entertainment are heavily laced with tobacco smoke. The cigarette dangling from the lip of the dancer, the gambler, the prostitute, and the drunk has come to symbolize the sophisticated worldling.

This is rightfully so. Hollywood has flaunted the use of nicotine as the "in" thing. The beautiful stars and starlets are shown with cigarettes poised seductively between their fingers or hanging limply from their lips, thus inviting millions of Americans to participate in this "chic" indulgence. Ironically enough, many of these actors and actresses who "turned America on" to the use of nicotine succumbed themselves to nicotine cancer.

THE CHRISTIAN AND VICTORY

The Gospel I preach is a Gospel of victory. Jesus Christ delivers men *from* sin, not *in* sin. If the Christian will not allow the Lord full sway within his life, then eventually any area of weakness will overcome him. As we have already said, God will be loving, kind, and long-suffering. He knows we are only flesh; He also knows the intent of our heart. However, I am duly concerned that if a Christian continues to use tobacco and does not make every effort to lay down this obnoxious weed, his disobedience in this one area will encourage disobedience in other areas as well — until that Christian is finally smothered and Satan drags him down to total defeat.

I will have to leave the final conclusion to God. I am not anyone's judge, nor do I wish to be. I can speak only what I believe to be the truth. But this one thing I do know: Jesus Christ can set the captive free. This is part and parcel of the power of God. The Lord breaks the bonds and the chains of sin. If the cigarette (or pipe, or cigar, or whichever) user will allow the Lord Jesus Christ full control within his life, that terrible bondage of iniquity can be broken. The testimony he so proudly bears of his wonderful conversion to the Lord Jesus Christ will then no longer be tainted and soiled.

The body is the temple of the Holy Spirit and is not to be defiled by poison. If a person will only prove God in this situation, he will know that God loves him so much. I realize that many of you reading this may say, "Brother Swaggart, I've tried everything I know, but seemingly to no avail." Keep believing; victory will be yours!

Come clean with God about it. Place the habit before the Lord. Tell Him that this thing is wrecking your testimony, that you are ashamed of it, embarrassed about it, and that you know it is not His will. Tell Him, even with tears, that you want victory. He is a God who answers prayer, and victory can be yours. Your body, as the temple of the Holy Spirit, will not be soiled, dirtied, and defiled by that which is so evil.

In respect to your problem, touch *Him*. He will say to you as He said to the woman long ago, *"Arise, go thy way: thy faith hath made thee whole"* (Luke 17:19).

AEROBIC DANCING

Can you imagine the confusion of the Bible students of the many centuries past if they had looked in their Bible and read, "Thou shalt not engage in aerobic dancing"? Because particular things are not named per se in the Word of God, certain individuals tend to take the position that there is no harm in the indulgence of same (whatever the issue may be). However, we must remember that Jesus Christ Himself taught the Pharisees (and us today) an invaluable lesson: the letter of the law is not as important as the spirit of the law. So, the spirit of the law being our guideline, let us ask ourselves, "Is what I'm doing pleasing to God? Does it bring glory to Him? Does it enable me to be a better witness and have a greater burden for lost souls? Does it enhance my relationship with Him?" Anything we do must be addressed after this fashion.

I feel that this particular "exercise" violates all of these questions concerning the will of God for our life. I will explain.

One, "dancing" is an appropriate name for the exercise thus called.

It is a counterpart of the dances engaged in by the world and which are about as evil as the mind of man can imagine.

Two, even though aerobic dancing goes under the guise of exercise, and I am sure it is that, a person could also say that regular dancing is exercise. To be frank, today's dancing is probably the best exercise in which a person could ever engage. We must quickly add, however, that Christians can exercise in ways more conducive to the Christian testimony than by participating in these licentious practices.

The spirit of the world is evident in the kind of music being played in the discos, honky-tonks, dance halls, and the like. And for Christians to get their aerobic exercise to the beat of what is passed off as Christian music is un-Christlike to say the least.

First of all, I cannot envision any knowledgeable Christian wanting to "bump-and-grind" to any kind of Christian music. I admit that many of the so-called Christian songs of today are Christian in name only and would probably be better used for the purpose of aerobic dancing than for worshiping God.

A Christian can exercise in many ways without exposing himself to this which is the twin brother of the modern dance, which is totally licentious.

Back to I Corinthians 3:16 — we are never to forget that our body is a temple of the Holy Spirit. For a Christian to place his temple of the Holy Spirit in a position of contortion to the beat of worldly music (which is little more than the modern-day dance, passing under the guise of exercise) is most unwise. This is another trick of the devil to lure Christians into a position that is embarrassing to the Holy Spirit.

In closing, I do not want to make more of this than should be made. Neither do I want to make less of it than should be made. As children of God we should watch as well as pray. We should be careful that we do not allow the spirit of the world to violate the principles that we must uphold in the Lord Jesus Christ. Let us always remember that we are *in* the world but we are not *of* the world (see John 15:19; 17:11, 16). We are to be set apart as special vessels used exclusively in the Master's service.

I realize that some persons will laugh at the answer I have given and determine they are going to do what they desire to do. They will say they feel no different after the aerobic dancing period is over than they did before except they feel better physically. However, we must remember that God loves us deeply and everlastingly. He does not depart from us when we make mistakes (thank God for that!). But the question must be asked in whatever direction it takes us: "Is this drawing me closer to God or farther from Him?" If we ask ourselves that question in total honesty, even though aerobic dancing may not be the sin of the ages, still it is not something that will draw us closer to God. We can simply get our exercise in another fashion and in other ways.

QUESTION:

IS IT BIBLICALLY WRONG TO JOIN THE MASONS OR OTHER SUCH SECRET ORDERS?

ANSWER:

Without going into a long dissertation on the methods and functions of these organizations, allow me to say that Christians should not participate in such things.

BELIEVER WITH UNBELIEVER

Naturally, the Word of God does not specifically condemn these kinds of organizations — for the simple reason that they were not in existence when the Bible was written. However, such secret orders do have difficulty with II Corinthians 6:14, where we are told that believers are not to be joined together with unbelievers. It is even difficult for a husband and wife to live together when one is saved and one is not. Of course, it is being done every day, and God somehow helps the saved partner to live the life he should live without weakening his testimony, but it is still difficult. Besides, most of the time marriage is a situation in which one party has control over the other. In the matter of secret orders, when a person voluntarily joins together with unbelievers, that person is constantly subjected to pressures that violate his conscience and the Word of God.

A QUESTION OF BALANCE

I realize these people do some good. I am not negating that fact;

but the Christian can involve himself with great and worthwhile projects without joining these particular orders.

Some persons may say they have need of, and enjoy, that kind of fellowship. There are two problems with that. First, Christians should neither want nor desire continued fellowship with unbelievers. This is not to imply that we are not to be friendly and kind to unbelievers, because we are. However, as far as building close ties of friendship and joining hands in a concentrated effort, it should not be done.

Likewise, no Christian businessman should join hands with an unsaved businessman in a business venture. Christians should not share close friendship with the unsaved. More often than not, the end result will see the unsaved friend pulling the Christian down, rather than the Christian lifting up the unsaved friend.

I could go into a long dissertation about the Masonic order, but that is not necessary. What I have stated is reason enough (scripturally) for a Christian to seek friendship and fellowship among those of like faith.

The Scripture still says, *"Be ye not unequally yoked together with unbelievers: for what fellowship hath righteousness with unrighteousness? . . . Wherefore come out from among them, and be ye separate"* (II Corinthians 6:14-17).

QUESTION:

IS IT WRONG FOR A CHRISTIAN TO ATTEND MOVIES, AND IS IT WRONG FOR A CHRISTIAN TO VIEW A CHRISTIAN MOVIE IN A MOVIE THEATER?

ANSWER:

The things I will say relative to movies will not in any way imply that Spirit-filled Christians today are any less consecrated than those of yesteryear. Rather, I feel that as a whole there are more consecrated and dedicated Christians than ever before; however, I do fear many are careless in their convictions. The problem is that we have too many Christians who attend churches that give no direction in matters of this nature; consequently, many Christians today think nothing of attending the movies. Many pastors simply assume that everybody knows better and preach sermons with which their people are more comfortable. Other ministers, I suppose, just do not see the harm in movies, so the subject never surfaces. The end result in either case is not good. It is wrong for Christians to associate themselves with worldly entertainment such as this, and I will give you the reasons why.

THE MOVIE INDUSTRY

There is nothing wrong with the equipment used in making movies (projector, camera, film). These tools have turned out to be some of the greatest inventions ever given man's ability to perfect; the problem is their use (or misuse).

I can say without fear of contradiction that movies get more sordid and raunchy all the time. The majority of films today are *filled* with profanity, obscenity, nudity, vulgarity, and the like. Moviemakers have been quoted as saying that the more colorful the picture, the more money it brings in. The gutter language, the outright filth, the illicit sex, and perversions have become the common denominator of the industry. The silver screen leaves nothing sacred today. The Bible and things of God are lampooned, ridiculed, and made light of. Filthy, immoral living is portrayed to be the standard norm of the day. These are the movies that win the Academy Awards. The world is sick!

Although I do not believe lightning would strike me if I went to a movie, I do feel that a Christian's time and money can be better spent. Also, I am of the opinion that if a Christian truly loves the Lord with all his heart, he will not desire this kind of thing.

Let us be sensible about the matter. Can we, in good conscience, spend our money to help some jaded actor or actress pay alimony to his fourth or fifth wife (or husband)? I think not. Our money is far too valuable to waste in such a way.

But some persons may say, "Brother Swaggart, I am selective in my moviegoing. I make sure that I only go to those that are clean and wholesome."

I agree that some few "clean" movies are made, and there may be nothing wrong with seeing these particular ones. However, I would find it disconcerting to buy a ticket for even a clean movie and have to sit through 15 or more minutes of previews for others that are not so clean. We should, rather, just avoid all movies. Then, our Christian testimony will more effectively show the world (by our abstinence) that, as a

Christian, there are things we cannot approve of. The Bible says, *"Prove all things; hold fast that which is good. Abstain from all appearance of evil"* (I Thessalonians 5:21, 22). I am concerned. Have we become so hard as Christians that anything goes and nothing is sacred anymore?

TELEVISION

You may say, "But movies come on television," and they do. Of course, I cannot answer for you, but even though I have a television set, there are many things I will *not* watch. I do not feel that I would backslide if I did, but the rottenness of most programs insults me. They insult my intelligence and, mostly, my morals. I realize that many of the things shown on television are bad enough; but still, they are not nearly as immoral and reprobate as what comes through the movie houses. As a Christian, regarding TV, you simply ought to refuse to watch the offensive material. Turn the set off. Some persons would even go so far as to say, "Take the television out of your house." If you cannot control it, then that may be your only recourse; but, at the same time, it is useless to fight the equipment.

Television can be utilized as one of the greatest evangelistic agents known to man. Thank God, it is being used today (in spite of everything the devil can do) to touch many souls for the Lord Jesus Christ. I am thrilled the Lord allows us to use television with the Jimmy Swaggart Telecast to go into multiplied thousands of homes and hearts across America and Canada.

I was sitting in my living room on one of those rare Saturday nights I had the occasion to be home. The television was playing and a program called *All in the Family* (I am glad it is not all in my family!) came on. The conversation in this particular program — the profanity, the innuendos, the sexual overtures — made me acutely aware of the nature of the program. I turned the trash off, and that program has not been aired again in our home. Now, I am certainly not to be patted on the back for that action (everyone should do the same thing); however, at the same time, I fear that little by little, as we continue to allow such programming into our home, we become more calloused than we realize. We offend the blessed Holy Spirit who resides in our heart and life.

Nevertheless, as bad as television is, we should not attempt to justify moviegoing by the television set. You can switch the program on the set, or turn it off. Too, you did not pay money to hear something that is offensive, ribald, and downright vulgar.

CHRISTIAN MOVIES

As far as a Christian movie in itself is concerned, there is nothing wrong with it. However, perhaps when pastors or other individuals encourage attendance at a movie theater to see what is purported to be a Christian movie, they may at the same time put somewhat of a sanction on theater attendance in general. I do not feel this is right. Christian movies would best be shown in churches or a suitable rental facility.

The attitude relevant to Christian movies in theaters, it seems, is that most kids of today will go to the theater anyway, so give them a Christian movie every once in a while so they can relate to something clean and wholesome.

I will say this to that theory. We do not encourage children to drink beer, hoping that will prevent their drinking hard liquor. We do not endorse cigarette smoking so that they will not smoke pot. I make my point.

DESIRE OF THE HEART

If a Christian loves the Lord with all his heart, he will not desire these forms of entertainment. There will be an abhorrence of things contrary to the Gospel of Jesus Christ. Actually, the bottom line of the things we have mentioned (drinking, smoking, entertainment, immodest dress, et cetera) is this: they are only a symptom of a more serious problem.

The Christian life still demands separation. We are called *out of* and *unto* (out of the world and unto salvation). Ours is an action life; we stand for something; we do not just lull our time while the world goes by at breakneck speed on its way to a devil's hell. By our life the world must have no doubt as to which side we are on. That is the Gospel I preach; that is the way I try to live my life; that is the way I interpret the Bible to teach.

"Be ye not unequally yoked together with unbelievers: for what fellowship hath righteousness with unrighteousness? and what communion hath light with darkness? And what concord hath Christ with Belial? or what part hath he that believeth with an infidel? And what agreement hath the temple of God with idols? for ye are the temple of the

living God; as God hath said, I will dwell in them, and walk in them; and I will be their God, and they shall be my people. Wherefore come out from among them, and be ye separate, saith the Lord, and touch not the unclean thing: and I will receive you, And will be a Father unto you, and ye shall be my sons and daughters, saith the Lord Almighty'' (II Corinthians 6:14-18).

CHURCH

- Where should I attend church?
- Is it wrong to offer items for sale in church?
- Could you explain to me the office of the deacon?
- Is the shroud of Turin valid, or is it a hoax?

QUESTION:

WHERE SHOULD I ATTEND CHURCH?

ANSWER:

This is a thorny question. However, I will at this particular time tread softly where angels fear to walk.

Hundreds of people have written and asked what church I would recommend. Consequently, we should address ourselves to this rather critical issue rather than ignoring it. Although some persons will not like what I say, I will as always deal with it in truths. Everything I say will have been digested, investigated, and looked at in the Holy Word of God for quite some time in respect to the particular answer. I make the statement continually over our Telecasts and in our crusades that a person may not agree with what we say, but he cannot disprove us by the Holy Word of God. If he can, I am always open-minded; I seek to learn; but I have always tried to make it a practice not to address a thing unless I can back it up with the Word of God. Anything else can be folly.

FOUNDATION OF THE CHRISTIAN MINISTRY

When I say church, I am speaking not of a particular denomination, but of the body of Christ, which includes all born again members regardless of denominational affiliation. This also includes every particular work and ministry of the Lord Jesus Christ and the Holy Spirit irrespective of the direction it takes. Although, being a broad statement, this affords much leverage. When you say church, most people think of the church on the street corner with the steeple pointing toward heaven. Because of the vagueness of definition, we will address ourselves to the simplicity of choosing a church that serves its people under the guidance of the Lord Jesus Christ.

I have the opportunity and privilege of ministering to several million people each week by television. (This is not some abstract figure I have conjured up; it is an educated figure derived from the rating systems.) I thank God for the opportunity and the honor of serving in this capacity. Yet, as I tell people all across the country, my work (be it television, missions, education, or whatever) must emanate from the local church; it can never be separate and apart from the church. When ministers function apart from the local church, the work of God in general is

33

hindered and hurt. We must work together. Unity brings strength in respect to labor for our Lord Jesus Christ.

There are good churches, not-so-good churches, and even some bad churches. Some churches would do just as well to go out of business; but at the same time, there are more good ones today than ever before in the history of the great work of God. The local churches (good ones) are the bedrock of this great Christian ministry. That does not mean the local church is to control every ministry in a dictatorial fashion, but in spirit it must be linked with it. This is what I teach and preach.

A PARTICULAR DENOMINATION

The Lord is moving today in such a gracious fashion that He is touching every denominational background with the mighty outpouring of His Holy Spirit. We thank God for that. Admittedly, some denominations stress the fullness of the Spirit and the moving of the Holy Spirit more so than others. At the same time, because of the great ecumenical move of the Spirit of God, this does not always hold true.

You must remember that when I say ecumenical, I am not speaking of the World Council of Churches. That particular body is not of God, has never been of God, and has little to do with God. I am speaking of the ecumenical effort brought about by the Holy Spirit, which is far different.

Forget the denomination. If you trust in a denomination to save you, you are in for a terrible surprise. Denominations are man-made. In essence, in a narrow confine, they are Spirit-directed; but at the same time, when a denomination lays down a policy that you have to belong to a particular church to be saved, that is satanic in concept and is not of God. If the leaders project the thought that other people may make it to heaven, but if you want to be on the right side of God you will belong to their particular denomination, this is satanic in concept, too. Actually, God has no interest whatsoever in denominations. He is interested in the moving of His Spirit in general wherever the needs of men are to be met.

Whenever I ask people if they are saved and they automatically respond, "I am Assemblies of God, or Baptist, or Methodist, or Catholic, or so forth," I question their salvation. These people are trusting in their denomination or particular church to save them; and of course it was not a denomination or a church that died on Calvary. Jesus Christ died on Calvary.

When I ask people if they are saved and they automatically look at me and say, "Yes, I have accepted Christ as my Saviour," or "Yes, I know the Lord," or "Yes, Jesus has come into my heart," I know they are saved. Yet when people speak of a denomination in respect to their salvation, I know they do not understand what salvation is all about. They may be religious, but they are not born again. There is a vast difference there and the sad fact is that millions of people are trusting in their religiosity; they are trusting in their denominational ties; they are trusting in their church work to save them — when none of these will.

TYPE OF CHURCH

The word "type" is a better word to use than "tag." You should first remember that there is no perfect church. As long as human beings comprise churches, they will not be perfect. God does not work with perfection; He works with human instrumentality. We fail at times, but through His mercy, grace, and love He helps us to continue to grow in grace. So if you are looking for the perfect church, that is difficult (or impossible, actually) to find. However, there are doctrinal criteria that a person should definitely consider. I make the statement many times: It does not make any difference what the name is over the church door, but it makes all the difference in this world and the one to come what they teach inside those doors. That is critical.

SALVATION

The foundation of any church should be a belief in being born again; that is, accepting Jesus Christ as one's own personal Saviour and being washed by His precious blood (Romans 10:9-13). The born again experience is not preferential; it is a must. The pastor should give altar calls in which people walk down the aisles to accept Jesus Christ as their own personal Saviour. By that I do not mean joining a church; I mean asking the Lord into their heart to wash away their sins by His precious blood and becoming a member of the body of Christ by being born again. There is a vast difference in the two.

The pastor should preach evangelistic messages that will touch the heart. There should be a spontaneity of praise flow through the congregation from time to time. If the church you attend frowns upon people worshiping God and lifting hands in praise and adoration to the Lord Jesus or saying "Amen" or "Thank the Lord" or "Hallelujah" or "Praise God," you are attending the wrong kind of church irrespective of the name on the door.

THE HOLY SPIRIT

Your church should also stress, preach, and teach the mighty baptism in the Holy Spirit with the evidence of speaking with other tongues as the Spirit of God gives the utterance (Acts 2:4, 19). A church without the operation of the mighty Holy Spirit is like a soldier without weapons. We are in a warfare; we are not playing spiritual tiddlywinks. Satan desires to destroy our effectiveness in this world, and the baptism in the Holy Spirit is the only power that God has given us over the powers of the enemy (Acts 1:8).

We believe and teach that the baptism in the Holy Spirit is an experience apart from salvation, a definite work of grace. I make the statement many times in my crusades that salvation is God's greatest gift to this world, but the baptism in the Holy Spirit is God's greatest gift to His children, the church. Without it a church is ineffective. It may gain many adherents, but it will not gain many true Christians according to the Bible's standards.

Even with the baptism in the Holy Spirit, a church encounters many problems, but without Him a true church is impossible. I realize the church of the Lord Jesus Christ is divided today. This is sad. Many people say there is nothing to the Holy Spirit with speaking in other tongues, that it is not for us today, that it never was for us, and that it is of the devil. I believe the particular churches that teach and adhere to this are by and large ineffective as far as the work of God is concerned.

Notice, I say *by and large*. There are some among them that stress and teach salvation by the blood of Jesus. I thank God for that. I pray for their continued success in this realm, but they will never have Christians in the confines of their churches, whoever and whatever they may be, who will grow to spiritual maturity in the Lord as they should.

At the same time, I realize many Spirit-filled churches are shallow in their experience. This is not the Spirit's fault, it is theirs. It is gross error when a person receives the baptism in the Holy Spirit and thinks that automatically he is going to become a spiritual giant. A person still has to study the Word of God, work, labor, and pray incessantly that the Lord will help him to grow. Satan will contest every step of that advancement, but with the Spirit of God, victory is ours.

THE VICTORIOUS, OVERCOMING CHRISTIAN LIFE

The pastor of a church must guide his people into seeking victory over this present world. Every effort must be made for them to live an overcoming life, free from the problems that bind humanity. It is a shame to see millions of church members bound by alcohol. There are those who cannot wait for Sunday School to end so they can go outside before the morning worship service to turn the air blue with cigarette smoke. This is terrible, and it is never of God.

When I speak of the overcoming life, I am not speaking of ritualistic attitudes that some persons have purported to be the work of God when actually they put people in bondage instead of trying to help them. We cannot legislate holiness. It has to come from the heart. Actually, the definition of "holiness" is "a sincere desire to please God in all respects of our earthly walk before Him." If a person loves the Lord Jesus Christ and is born again, he will have no desire to imbibe alcoholic beverages. There will be no desire to frequent the movies that indulge in profanity, filth, and obscenity. There will be no desire to smoke cigarettes or pot or to engage in 101 other things not so obvious but just as deadly, such as jealousy, envy, and so forth.

One of the chief ministries of the local church is to produce strong Christians who are anchored in the Word and matured in the Lord. A great soul-winner desiring to lift up Jesus Christ must be a witness at all times for the Master — in word and in deed. The victorious, overcoming Christian life is a must. We all realize that in every church, regardless of how strong and spiritual it may be, there are certain members who are weak. There are those who indulge in things irrespective of the pastor's efforts to preach and teach the great Full Gospel, overcoming message. However, the overall picture must be one of power, virtue, strength, holiness, and dedication to the Word of God.

DIVINE HEALING

Any church that endeavors to follow the New Testament pattern should be a church that believes and teaches that Jesus Christ heals the sick (James 5:14). There should be special times when the pastor and the elders of the church call for those who need prayer and anoint those people with oil according to the Word of God and believe for them to be healed. They should expect healing; they should expect miracles. Actually, any church that is following the New Testament pattern will see these things in their regular services.

Many times evangelists who labor in the field of praying for the sick and believing God for miracles receive much attention regarding this matter; but there are scores of Godly pastors who never write books or publish monthly magazines or anything of this nature who see just as many healings, just as many miracles, as some evangelists. They do so simply because they follow the Word of Almighty God and are reaping its eternal and gracious benefits. If your church insists that these things are not for today and it neither practices or desires them, you should find another church home.

SOUL-WINNING

The church you attend should be a soul-winning church, making every effort to rescue the perishing and care for the dying. There is tremendous benefit in any church that has a concern for souls having a bus ministry. Many times the children that are brought in (besides the adults) have the only opportunity of their life to hear the Gospel of Jesus Christ. Thank God for every dollar that is spent on any available means to bring people in to hear the greatest message man has ever heard. A church may enjoy the fruit of the gifts of the Spirit. The people may brag and boast of the way the power of God moves in their services. All this is great, well, and good. Yet if, at the same time, that church is making no more effort to get people saved than by putting a sign on the front lawn announcing the time of their services, they are failing God greatly in this respect.

I thank God for men that I could name across this great nation who are working day and night to get people saved by the blood of Jesus. A strong soul-winning church with heavy emphasis on the mighty baptism in the Holy Spirit is an unbeatable combination. Often, great Full Gospel churches have let down in soul-winning. They somehow feel they do not need to work quite as hard to get people saved because they have the moving of the Holy Spirit. This, I feel, is error on their part. A church must be a soul-winning church, and its people must be involved.

OUR LORD'S IMMINENT RETURN

Every church must preach it, every pastor must preach it, every Christian must look for that moment when our Saviour shall come back. His coming is imminent; it could happen at any moment. When our Lord returns, He is coming back according to I Thessalonians 4:16, 17. We call it the rapture. The word "rapture" is not actually used in the Holy Scripture, but it is derived from "caught up," which means "great ecstasy of joy, rapture." We believe that every saint of God who has ever lived and died trusting Jesus Christ and those *"which are alive and remain"* who are ready at that moment *"shall be caught up together . . . to meet the Lord in the air: and so shall we ever be with the Lord."* This should be preached, it should be believed, it should be adhered to in the church that you attend. Actually, this, too, is a must.

DIVINE GUIDANCE

I feel in my spirit those things we have brought to your attention are the criteria for selecting a good church. You may have to drive a number of miles to get there each Sunday morning or Sunday night or whatever particular nights the services convene. It would be well worth it. People who attend a church solely on the basis that it is close or they like the way the preacher parts his hair or the way he sings or the architecture of the building — or even the fact that their grandparents attend there or they have invested money on the building — irrespective of what it teaches — are foolish indeed.

Most men go to great lengths to find a good garage to work on their automobile. Most ladies will shop extensively to find the best cuts of meat for their family's nutritional needs. Should man do less for his eternal soul? Our attendance and laboring in a local church should never be for social position. It should never be that our parents belong there or that we feel obligated. It should be for one purpose, and that is to enrich our life in the Lord Jesus Christ. The Word still admonishes us, *"Not forsaking the assembling of ourselves together, as the manner of some is; but exhorting one another: and so much the more, as ye see the day approaching"* (Hebrews 10:25).

You may have to look at length for a church such as I have discussed. You may have to visit several. Do so prayerfully with an open mind and heart. Forget the name on the door, and ask the Lord to lead you. Question the pastor as to what he believes. It is extremely important.

Many churches (sadly) are not living up to what they should; some do not preach the Gospel at all. Yet, thank God, there are many today that are preaching this great Gospel of Jesus Christ as never before. Lives are being changed; believers are being filled with the Spirit; sick bodies are being healed; miracles are being performed. Bondages of darkness that bind humanity are being broken as men of God pray the prayer of faith and the people believe God to move. It is a common occurrence for the Spirit of God to "fall" in the services to bless, stir, and encourage the heart. This is the kind of church you want to attend. It may be a stately cathedral or maybe an old, small building on the outskirts of town. Forget about its location, forget about its appearance, and look for what it teaches, proclaims, preaches, and practices. This is critical to your eternal soul.

QUESTION:

IS IT WRONG TO OFFER ITEMS FOR SALE IN CHURCH?

ANSWER:

I have found in my years of dealing with people that most of the time they are honest and sincere in their questions, and so I will do my best to answer with the sincerity in which this particular question is asked.

This question is derived from John 2:13-17 where we read the story of Jesus overturning the money-changing tables and driving the money-changers out of the temple. Let us see what was actually happening.

The Jews in that day had so twisted the law of Moses until it was hardly recognizable. They had perverted it to benefit themselves financially and to work great hardship on the people.

This is how they worked it. When the people came into Jerusalem to offer their sacrifices, frequently the high priest would not accept the lamb or dove (or whatever) they had brought. He would find fault with it, telling the people even though he could not accept that one, he had a friend right out back who could sell them just what they needed. Of course, the sellers would charge the poor people several times the price for the animal (which would be identical). When the people would start to pay for the animal, the sellers would tell them that only temple money could be used. The people would go into the temple to the money-changers and be ripped off again. There would be several tables of money-changers, each one shouting over the crowd promising better deals than the others. All this commotion was going on in the temple where people were supposed to be worshiping God. Actually, it had ceased to be a place of worship at all, which is why Jesus said, *"My house shall be called the house of prayer; but ye have made it a den of thieves"* (Matthew 21:13). *"Take these things hence; make not my Father's house an house of merchandise"* (John 2:16). They were selling sheep and oxen right in the temple (John 2:14).

(Actually, the biblical temple has no relationship whatsoever to the modern-day church.)

THE HOUSE OF GOD

During the Lord's day (when He was on earth), the temple was the house of God, or rather was supposed to be. God presently does not dwell in a house made by hands, but actually our body is a temple of the Holy Spirit (I Corinthians 3:16). So when people say, "You mean you 'sell' records in the house of God?" they do not know what they are talking about. The church building is not the house of God, but a place to keep out the weather, et cetera. Of course, many people do not realize this. They somehow think a church building is different, when it is not. Some persons may say, "But our church building is dedicated to God," and it certainly should be. Everything you have should be dedicated to the Lord — your home, car, clothes, et cetera.

I remember, sometime ago, I received a letter from a lady who mentioned how difficult it had been finding a good church to attend, but then she said she finally found one. She told me how she had been blessed, how the preacher had preached such a great message, seldom had she been in such a good service. Then she went on to say,

"Immediately after the service was over, as I was walking out a side entrance, thankful in my heart I had finally found a good church, I looked through an open door which led to the side and saw a kitchen." She said, "Brother Swaggart, all the joy seemed to drain out of me. I had finally found a good church; but when I saw this kitchen, I knew I could not come back. How could anyone eat food in the house of God?"

By now you realize how foolish that was. This woman was completely forgetting the moving of the Holy Spirit that had taken place in the services. Evidently she had been taught (erroneously) that it was wrong to have a kitchen in the church. Consequently, she would miss the privilege of attending a great church because of some ridiculous notion. No, it is not wrong to have a kitchen in the church; and when you realize that the church building is not the house of God but just a meeting place, you then see how foolish are these petty rules.

Actually, the early church (in New Testament days) had few church buildings as we have today. Most of their worship was conducted in homes, and the homes had kitchens in them, did they not? (Compare Acts 2:46; 20:20; Romans 16:5.)

The devil will do everything he can to get us sidetracked from the true purpose of God's intentions.

MOTIVE

Now, if anyone is selling records, books, Bibles, and the like in church services for the sole purpose of making money, then the motive is wrong and it should not be done. The items should be to help the individual doing the purchasing. Of course, I cannot answer for all other records, but I am thankful for the way the Lord has used our albums to bless and help untold thousands of people. That has always been our purpose, and the Lord has honored that. Now, would it not be a little foolish to say the records are good enough to be anointed by the Holy Spirit but not good enough to be offered to the people in the same church building?

Many evangelists receive a meager income, and some suffer because of a lack of finances. I know when Frances and I first went into evangelistic work, there were nights when we went to bed hungry because we had no money to buy food. Then, as the Lord blessed us in helping us to make records, the added income from the records meant the difference in poverty and in being able to do what we should do for the Lord. Actually, today, all of my records belong to the Jimmy Swaggart Ministries. My family does not receive a royalty from their sales or any part of the income derived thereon. All the monies in total go to promote the Gospel of Jesus Christ over radio and television.

SELLING ON SUNDAY

What I am about to say is going to come as a shock to some of you, but as far as God is concerned, Sunday is actually no more than Monday. The Christian is supposed to keep every day holy. The old Jewish Sabbath (Saturday) has been done away with. You can read where Jesus Christ blotted out the ordinances and nailed them to the cross (Colossians 2:14-17) and that includes the Old Sabbath Day. Most Christians meet on Sunday because this is the day the Lord rose from the dead (Luke 24:1; Acts 20:7; I Corinthians 16:2). We are admonished by the Holy Spirit not to make a religion out of Sunday or any other day but to keep every day holy unto the Lord (Romans 14:5-14). When it comes to work, Sunday is probably the hardest day the preacher has. America's custom of keeping Sunday is an excellent custom and one that is honored by the Lord. However, when we start making rules and regulations, such as whether it is proper to offer records for sale on Monday but not on Sunday, or something of this nature, we are doing wrong. Why could not a record that is anointed by the Holy Spirit be a blessing to someone if it was purchased on Sunday *or* Monday? Let us not add to the Word of God, or take away from it.

QUESTION:

COULD YOU EXPLAIN TO ME THE OFFICE OF THE DEACON?

ANSWER:

The office of the deacon is important in any church. The Bible bears this out, laying down specific qualifications for the individual who serves in this capacity. In some instances over the past few years, however, the office of the deacon has fallen into disrepute. There is a basic reason for this.

In recent years many churches or deacon boards have felt that the *boards* should "run" the church (that is, take charge of administration) and "hire" the pastor to fill the pulpit. Such cases find the pastor becoming little more than a hired hand whose position is subject to the good favor of the board. This is not in accordance with Scripture. This distorted kind of hierarchy does disservice to the work of God and to the growth of the churches following such practices. Let us look at the office of the deacon from a biblical perspective and do our best to define his position.

DEACONS IN THE NEW TESTAMENT

The office of the deacon is designated by the Greek word *diakonos,* which means "servant." *Diakonos,* in the New Testament, is used to denote various kinds of servants, including anyone who serves Christ. Concerning the latter note: *"Are they ministers of Christ? (I speak as a fool) I am more"* (II Corinthians 11:23). Here *diakonos* is translated *"ministers"*; namely, those servants of Christ involved in the work of preaching and teaching the Gospel. Our concern, however, will be locating those passages of Scripture where *diakonos* refers to the office of the deacon, as we define the term "deacon" today.

To pinpoint those Scriptures where the office of deacon is referred to, however, we must realize that the deacon is only one of many offices and positions named in the New Testament. At the time of its writing there were apostles, or those who had received their ministry calling directly from Christ. Also designated were bishops, elders, and, of course, the saints — all of those within the church who comprised the body of Christ.

Each office and position in the church had its own requirements and duties, as spelled out in the Scriptures. Today we use these guidelines in establishing church offices and in selecting those who fill them.

There are three places in the Word of God where the office of deacon is clearly designated — Acts 6:1-7; Philippians 1:1; and I Timothy 3:8-13.

DEACONS IN ACTS 6

Although the word "deacon" is not mentioned specifically in the King James translation of Acts 6:1-7, I believe that our idea of deacons was intended here. This may be seen by the kind of office the apostles established in this passage and the service that was to be performed by those who were selected to fill that office. Let us examine this further by reviewing three qualifying points.

First of all, if these chosen men were not deacons, then what were they? Their role was that of offering practical service to the church members. Remember, the Greek word for "servant" is *diakonos*, which we translate "deacon."

Second, if these men were not deacons, then we are left with no information as to when deacons were first elected. Paul, in his letter to the Philippians, addressed the saints who were there *"with the bishops and deacons"* (1:1). Paul also set forth the requisites for deaconship in I Timothy 3:8-13. From these two references it is obvious that the office of deacon was already established in the early church at the time of their writing and that it was an important position. It is therefore reasonable to expect the New Testament to give us an account of the initiation of deaconship in the church. Acts 6 is the only place that relates a happening that can be interpreted as such.

Third, the original Greek gives us clear insight as to the meaning of this passage. *"Ministration"* (Acts 6:1) is a translation from the Greek word *diakoniai,* which means "the office and work of a *diakonos,* or servant" — the word "servant" better rendered "deacon." *"Serve"* (verse 2) is a translation from *diakonein,* which means "to provide the necessities of life" or "to take care of." *"Ministry of the word"* (*diakoniai tou logou* in the Greek) means "the deaconship of the Word" (verse 4). This suggests the work of preaching elders — those responsible for ministering in spiritual matters — and therefore has nothing to do with our concept of deacons.

The kind of deacons we are concerned with here is those who hold the office of deacon in the local church and who serve much like business elders. In other words, the kind of minister referred to in verse 4 ministers the Word, and the kind of minister referred to in verses 1 and 2 ministers material things to the people.

SELECTION OF DEACONS

The apostles instructed the church to choose men *"full of the Holy Ghost and wisdom, whom we may appoint over this business"* (Acts 6:2, 3). It seems, in effect, that the apostles appointed the deacons themselves. Consequently, what I am about to say will fly in the face of most churches today.

Even though the people may have presented the individuals to them whom they felt were full of the Holy Spirit and wisdom, the apostles were the ones who actually made the choice. It may be inferred from the Scripture reference that the only reason the people were given the task of selecting the individuals to serve in this capacity was to save time for the apostles, who did not have time to do the investigation of individuals, et cetera. It must be remembered that there were several thousand people in this final analysis — the people had no choice in whom the apostles selected.

From this account, it is improper for local churches to vote for deacons. In other words, the selection of deacons should be made by the pastor. The pastor knows the individuals in his church better than anyone else — he knows the consecration and dedication of every member in the body. His whole life is given to the local church, therefore he is in a better position than anyone to select those individuals who will serve as deacons and further the work of God. This is the scriptural position that should be taken.

FUNCTION OF DEACONS

The deacons were to be appointed over the business of serving tables. Since the term *"serve tables"* (Acts 6:2) is a deceptive one, let us go on to clarify it.

Serving tables had nothing to do with a waiter serving food at a table. In the early church collection plates were put on tables; hence, the tables referred to were tables of collection where money was given and distributions made to those people who needed help. The deacons were to attend to this business in whatever disposition was made, making certain that no one in need was overlooked.

In regard to serving tables, one thing must be noted. The deacons were to attend to this business under the guidance and direction of the apostles (the Twelve). They were to do nothing on their own. They were appointed by the apostles and were told what to do by the apostles. Their task was to handle practical matters and so relieve the load of the apostles, enabling them to accomplish the spiritual work that God had called them to accomplish.

A DIFFERENT SCENARIO

Now this is a completely different scenario than is taking place in most churches today. What is happening in most churches is hindering the growth of the local church and actually hindering the work of God. This does not mean that modern-day deacons are individuals of lesser stature than those in early church days. It does mean that, in many cases, they are occupying a position that they are not scripturally supposed to occupy.

The unseemly position that most churches have fallen into, where the deacon board "runs" the church and "hires" the pastor, is not only unscriptural, but has the correct scriptural and spiritual order in reverse. Such a position is unreasonable — there is no legitimate defense for it.

Without a doubt, the pastor should run the church. He should seek the counsel, guidance, and help of the deacons, but ultimately he should make the decisions. It is the deacons' business to do what the pastor wants done and to do it to the best of their ability. They are to lighten the pastor's load so that the ministry and work of God may go forward and prosper. (Compare the story of Moses and Jethro in Exodus 18:13-26.)

Who is it that has the burden for the local church? Naturally, all of its members should have a burden; everyone should labor and do all that is within his power for the church's welfare. Even though this stands true, however, we all know that God appoints and anoints *a man*. He does not anoint boards, committees, groups, et cetera. Admittedly, these bodies of people may experience the blessings of God; but according to Scripture God always calls individual men to a ministry, to perform a certain task.

Furthermore, if a minister's hands are tied by persons that have placed themselves unscripturally in authority over him, then he is in an awkward position. It is difficult to accomplish a God-ordained task when trapped in a faulty power structure. The only one who is scripturally in authority over the minister of the Gospel (in this case, the pastor) is the

Holy Spirit. To be certain, a Godly pastor will answer to the church and do everything possible to be a good shepherd, but just because there are some immoral shepherds and some pastors who lack wisdom does not mean that the office of pastor and deacon should be reversed.

ATTITUDE OF DEACONS

If the deacon feels the pastor of the church is not conducting himself forthrightly or that his vision is too great or whatever the case may be, that deacon should pray for the pastor. He should not lead factions in the church against the pastor or try to instigate some kind of effort to remove him. This should be left to God.

If the deacon feels he can no longer sanction the conduct of the pastor, he should resign his position; and if that is not enough, he should attend another church. Never should he take it upon himself to be the authority over the pastor.

The wise pastor, however, will seek the counsel and guidance of the deacons he has chosen. He will lean heavily on them, realizing they are never to be looked upon merely as "performers of menial tasks." Also, the deacon must understand that whatever task he performs, he is to perform that task according to the position God has given him — a position calling for one that is of *"honest report, full of the Holy Ghost and wisdom"* (Acts 6:3).

I strongly emphasize that the deacon is never to serve as an administrator in church affairs. The administrative role of the pastor is set forth in Hebrews 13:7 and 17, and the local church should not deviate from this scriptural precept.

LIFE-STYLE OF DEACONS

As we have already stated, the qualifications for the office of deacon are *"men of honest report, full of the Holy Ghost and wisdom"* (Acts 6:3). First Timothy 3:8-13 takes this a step further by setting forth the kind of life-style that must be followed after a person has been appointed deacon. These are the guidelines for the deacon as he serves the local church:

One, he is to be *"grave,"* which actually means bearing qualities of honor and honesty (verse 8).

Two, he must not be *"doubletongued,"* but have the courage to abide by the truth irrespective of circumstances (verse 8).

Three, he is to be temperate, meaning not overindulgent in anything, and *"not given to much wine"* (verse 8). If a person were to consider the meaning of wine in our society, he would abstain from it to avoid even the *"appearance of [the] evil"* (I Thessalonians 5:22) of alcoholic beverages.

Four, he must not be *"greedy of filthy lucre"* (verse 8). He may be an excellent businessman (or possibly not), but his total purpose in life must be the furtherance of God's work, not making money, even though success in business is not wrong.

Five, he must hold *"the mystery of the faith in a pure conscience"* (verse 9), which means belief in and promotion of a correct doctrine respecting the work of God and the Word of God, and that from a sincere heart.

Six, his life is to be *"proved"* and *"blameless"* (verse 10). In other words, no novice should serve as a deacon. A deacon's Christian life should be of sufficient length to prove his consecration and dedication.

Seven, he should be *"the husband of one wife"* (verse 12). There is some controversy over what this means. I will explain.

Some persons say it refers to divorce and remarriage; others, polygamy. I believe Paul was speaking here of polygamy in the early church and not of divorce. In other words, individuals in the early church days, coming from a heathenistic society, often had more than one wife at a time. This practice was being stamped out, and the Apostle Paul was telling the church that no deacon could practice polygamy.

When it comes to a divorced person serving as deacon, each situation must be considered according to its own merit or lack of merit. For instance, did the man (or woman) experience this difficulty while living in sin (before conversion) or did this happen after he was saved? It is difficult to make a pat decision respecting these problems. Each case should be considered individually.

Eight, he must rule his children and house well (verse 12). The manner in which a person provides spiritual leadership for his own household serves as a guide for the position he will hold in the local church. If he cannot fill this role in the home, how can he do so in God's church?

Actually, the deacon is a servant, but his position is one of respect and honor. If this position is correctly filled, God will be glorified, the local church built up, and the pastor aided and abetted in his work.

FEMALE DEACONS

It is the opinion of many men of God that women may serve as deacons, and I believe this is scriptural. Romans 16:1 refers to *"Phoebe our sister"* as *"a servant."* The Greek word used here for "servant" is *diakonan.* This is the same word used to denote the office of deacon. It seems that in I Timothy 3:11 the word "deaconesses" may be implied. Paul was here describing the requirements of a deacon's wife and could also have been referring to women deacons.

FAITHFUL DEACONS

First Timothy 3:13 concludes the discourse on deaconship by setting forth the rewards of that deacon who has executed his office faithfully.

First, he purchases to himself *"a good degree,"* or position of respect. He is looked to with honor by other Christians.

Second, he receives *"great boldness in the faith"* to proclaim the Word of God and stand tall in the realm of Godliness and consecration.

That deacon who remains aware of the purpose, duties, and standards of his office will prove an invaluable asset to the pastor and the local church. Truly, the successful deacon — the one who fills his role as Scripture dictates he fill it — is the one who has come to realize that supporting and serving is not only an honor, but a vital function in the local church and in the overall body of Christ.

QUESTION:

IS THE SHROUD OF TURIN VALID, OR IS IT A HOAX?

ANSWER:

I will tell you at the outset that the shroud of Turin is a hoax, but let us look at it a little more closely.

On the face of it, the shroud of Turin is an unlikely object for serious scientific study or religious edification: it is simply an old linen cloth, stated by some to be the burial shroud that Joseph of Arimathaea and

Nicodemus draped around the body of Jesus before they laid Him in the tomb (John 19:38-40). The cloth is imprinted with an image, an image that is ghostly dim.

MEDIEVAL TIMES

The shroud of Turin became known about A. D. 1357 when it was exhibited in a small wooden church in the sleepy French provincial town of Lirey, about 100 miles southeast of Paris. The shroud's owner, Geoffrey de Charny, had been killed the previous year by the English at the Battle of Poitiers. Impoverished by her husband's death, his widow, Jeanne de Charny, hoped to attract pilgrims (and their monetary offerings) by exhibiting what was purported to be Jesus' burial garment in the local church.

No one was ever able to explain how this family came into its possession. It seems that people in these medieval times did not give any credence to Madame Charny's claims, and it was only when the shroud came into the possession of the powerful House of Savoy that it was accepted in some ways as the true shroud of Christ. It seems that now, in the twentieth century, some so-called scientists accept the shroud's authenticity more readily than it was accepted in the past.

RESEMBLANCE

It is said that the image of the face of the man buried in the shroud closely resembles the standard artists' renderings of the face of Christ — and that people immediately recognize it as the face of Christ precisely because it is the standard face of Jesus in art.

Around A. D. 1464 Pope Sixtus IV let it be known that he regarded the garment as an authentic relic.

In A. D. 1578 the shroud was moved to Turin, Italy. It has remained there ever since, except for a six-year period in World War II when it was safeguarded in a remote abbey in the mountains of southern Italy.

I personally do not believe that the shroud of Turin is the burial shroud of Jesus Christ. There are several reasons why I have drawn this conclusion, and I will use the remainder of this article to share them with you.

TOO MANY RELICS

Even though I am not certain that the Catholic church considers the shroud to be genuine, I do know that the Catholic church is notorious for coming up with all kinds of relics, each reported to be some miracle object which, in their thinking, gives some kind of authenticity to the Catholic church.

When Martin Luther first saw Rome, one of the things that started him thinking that something was amiss was his expectation of viewing a city ablaze with the glory of God, but instead seeing something that sickened him and turned his stomach. As he stood on a hill overlooking the city, he saw a multitude of wagons coming in, many of them filled with bones and going to particular churches purporting to carry remains of apostles or saints who had died. Any church that could conjure up one of these so-called remains was thought to be more holy than other churches, et cetera. But for all these bones to have been authentic, there would have had to have been several tens of thousands of apostles. So a person can see the amount of fakery that accompanied all of this activity. This has gone on down through the centuries and is happening even today.

I was conducting a crusade in Manila (in the Philippines) when the "Madonna" was scheduled to make its appearance in the city. Thousands of people lined the roadside as the object was carried off the plane and made its tour of the city. For you see, this "Madonna" is an object made to look like the Virgin Mary (or rather, what somebody thought the Virgin Mary looked like). It is supposed to, at times, cry real tears.

Constantly, these kinds of sightings and observations are going on within the Catholic church. Most of the time the Catholic priests do not deny them or accept them; they merely use them. In other words, each is another relic that is given to the people with a slight suggestion that God gives these kinds of things only to the "true" church.

Consequently, it behooves all of us to be suspicious of any object, relic, or whatever that is purported to be some form of "miracle" coming from the Catholic church. This is certainly not to say that God cannot perform a miracle — He is a miracle-performing God — but, at the same time, all of these sightings and observations are spurious indeed. They always have been, and they are today. I believe the shroud of Turin falls into the same category.

THE DISFIGUREMENT OF CHRIST

Jesus took a terrible beating, and, considering the disfigurement the beating caused, I seriously doubt that any shroud or cloth would have left any kind of identifying mark. The Word of God attests to this: *"I gave my back to the smiters, and my cheeks to them that plucked off the hair: I hid not my face from shame and spitting"* (Isaiah 50:6). Here it says that His beard was plucked off. This within itself would have caused horrible swelling and disfigurement, as well as the loss of some blood.

"And they clothed him with purple, and platted a crown of thorns, and put it about his head" (Mark 15:17). As is commonly known, the scalp of a human being is most tender. If it receives any kind of blow or any kind of puncture wound, it swells almost immediately. We are told that the kind of thorns used in the makeshift crown that went upon Jesus' head were "victors' thorns." These thorns are said to be about six inches long and are strong and sharp. This kind of mat placed down upon His head, if it was done that way, would have penetrated His scalp and caused tremendous swelling almost immediately.

Also *"they smote him on the head with a reed"* (Mark 15:19). "They" could have been as many as 600 men, because verse 16 says they called together the whole "band." The Greek word for "band" is *speira*, meaning a company assembled around a standard. It was a whole company of Roman soldiers, which was usually about 600 men. If all of these men — or even a small portion of them — hit Jesus over the head with a reed, you can well imagine what this did to Him, considering that thorns were pressing on His brow and the reed hitting the thorns was pressing them even deeper. More than likely His head swelled far beyond its normal size.

MARRED MORE THAN ANY MAN

Scripture says Jesus was marred more than any man: *"As many were astonied at thee; his visage was so marred more than any man, and his form more than the sons of men"* (Isaiah 52:14).

The Hebrew word for "marred" is *mishchath*. The idea is that in His sufferings the Messiah was so bruised, beaten, marred, disfigured, stricken, mutilated, injured, spat upon, and torn that His outward appearance was terrible to behold. His suffering was so great that even the most wicked of hardhearted men shuddered with shock at the treatment heaped upon Him by His enemies. Jesus became so disfigured and destitute of His natural beauty and handsomeness that men were stricken with amazement, disgust, and heartsickness at what they saw. The perfection of His body made the marring He suffered seem even more severe.

When a person considers all the things that the Word of God says about the terrible disfigurement of Jesus' countenance (*"visage"*) and the horrible death He died, it seems highly unlikely that any garment placed upon His face would have left any imprint even remotely resembling that of a human. It seems from Scripture that Jesus' countenance was grotesque after the pulling of His beard, the placing of the crown of thorns, and the beating by so many men upon His head. Considering that the Scripture says His *"visage [face] was so marred more than any man,"* I think the evidence is fairly conclusive. Any garment placed over Him would have left no recognizable imprint.

No, the shroud of Turin is not real. It is but another relic (possibly) produced by the Catholic church to deceive a gullible public into believing that the Catholic church is the "true" church and that, in some small way, things of this nature add to its prestige and authenticity.

QUESTION:

CREMATION

■ Do you believe that the practice of cremation is scripturally wrong?

QUESTION:

DO YOU BELIEVE THAT THE PRACTICE OF CREMATION IS SCRIPTURALLY WRONG?

ANSWER:

Yes, I feel cremation is wrong, but I will qualify my answer.

First of all, it is not clearly forbidden in the Bible. We all know that in times of war men's bodies are sometimes blown to bits, drowned at sea, eaten by fish, burned beyond recognition, and so forth; and in any event, every physical body will go back to the dust of the earth after burial. I will give the reasons, though, that I think cremation is wrong.

A PROBLEM OF ATTITUDE

First of all, I feel it is irreverent. It is not clearly forbidden in the Bible, and, of course, God could gather the ashes of a cremated body as well as those torn to pieces in war, just as He will gather the dust of those who have long since died. So that is no problem to Him; the wrong is the attitude causing a person to desire cremation.

All through the Christian life the physical body is to be treated with respect. That is the reason the Christian has certain codes of modest dress. We should present our body as *"a living sacrifice, holy, acceptable unto God, which is [our] reasonable service"* (Romans 12:1). The body is the temple of the Holy Spirit and, consequently, in spiritual form (the glorified state) will house the soul and the spirit forever. So it is important to God. When people purposely have their body cremated, they are in essence refuting these things I have just mentioned.

Basically those people who desire their body to be cremated are unsaved people who do not look for the resurrection. Since the body will be resurrected, it should be laid away with reverence. That simply means this: in everything we do, we should be looking forward to the resurrection. The Christian burial is one of respect and reverence simply because we expect that one day the trump of God will sound. This life does not end it all. There is another day coming.

The statement I made in the previous paragraph is another point. People who desire their body to be cremated feel that this life embraces everything. In other words, there is no hereafter — no soul, no spirit, no judgment, no standing one day before God to give an account. Their desire to be cremated means, in essence, they are saying these very things.

A MATTER OF RESPECT

So even though there is no express command in the Bible against cremation, for the reasons given, I feel it *is* wrong. I must, however, add this: if a person had recently come to the Lord but had requested in some earlier will or statement that cremation be performed (the comments I have thus far made having never been brought to that individual's attention), and if, in fact, the act was carried out after death, God would overlook such a thing, I believe, because it would have been done in ignorance. Yet those people who love the Lord Jesus Christ with all of their heart are looking forward to the resurrection. Consequently, they would want to treat their body with respect, not only in this life, but also after their death.

"Behold, I shew you a mystery . . . . In a moment, in the twinkling of an eye, at the last trump: for the trumpet shall sound, and the dead shall be raised incorruptible, and we shall be changed. For this corruptible must put on incorruption, and this mortal must put on immortality. So when this corruptible shall have put on incorruption, and this mortal shall have put on immortality, then shall be brought to pass the saying that is written, Death is swallowed up in victory" (I Corinthians 15:51-54).

DEPRESSION

■ I'm bothered terribly with the problem of depression. Is there anything that can be done about it?

QUESTION:

I'M BOTHERED TERRIBLY WITH THE PROBLEM OF
DEPRESSION. IS THERE ANYTHING THAT CAN BE
DONE ABOUT IT?

ANSWER:

Yes, there is something that can be done about it.

Martin Luther (the great reformer) suffered from acute depression. In one of his worst, and possibly the last, times he moped around the house for days, even to where his wife, it seems, could make little or no headway toward encouraging him. At that point, she decided that a drastic problem required drastic action, so she dressed up in black mourning clothes — including black hat, black veil (the works), in funeral attire. He finally noticed her and asked, "Who died?" She, with a straight face, replied, "God." He opened his eyes wide in astonishment and exclaimed. "Woman, what do you mean — God cannot die!" To which she replied, "Well, why are you acting as if He is dead?"

He caught the point and snapped out of the terrible depression. When a child of God allows depression to rule his life — and rule it, it will, given the opportunity — he is acting as though God is dead.

COMMON TO MAN

Depression just may be one of the worst problems in the world today, attacking Christian and non-Christian alike. It shows no favoritism. *"There hath no temptation taken you but such as is common to man"* (I Corinthians 10:13). Depression can range all the way from mild (which hinders a person's daily routine) to paralyzing (which sometimes causes a person to be submitted to electroshock therapy). Of course, the questions are asked repeatedly: What is depression? What causes it? How can a person overcome it to where it does not bother him anymore?

There are answers to all of these questions. Admittedly, medical science, even psychiatry, has little or no answer for these questions. In all honesty, I cannot recommend the medical profession respecting the problem of depression — simply because most doctors treat depression with mood-altering drugs such as valium. Granted, these drugs may give momentary relief, but the result will be only a double-barreled problem of depression *and* drugs.

Likewise, I cannot recommend secular psychologists or psychiatrists, again for the simple reason that most of these individuals exclude God from their therapy. The psychiatrist not only will recommend drugs, but will (most of the time) also delve deeply into a person's mind and spirit, getting the individual to zero in on himself, which is actually the worst thing the person can do.

Admittedly, there are some kinds of nutritional difficulties and some kinds of chemical or hormone imbalances that can cause depression in the human body. In respect to these particular problems, naturally a physician may need to be consulted. However, for the most part, depression is not caused by physical or biological difficulties; depression is a problem of the spirit, and God has His own psychiatry for it.

TWO KINDS OF DEPRESSION

There are basically two kinds of depression mentioned in the Word of God; we will attempt to address ourselves to both of them, respecting the cause and the cure.

I suspect that psychiatry would clinically diagnose *many* kinds of depression, but the *two* outlined in the Word of God basically cover the gamut of human psychology as God sees it. God, having made man, should know the psychology of man better than anyone else. In the Word of God, as with most things, God gives the answer (and cure) for these particular problems. Make no mistake about it: depression can be a debilitating force in a person's life, making life miserable and a literal hell on earth. It has robbed millions of people of their joy and has caused many even to attempt or to commit suicide. However, through the Word of God, not only can depression be controlled, but the individual can gain total and complete victory to where there is not even a sign of an occasional lapse into this life-threatening difficulty.

SITUATIONAL DEPRESSION

The first kind of depression is brought about by what seems insurmountable difficulties. An account of this is given in I Samuel 30. David was soon to become the great king of Israel . . . . But before I get into the difficulty that brought on this acute depression, which not only affected David but continues to affect millions of people today, let us take a little eye-witness view of this man whom God had called.

Nearly 12 years previously, when David was just a young boy, he had experienced the anointing of the Holy Spirit by Samuel, the great prophet, telling him that he (David) would be the king of Israel. Tremendous victories followed for David, such as his slaying the giant and becoming the people's favorite, but still David witnessed the rage of Saul because of jealousy and envy against him. This jealousy and envy were so acute that Saul had become demon-possessed and was endeavoring to kill David. Consequently, David was now being billed as the most-wanted criminal in the country of Israel (actually, he was no criminal, but was labeled such by a jealous king). Even the people that tried to befriend David were murdered by the jealous Saul. It appears at first glance that this call of God on David's life had brought not victory, but trouble. Now he faced the most difficult problem of all.

David now had been made to flee from his own country, had been placed in the position of a vagabond, and had been surrounded by men of like circumstances. His lot in life was not easy; it seems there was no letup. The question could have been asked, "Will God ever bring the prophecy given to Samuel so long ago to its completion?" It did not look like it.

David was now in the land of the Philistines, Israel's hated enemy, and he returned with his men to the city of Ziklag. He had been away for some time. His family was stationed in Ziklag, as were the families of all of his men. While he had been gone, the Amalekites had invaded Ziklag and had *"burned [it] with fire"* (I Samuel 30:3). They had taken all the women and children captive (howbeit, they had not killed any of them) and had burned the city. When David and his men saw this debacle before them, they *"lifted up their voice and wept, until they had no more power to weep"* (verse 4). *"David was greatly distressed"* (verse 6).

Now, this was acute depression brought on by insurmountable difficulties! The situation was so bad, the Bible says, that not only did David lose his wife, his children, and his belongings, but his own men now spoke of stoning him. Yet David refused to be destroyed: *"[he] encouraged himself in the Lord his God"* (verse 6).

Of course, the Scripture goes on to tell that David pursued these men. He overcame the Amalekites and rescued his family as well as the families of all the other men, without losing a single person, because *"[God] answered him, Pursue: for thou shalt surely overtake them, and without fail recover all"* (verse 8). (Incidentally, there were 600 men with him.)

THE CHRISTIAN'S ANSWER

There is an old adage that says, "Into every life a little rain must fall." I realize there is much teaching abounding today that states just the opposite of this. However, irrespective of *how close to God* a person may be, there will possibly come times of acute difficulty and problems. Irrespective of *how much faith* an individual may have, problems and difficulties will at some point come, at times becoming so severe that a person will think he is going to be totally overcome by them.

At these times the unsaved person reaches for drugs or alcohol (or immerses himself in some other vice). However, we all know this does not help; it only makes the matter worse. If a Christian will *"encourage himself"* in the Lord, victory can be his. There is an old song that says this:

"When your body suffers pain
And your health you can't regain,
And you try to get along on meager fare;
Just remember in His Word,
How He feeds the little birds,
Take your burdens to the Lord and leave them there."

This is exactly what David did: *"[he] encouraged himself in the Lord his God."* As Martin Luther's wife so vividly portrayed to the great reformer, we cannot keep the difficulties from coming our way, but that is not reason to act as if God is dead. God is alive!

Financial reverses will come to most Christians; no one is exempt from physical problems. Satan will take every advantage to make us feel there is no hope. Acute depression will set in like a black cloud. It may look as if there is no way out, but an attitude of gloom is one that reckons without God. *"With God all things are possible"* (Mark 10:27). Do not look at that which is, but look at that which can be. *"David encouraged himself in the Lord,"* and the blackest hour in that terrible experience was truly just before dawn. This was one of Satan's last gasps, for in a short time David would fulfill the prophecy foretold by Samuel — he would become the king of Israel.

When reverses come our way, bringing with them acute depression, we must remember two things:

One, God will vindicate us; God will bring us out of it; God has the answer.

Two, even if we are not brought out of it now in the way we would desire, and even if it looks like defeat not only to us but to the world, there will come an hour when *"we shall be like him: for we shall see him as he is"* (I John 3:2).

Some individuals may say, "But, Brother Swaggart, my child (or other loved one) was not healed; he died. That has to be nothing but defeat." No, it is not defeat. If your child died in the Lord Jesus Christ (and certainly all children do if they die prior to the time they are of the age they can be held accountable unto God), then you will see him again. The same is true with the death of other Christian loved ones. There will be a reunion. There will be no sickness there. So the final end will be victory. Encourage yourself in the Lord — that is the answer.

SPIRITUAL DEPRESSION

The second kind of acute depression is caused by demonic power. This is the area where medical science breaks down. Even secular psychology and psychiatry do not understand it, simply because it *is* spiritual. We are told, *"God hath not given us the spirit of fear; but of power, and of love, and of a sound mind"* (II Timothy 1:7).

The spirit of fear causes acute depression. Satan is the author of this spirit of fear; it does not come from God. It attacks the individual without warning. This kind of depression has nothing to do with accumulating difficulties and problems — oh, it may have, but it is not necessarily so. It is like, as we mentioned earlier, a cloud that descends upon the individual, causing everything to look completely hopeless. It is as if a 100-pound weight is pressing on his back.

During this time the individual does not have complete control of himself. He functions as if he is walking through water and every step is laborious; he feels he is suffocating. Irrespective of what anyone says to him or what happens, he cannot see any way out. The problem can become so severe that the individual will just sit in a chair and stare. This is, of course, the worst kind of depression. Electroshock therapy is applied to some individuals to try to jar them out of this terrible malady.

Most people who are troubled in the extreme by acute depression have suicidal tendencies. Even though they may never voice such to their loved ones, the thought fills their mind continuously. The situation is demon-induced and demon-inspired. However, and please get this, it does *not* mean the person is demon-possessed. I would even suggest that most depressed persons are *not* demon-possessed, simply because this acute depression can engulf any Christian — even the most Godly. Yet it is definitely caused by a spirit of fear. Now, how can it be overcome?

Of course, the world's answer is drugs — prescription drugs, legal drugs, illegal drugs, alcohol, whatever is readily available. Other than this particular false strength, about the best that secular counselors or others can do or say is simply to try to get your mind off of it, take up a hobby, et cetera; but that is like trying to put a Band-Aid on cancer.

God's Word has the clear and concise answer. It is given to us in Philippians 4:4-19. I will outline it briefly. I will also say at the outset: the answer to depression does not come easily.

Even though people in the state of acute depression do not want to be this way, most of them do not have the strength or the spiritual integrity to climb out of it. It is as though they are bound. They want someone else somehow to do it for them, but there is nothing or no one that can. Such a person can be anointed with oil or prayed over, and preachers can even rebuke the spirit. Still, even though these things may help momentarily, they will not last simply because the individual's state of mind has not changed. The Christian's life must change in the sense of his faith and of his believing God, plus doing what God said to do to overcome this problem. Only the afflicted individual can do it; no one else can do it for him.

"Rejoice in the Lord alway: and again I say, Rejoice" (verse 4). Look at this closely: the Apostle Paul did not say to rejoice when good things happen to you, but he said to *"rejoice in the Lord."* Then he added one other word: *"alway."* This means the Christian should live in perpetual joy; we should be thanking the Lord constantly. When we do this, we give *"[no] place to the devil"* (Ephesians 4:27) to come in with the spirit of fear.

Joy is something that must be practiced. By this I mean that Christians should smile, we should square our shoulders, and we should stand tall whether or not we feel like it. It is not a question of "I feel good"; it is a question of *rejoicing* whether or not I feel good. This is a *must* for the child of God. Once a depressed person starts doing this, he is on the road to complete victory.

"*Let your moderation be known unto all men. The Lord is at hand*" (verse 5). This Scripture is dual in meaning. First, the word "moderation" means "meekness and gentleness." It also means "mildness, patience, and kindness." These are attributes of the child of God that include the fruit of the Spirit. We should practice these things.

The Scripture tells us, "*perfect love casteth out fear.*" It does not tell us that perfect *faith* casts out fear; it says that perfect *love* casts out fear. All of the attributes mentioned above — summed up in the one word "moderation" — are outgrowths of love. They will overcome fear, for "*there is no fear in love; but perfect love casteth out fear: because fear hath torment. He that feareth is not made perfect in love*" (I John 4:18).

The second portion of this verse, "*The Lord is at hand*" (verse 5), simply means that whatever is happening, the Lord is there to help us. It also means that the Lord is coming again, that His second coming is near. So we do not have to feel we are bearing the cross alone; we do not have to feel we are facing the difficulty by ourselves — Jesus is at hand. Jesus is near.

"*Be careful for nothing*" (verse 6). This simply means, do not worry about anything. It is a command, not a request. As children of God it is a sin to worry, and we should not allow worrisome things to cross our mind. We should "*be careful for [anxious about, worried about] nothing.*" Paul went on to say, "*In every thing by prayer and supplication with thanksgiving let your requests be made known unto God*" (verse 6).

Paul was telling us here that we have the privilege of seeking God and personally making supplication to Him. We are first to thank Him for all the things He has done and then to tell Him what we have need of, knowing He is a prayer-hearing, prayer-answering God. Then we will find the key to victory over depression: "*And the peace of God, which passeth all understanding, shall keep your hearts and minds through Christ Jesus*" (verse 7). According to God's Word, if we do these things we have mentioned, we will have peace; depression will find no place within our heart and life. Our mind will be "kept" through Christ Jesus.

"*Finally, brethren, whatsoever things are true, whatsoever things are honest, whatsoever things are just, whatsoever things are pure, whatsoever things are lovely, whatsoever things are of good report; if there be any virtue, and if there be any praise, think on these things"* (verse 8). This Scripture is clear; it is the secret of a happy life and of overcoming depression. Our thinking must be straight. We should not allow our mind to dwell in the garbage or on defeat. We should not look at every cloud as if it were black. Stated clearly and simply, we are to think on things that are honest, just, pure, lovely, and of good report. Let us talk of virtue and of praise. This will channel our mind in the right direction, and the Holy Spirit will help us to do it.

GOD'S PSYCHIATRY

I have outlined, as I see it in the Word of God, the cause of two kinds of depression. Satan will hit us with both kinds. However, as children of God, we can so acclimate ourselves to the Word of God and doing what God says that the attacks of acute depression not only will become further and further apart, but will eventually disappear altogether. Satan will finally know our mind is no longer fertile ground for his spirit of fear. This is our victory; this is our peace. Now, let us walk in victory in the Lord!

I will close by saying this: it will not be easy; nothing worthwhile ever is. The hardest attack will be the first one; but once these scriptural guidelines become our life-style, there will be no place for the spirit of fear that causes depression. Victory is ours in the Lord Jesus Christ.

DOCTRINE

■ What is meant by the term "sound doctrine," and how do I know if my church is preaching and practicing sound doctrine?

■ How can a person tell if the doctrine he lives by is true?

■ Is the ministry of Herbert W. Armstrong, who has preached for many years over radio and now over television, a creditable, scriptural ministry?

■ What is the millennial reign? Will it be a literal kingdom? Exactly what will it be like?

QUESTION:

*WHAT IS MEANT BY THE TERM "SOUND DOCTRINE,"
AND HOW DO I KNOW IF MY CHURCH IS PREACHING
AND PRACTICING SOUND DOCTRINE?*

ANSWER:

This is a question that is somewhat thorny, to say the least, but I will attempt to address myself to it as best I can.

"Doctrine" means "something that is taught, a principle or position, or the body of principles in a branch of knowledge or system of belief." The Apostle Paul said, *"For the time will come when they will not endure sound doctrine; but after their own lusts shall they heap to themselves teachers, having itching ears"* (II Timothy 4:3). Jesus Himself said, *"My doctrine is not mine, but his that sent me. If any man will do his will, he shall know of the doctrine, whether it be of God, or whether I speak of myself"* (John 7:16, 17).

So, there is such a thing as false doctrine and there is such a thing as sound doctrine. Sound doctrine is simply what is preached and practiced according to the Word of God by preachers and teachers who have rightly divided the Word of Truth.

ERROR

The second part of the question is what causes the most controversy. The place where a person attends church is probably the singlemost important thing in his life. By that I do not mean the denominational tag, but what is taught and preached in that particular church.

Millions of people today believe error. Satan has infiltrated the pulpit, the ministry, and the church of the Lord Jesus Christ. He endeavors to twist, to distort, the Word. Alas, demon spirits instigate false doctrine, and millions believe it — taking it for Gospel. Consequently, they suffer defeat in their life. Many churchgoers even die lost.

Many people believe a particular doctrine because their preacher said it. It sounds good; it looks good. Or it is easy to believe. In other words, it requires little or nothing of them. Millions of "good people" will die lost because of the erroneous path they trod.

71

SOUND DOCTRINE

I wish I could say that all churches are preaching the truth, but, sad to say, they are not. Some are preaching some truth and some error. Some are preaching a little truth and a lot of error. Some are preaching a lot of truth and a little error; and some may be preaching all truth — as far as they know it. However, there is a way to prove if a doctrine is true to the Word of God.

One, is it scriptural? It is possible to take one or two Scriptures out of context and base a doctrine on those particular Scriptures. However, for a doctrine to be correct, it must be compatible from Genesis to Revelation. If it is true doctrine, it will stabilize and teach the same thing all the way through the Bible and will not leave questions unanswered or Scriptures unexplained.

There is a little problem with this. Every preacher I have ever heard says that whatever he teaches is Scripture. In other words, one man may preach the exact opposite of the other, and both men will claim to be scriptural. That oftentimes leaves the layman in a quandary. Both claim to be scriptural, and yet one (or both) may be wrong.

Two, is it profitable? *"All scripture is given by inspiration of God, and is profitable for doctrine, for reproof, for correction, for instruction in righteousness: That the man of God may be perfect, throughly furnished unto all good works"* (II Timothy 3:16, 17). In other words, you can judge doctrine by its results. If it fosters slack living or does not bring man up to his ultimate in God, then something is wrong with that doctrine. True doctrine, sound doctrine, will always bring forth right living and good works.

Jesus Himself provided the test of true doctrine. He said, *"My doctrine is not mine, but his that sent me. If any man will do his will, he shall know of the doctrine, whether it be of God, or whether I speak of myself. He that speaketh of himself seeketh his own glory: but he that seeketh his glory that sent him, the same is true, and no unrighteousness is in him"* (John 7:16-18).

He said, in essence, "If I am a self-seeker for my own glory and secular interest, then reject me; but if I promote God's glory, induce men to serve Him, propose nothing contrary to the Scripture or the fulfillment of it, then judge me a true prophet and my doctrine to be sound." He challenged His enemies to judge His doctrine on this basis.

As the Master in essence said this about Himself, I think it holds true for every particular church and for every minister of the Gospel too.

QUESTION:

HOW CAN A PERSON TELL IF THE DOCTRINE
HE LIVES BY IS TRUE?

ANSWER:

Unfortunately false prophets and false doctrine do exist. *"Now the Spirit speaketh expressly, that in the latter times some shall depart from the faith, giving heed to seducing spirits, and doctrines of devils"* (I Timothy 4:1). *"In the last days . . . men shall be lovers of their own selves . . . having a form of godliness, but denying the power thereof . . . ever learning, and never able to come to the knowledge of the truth . . . reprobate concerning the faith"* (II Timothy 3:1-8). *"Evil men and seducers shall wax worse and worse, deceiving, and being deceived . . . . From such turn away"* (II Timothy 3:13, 5).

Millions of people today (sadly) believe error. Satan has infiltrated the pulpit, the ministry, and the church of the Lord Jesus Christ. He endeavors to twist, to distort, the Word. Also, demon spirits instigate false doctrine, and millions of people believe it — taking it for Gospel, consequently suffering disastrous defeat in their life — many even dying lost.

Most people believe whatever they believe because their preacher said it. Now even if he tells you the truth, it is a sad thing to believe something just because someone else said it. Get into the Word yourself — study it to prove it — and let it be anchored in your own heart. We are told to *"meditate therein day and night"* (Joshua 1:8). Sadly enough, so many people believe what they believe because it sounds good, it looks good, or it is easy-to-believe. In other words, it requires little or nothing of them.

YOUR BELIEFS

What you believe is extremely important; it can "make" you or "break" you. So many Christians just blunder along, believing a lie instigated by Satan — never understanding why they stagger from one defeat to the next. It is not easy to admit you have been wrong about something, especially what you have been taught respecting the Word of God. However, I doubt there is a person in this world who, when he earnestly began to seek God and His Word, has not found that at one time or another he was believing something wrong. Under these circumstances, a person must renounce the error and align his thinking and believing with the Word.

The Bible issues some strong warnings against error. *"For there are certain men crept in unawares . . . ungodly men, turning the grace of our God into lasciviousness, and denying the only Lord God, and our Lord Jesus Christ . . . . These are murmurers, complainers, walking after their own lusts; and their mouth speaketh great swelling words, having men's persons in admiration because of advantage. But, beloved, remember ye the words which were spoken before of the apostles of our Lord Jesus Christ; How that they told you there should be mockers in the last time, who should walk after their own ungodly lusts. These be they who separate themselves, sensual, having not the Spirit"* (Jude 4-19).

"There shall come in the last days scoffers, walking after their own lusts . . . even as there shall be false teachers among you, who privily shall bring in damnable heresies, even denying the Lord . . . . And many shall follow their pernicious ways; by reason of whom the way of truth shall be evil spoken of. And through covetousness shall they with feigned words make merchandise of you" (II Peter 3:3; 2:1-3).

THE ACID TEST

Thank God there is an acid test to prove your doctrine to be true, and this is the heart of the answer to your question.

One, does your doctrine harmonize with Scripture? To harmonize with Scripture, the doctrine must be compatible from Genesis to Revelation. True doctrine will stabilize and teach the same thing throughout the Bible and will not leave gaping holes, questions unanswered, and Scriptures unexplained. However, there is one problem with this (and many persons have told me this): Just about every preacher everywhere says whatever he teaches is Scripture. In other words, one person may teach the exact opposite of the other, and both claim to be scriptural. That leaves the layman confused. One (or both) must be wrong. However, there is a second test that is foolproof and will never fail in regard to true doctrine.

Two, does your doctrine bear good fruit? You can judge doctrine by its fruit (Matthew 7:20). For instance, look at the doctrine of unconditional eternal security. What kind of fruit does it bear? It fosters slack living, giving vent to gross error. Millions of people today make no pretense at living for God yet think they are saved because someone once told them that once they were saved they could not lose their salvation. These people are of no service whatsoever to the work of God, their life being an example of unrighteousness instead of righteousness. Millions of individuals are in hell today because of this particular doctrine. This is what I mean when I say you can judge a tree (doctrine) by its fruit. No doctrine given by the Holy Spirit lends credence to iniquity, sin, and unbelief. I could go on and on in this vein and name many doctrines that do not coincide with the Word and do not bear good fruit.

I pray that every one of you reading this will examine what you believe in the light of these two points: Does your doctrine harmonize with Scripture? Does your doctrine bear good fruit? If it does not, ask God to forgive you for believing a lie, denounce it, line up with the Word of God, and receive its vast benefits.

QUESTION:

IS THE MINISTRY OF HERBERT W. ARMSTRONG, WHO HAS PREACHED FOR MANY YEARS OVER RADIO AND NOW OVER TELEVISION, A CREDITABLE, SCRIPTURAL MINISTRY?

ANSWER:

I will start this answer by stating the words of Jesus: *"And many false prophets shall rise, and shall deceive many"* (Matthew 24:11). No, I do not believe that Herbert W. Armstrong's ministry has ever been a creditable or a scriptural ministry. As much as I am sorry to say it, I feel this individual would have to be classified as a false prophet. I will explain.

This man's radio ministry, started in 1934, quickly blanketed the United States as well as other parts of the world. He was an intelligent individual, and that, coupled with the fact he had a pleasant voice, caused the skyrocketing success he enjoys even today.

When Herbert W. Armstrong semiretired, his son, Ted, took up the reins. He was equally brilliant respecting the delivery of radio messages and the like. However, there came a division between father and son not too long thereafter, no one quite knowing what precipitated that breakup. In time the story surfaced that the 90-year-old Herbert W. Armstrong was being divorced by his wife of many years his junior. Now let us see what this man preaches. For reference we will quote from his own book, *Why Were You Born?*

EXCLUSIVISM

One, he teaches that the Herbert W. Armstrong way, better known as the Worldwide Church of God, is the only source of salvation in the world. This is always the first mark of a cult, as cult leaders totally ignore the sacrifice paid by the Lord Jesus Christ for our salvation.

Mr. Armstrong made this statement: "I'm going to give you the frank and straightforward answer. You have the right to know all about this great work of God — and about me. First, let me say — this may sound incredible, but it's true — Jesus Christ foretold this very work — it is, itself, the fulfillment of His prophecy." He was speaking of the Worldwide Church of God. He also stated: "There is no other work on earth proclaiming to the whole world this very same Gospel that Jesus taught and proclaimed." He went on to say that his work was the most important activity on earth today.

In dissecting this man's teachings, I find he reflects a strange mixture of many false sects and isms. His sensational teaching adheres in many respects to some of the prominent doctrines of Seventh Day Adventism, British Israelism, and the Jehovah's Witnesses, plus there is even a touch of Mormonism in his insistence that it is possible eventually to become God.

He is totally unreliable and untrustworthy in biblical matters. His teaching is not recommended by those who would truly follow the Lord.

LEGALISM

Two, he teaches what appears to be types of Old Testament "holy days." These are his words: "Passover, the days of unleavened bread, Pentecost, and the holy days God had ordained forever were all observed by Jesus, and the early apostles, and the converted Gentile Christians." However, in checking his references, a person immediately observes that there is not the slightest information in them that Jesus, the early apostles, or the converted Gentile Christians observed these "holy days." Actually, the early Christians were told by the Apostle Paul not to *"turn . . . again to the weak and beggarly elements"* (Galatians 4:8-11).

Three, he also teaches observance of the old Jewish weekly Sabbath — Saturday. He said: "The New Testament reveals that Jesus, the apostles, and the New Testament church, both Jewish and Gentile — observed God's Sabbath, and God's festivals — weekly and annually." It seems he ignores completely the New Testament teachings that we are not bound by any ceremonial sabbaths (Colossians 2:14-17).

GOD — AUTHOR OF SIN

Four, Mr. Armstrong's teachings imply that God planned to wreck His creation by sin; in other words, God was directly responsible for Adam's sin and the failure of mankind. This is what he said in *Why Were You Born?* "Now if Satan did not succeed in thwarting God's will, wrecking God's perfected and completed creation, then the only alternative is to say that it all happened according to God's will — exactly as God Himself originally planned" (page 8). Again, "Satan did not break into the Garden of Eden in spite of God — did not do one single thing contrary to God's great purpose! All that has happened has been planned before of God — and all is progressing exactly as God wills" (page 9).

SALVATION BY WORKS

Five, he teaches salvation by works. In the booklet we have been quoting from he quotes the Scripture, *"By grace are ye saved through faith . . . for we are his workmanship, created in Christ Jesus unto good works, which God hath before ordained that we should walk in them"* (Ephesians 2:8, 9). He leaves out the *"not of works, lest any man should boast"* and adds this: "Notice there are GOOD WORKS to salvation" (page 11).

Obviously no one denies that "good works" are God's plan for the Christian once he has been saved by grace through faith. Yet those good works certainly do not make a person a Christian; and, actually, the two cannot possibly be interdependent since the Word of God tells us, *"And if by grace, then is it no more of works: otherwise grace is no more grace. But if it be of works, then is it no more grace: otherwise work is no more work"* (Romans 11:6).

SALVATION BY PROCESS

Six, he also teaches salvation by process (that none are saved now). So if this man does not believe in salvation by grace through faith, he really cannot offer assurance of salvation for himself or anyone else. He is compelled to teach in his writings, "Salvation then is a process! But how Satan would blind your eyes to that! He tries to deceive you into thinking that all there is to it is just 'accepting Christ' — with 'no works' — and presto-chango, you are pronounced 'saved'!" Then he goes on to say that the Bible reveals that *none* are yet "saved" (page 11).

JESUS HIMSELF BORN AGAIN

Seven, he teaches that somehow Jesus Himself got saved — a most amazing declaration! He says: "Jesus, alone, of all humans, has so far been saved! By the resurrective power of God! When Jesus comes, at the time of the resurrection of those in Christ, He then brings His reward with Him" (page 11). He then goes on to say, "Jesus is the author of our salvation — He wrote that salvation by His experience, and that was the first writing of it — He was the first human ever to achieve it — to be perfected, finished as a perfect character!" (page 14).

He so carefully omits that if Jesus needed salvation, then He would have had to have been a sinner. Of course, the Bible repeatedly and emphatically denies this, describing the Master as One who was *"in all points tempted like as we are, yet without sin"* (Hebrews 4:15). It is one more strange doctrine or strange religion that requires that Jesus "get saved."

DIVINITY OF MAN

Eight, Herbert W. Armstrong also believes and teaches that man can eventually become God — a doctrine strangely peculiar to Mormonism. Here is what he said on this subject: "The purpose of life is that in us God is really recreating His own kind — reproducing Himself after His own kind — for we are, upon real conversion, actually begotten as sons of God; then through study of God's revelation in His Word, living by His very Word, constant prayer, daily experience with trials and testings, we grow spiritually more and more like God, until, at the time of the resurrection, we shall be instantaneously changed from mortal to immortal — we shall then be born of God — *we shall then be God*!"

He went on to say: "Do you really grasp it? The purpose of your being alive is that you be born into the kingdom of God, when you will actually be God, even as Jesus was and is God, and His Father, a different person, also is God" (pages 21, 22).

I suspect that many professing Christians who have listened to and supported this man's broadcast would stop immediately if they realized the abominable heresy of his doctrine.

BRITISH ISRAELISM

Nine, Mr. Armstrong follows the fanciful folly of British Israelism, claiming Great Britain to be Ephraim and America to be Manasseh. He basically states that these two countries are the two lost tribes of Israel, quoting the Lord's words, *"Ye shall be hated of all nations"* (Matthew 24:9), and identifying Britain and the United States as "ye" — meaning that the world would hate the United States and Great Britain, thus "proving" that these are the two lost tribes of Israel. Of course, this is foolishness.

FALSE PROPHET

This man is a false prophet beyond any question, because that which he teaches is a gospel contrary to the Word of God. His doctrine is wrong regarding the person and work of Jesus Christ; hence, it is not Christian doctrine.

It has never merited, nor does it merit now, the support, the prayer, or the interest of Christian people. Money sent to this individual actually finances Satan's program of warfare of God's Word and of His dear Son, Jesus Christ. Anyone who would aid in this slander against the person and work of Jesus Christ becomes a *"partaker of his evil deeds"* (II John 11). You should not listen to his radio broadcasts or television programs or read his magazine called *Plain Truth*. It is freighted throughout with false doctrine and will lead a person astray according to the proof that we have given you in this article.

I realize many persons will take umbrage at me for exposing this, but many Christians are led astray by individuals who sound plausible and scriptural, when in reality they are just the opposite. *"Whosoever is deceived thereby is not wise"* (Proverbs 20:1).

"Beloved, believe not every spirit, but try the spirits whether they are of God: because many false prophets are gone out into the world. Hereby know ye the Spirit of God: Every spirit that confesseth . . . Jesus Christ . . . is of God: And every spirit that confesseth not . . . Jesus Christ . . . is not God . . . . Hereby know we the spirit of truth, and the spirit of error" (I John 4:1-6).

QUESTION:

WHAT IS THE MILLENNIAL REIGN? WILL IT BE A LITERAL KINGDOM? EXACTLY WHAT WILL IT BE LIKE?

ANSWER:

You have asked several questions in one, and I will do my best to answer.

First of all, the word "millennium," of which "millennial" is a form, is not found in the Bible, but it simply means "1,000 years" — and that term is repeated six times in Revelation 20:1-7.

MILLENNIAL REIGN

The 1,000-year millennial reign will start when Jesus Christ comes back with all of the saints, interrupting the Battle of Armageddon, and sets His feet upon the Mount of Olivet and sets up His kingdom in Jerusalem. At that moment the millennial reign will begin.

We know that Satan must first be bound (Revelation 20:1-10), for we read in Revelation 20:3 that Satan will be bound during the millennium. Also, Revelation 20:5 tells us that the tribulation martyrs will have a part in the first resurrection, which takes place before the 1,000 years and includes all the different companies of the redeemed and every individual saved — from Adam to the binding of Satan. This verse also implies that the tribulation saints will be the last redeemed company resurrected and translated. The first resurrection ends with the rapture of this company and the two witnesses.

Yes, it will be a literal kingdom, with Jesus Christ reigning in Jerusalem. This is what confuses a lot of people — but as all preceding kingdoms have been literal, so this one will be literal as well (Isaiah 9:6, 7; Daniel 2:44, 45; 7:13; Zechariah 14; Revelation 17:8-18). In the following statements we will prove this from the Word of God and give some particulars as to exactly what it will be like.

First of all, the millennial reign is called several different things. I will not attempt to give all the Scriptures, to conserve space, but I will give some of the names by which it is referred to in the Word of God.

- The 1,000-year reign of Christ
- The dispensation of the fullness of time
- The day of the Lord
- That day
- The age to come
- The kingdom of Christ and of God
- The kingdom of God
- The kingdom of heaven
- The regeneration
- The times of the restoration of all things
- The consolation of Israel
- The redemption of Jerusalem

As already stated, the expression "thousand years" is mentioned six times in Revelation 20:1-7. So we know from this that it will last 1,000 years. It will last until the loosing of Satan, the last rebellion, the renovation of the earth by fire, and the Great White Throne Judgment (II Peter 3:8-13; Revelation 20:11-15).

Man will have a beginning more favorable at this time than in any other dispensation: the God of heaven for a ruler and all the privileges that such rulership will bring.

ESTABLISHMENT OF THE KINGDOM

- The kingdom will be established at the return of the King from glory (Isaiah 9:6, 7; Daniel 2:44, 45; Matthew 25:31-46) after the church is raptured (I Corinthians 15:51-58; I Thessalonians 4:13-17).

• The church will come back with Christ to help Him set up the kingdom and reign over the nations (Zechariah 14:1-5; Jude 14; Revelation 1:4, 5). We know from II Thessalonians 2:7, 8 that the church is raptured before the revelation of the Antichrist, and the Antichrist will be revealed before Christ comes (II Thessalonians 2:1-6). So the kingdom cannot be set up until after these events take place.

• After the future tribulation, then, the Lord will come to the earth with the saints (Daniel 12:1-13; Zechariah 14:1-21; Matthew 24:15-31; Revelation 19:11-21).

• The Antichrist will be destroyed at Christ's coming, so he must be here when the Lord comes (Daniel 7:18-27; II Thessalonians 2:1-12; Revelation 19:11-21).

• At the time the Antichrist is destroyed, Satan will be bound for 1,000 years (Revelation 20:2, 7). Christ will reign on the earth during that time. Realizing that Satan will be bound during that 1,000 years and knowing that he is now loose, we know we are still living in the Church Age and will be until Christ comes to bind the devil, at which time we will enter into the great millennial reign.

• The kingdom will be set up when Ezekiel's temple is built, which will be on the site of Solomon's temple, as recorded in Ezekiel 41 through 43.

THE FORM OF GOVERNMENT

The government will be not monarchic, democratic, or autocratic, but theocratic — which simply means that God will reign through the Lord Jesus Christ (Matthew 25:31-46; Luke 1:32-35; Revelation 11:15) and through David, who will actually rule the nation of Israel (Jeremiah 30:9; Ezekiel 34:24; Hosea 3:4, 5).

God will also rule through the apostles and all saints from Adam to the millennium. All saints that have ever lived will be judged and rewarded according to the deeds done in the body, and will be given places of rulership according to their rewards — not according to the company of redeemed of which they are a part or the age in which they were redeemed or lived.

To give you an example, David will have a greater rulership than any one of the apostles. He is to be king over all Israel unto Christ, while the apostles will have only one tribe each. For instance, some of the Old Testament saints did much more for God and had more power than the average New Testament saint, and they will be given authority commensurate with what they did while on this earth (Psalm 149:5-9; Romans 8:17; I Corinthians 4:8; Ephesians 2:7; II Thessalonians 1:4-7; II Timothy 2:12).

Jerusalem will be rebuilt and restored to a greater glory than ever before and it will be the seat of government, the world capital, and the center of worship forever (I Chronicles 23:25; Psalm 48:8; Isaiah 2:2-4; Jeremiah 17:25; Joel 3:17-20; Zechariah 8:3-23).

THE EXTENT OF THE KINGDOM

The millennial kingdom will be worldwide and will forever increase in every respect just as every other kingdom — except that it will not have sin and rebellion (Psalm 72:8; Isaiah 9:6, 7; Daniel 7:13, 14; Zechariah 9:10; Revelation 11:15).

All nations now in existence on the earth, and who will be living when Christ comes, will continue as such in the kingdom forever and ever. All people, nations, and languages shall serve Him. *"His dominion is an everlasting dominion, which shall not pass away, and his kingdom . . . shall not be destroyed"* (Daniel 7:14).

After the Battle of Armageddon and the judgment of the nations at the return of Christ, there will be many of all nations left who will go up from year to year to worship the Lord of Hosts and keep the Feast of Tabernacles (Zechariah 14:16-21; Matthew 25:31-46; Revelation 11:15).

LAW OF THE KINGDOM

There will be law in this kingdom, and it will be for the same purpose as in any other kingdom. The kingdom will be a literal, earthly one with earthly subjects, many of whom, sad to say, will be rebels in heart against the rule of Christ and will openly rebel at the first chance they get when the devil is loosed out of the pit at the end of the 1,000 years (Revelation 20:1-10). However, *anyone* truly born again and baptized in the Holy Spirit, and who enjoyed fellowship with God during the 1,000 years, certainly will not rebel with Satan at that time.

That there will be sinners here during the millennium is clear from Isaiah 2:2-4; Micah 4:3; Zechariah 14:16-21.

Many unsaved people will be permitted to live and go through the millennium because of keeping the outward law of the government, but, sad to say, in their heart they will be rebellious against the government. On the other hand, some will be executed during the millennium because of committing sins worthy of death (Isaiah 11:3-5; 16:5; 65:20).

The law of God revealing His will in detail, as given by Moses and Jesus Christ, will be the law of the kingdom. This will include the law of both the Old and New Testaments. It seems from Isaiah 2:2-4; Ezekiel 40:1 through 48:35; Micah 4:2 that the law of Moses will again become effective during the millennium and forever. And of course, as stated, the law of Jesus Christ as laid down in the four Gospels will also be paramount; neither will conflict with the other.

Christ and the glorified saints who have been made kings and priests will execute the law of God forever.

THE DIFFERENT NATIONS

The Gentile nations will perhaps live in the same place as they do today, with the exception of those who live in the lands promised to Abraham and his seed (Israel) for an everlasting possession. The Promised Land, as given by God, extended from the Mediterranean Sea on the west to the River Euphrates on the east, taking in all the Arabian Peninsula and possibly Syria as well, and including the wilderness countries south and east of Palestine. So it seems that all the nations of the world will basically remain as they are, with some minor exceptions, understanding that Israel will incorporate what God promised in the beginning and was never fully realized. Consequently, some parts of the nations of Syria, Lebanon, Jordan, and Saudi Arabia possibly may be eliminated (Genesis 15:14-18; Exodus 32:13; Deuteronomy 4:40; Joshua 14:2-9; Ezekiel 47:13-23).

THE TEMPLE

Yes, the Jews will have a temple during the millennial reign. It will be located at the site where Solomon, Zerubbabel, and Herod built their temples — all of which were situated successively on the same site.

However, it must be understood that this temple will not be the one that will be built in the last days before the second coming of Christ, in which the Antichrist will sit during the last three and one-half years of the tribulation period. The millennial temple will be built by Christ Himself when He comes to the earth to set up His kingdom (Zechariah 6:12, 13). It will be the place for Christ's earthly throne forever (Ezekiel 43:7).

There will be a literal river flowing out from this temple eastward and from the south side of the altar (in Jerusalem). Half of it will flow into the Dead Sea and half into the Mediterranean. The Dead Sea will be healed so that multitudes of fish will be found in it (Ezekiel 47:1-12; Zechariah 14:8). Actually, when the Lord comes back and sets His feet on the Mount of Olives with all the saints, there will be a great earthquake, and the whole country will be changed (Zechariah 14:4, 5). The Dead Sea will be raised so that it will have an outlet to purify the stagnant waters that have been shut up for all these centuries. There will also be trees on both sides of the river whose leaf shall not fade, neither shall the fruit be consumed. The trees shall bring forth new fruit according to their months, which shall be for meat and preservation of natural life for the nations. It could be that these trees will be similar to the tree of life that existed in the Garden of Eden.

THE SPIRITUAL CONDITION

We are told that the Holy Spirit will be poured out as never before in the millennial reign (Joel 2:28-32). God's promises to this world, even with the salvation of millions of people and the infilling of the Holy Spirit by the millions, have not been fully realized as of yet and will not be realized until the great millennial reign. Then, multiple hundreds of millions of people will be saved by the blood of Jesus Christ — exactly as they are today. Then, millions of people will be baptized in the Holy Spirit according to Acts 2:4 — exactly as they are today. In other words, what was received by the early church is being received today and will be received in a greater way throughout all eternity from the time the Messiah comes to bring universal peace and prosperity to all. But you must understand: this includes only the *natural* people who are on the earth. All the saints of God who have lived from the time of Adam to the millennium will have glorified bodies and will, of course, not need to be saved because they already will have been saved.

There will be universal knowledge, as outlined in Isaiah 11:9; Zechariah 8:22, 23; Habakkuk 2:14. This means that all people will know of the ways of the Lord. There will not be people ignorant of His ways as they are today. Sad to say, most of the people on this planet today do not know of the ways of the Lord, but then *"the earth shall be full of the knowledge of the Lord, as the waters cover the sea"* (Isaiah 11:9).

The term Jewish missionaries may sound strange, but actually there will be Jewish missionaries in that day. The Jewish people will become the missionaries of the Gospel and the priests of the law during this age and forever. Of course they will be aided and abetted by the glorified saints and others, but it will be they who will primarily serve in the capacity of missionaries because they will be natural people in a natural setting (Isaiah 2:2-4; 52:7; 66:18-21; Zechariah 8:23).

It will become popular then to serve God and the Lord Jesus Christ. There will not be all different types of faiths and religions; there will be only one and that will be the religion of the Lord Jesus Christ or, better said, the salvation of the Lord Jesus Christ (Isaiah 2:2-4; Jeremiah 31:31-36; Joel 2:28-31; Zechariah 14:6-21; Malachi 1:11). All the teachings of the Lord, of course, will be based on the Word of God.

THE LIVING CONDITIONS

Satan will be bound. There will be no tempter (Isaiah 24:21, 22; Revelation 20:1-10).

There will be universal peace. This means there will be no taxation to keep up large armies and navies. The universal conversation will be not about war, treaties, armament, depression, varied religions and forms of government, but about the goodness and greatness of God and the wonder of His reign. People will be fully satisfied in peace and prosperity (Isaiah 2:4; 9:6, 7; Micah 4:3, 4; Malachi 1:11).

There will be universal prosperity. We are told this in Isaiah 65:24 and Micah 4:4, 5. All investments will be safe. Everybody will have his needs met. There will be no financial crises to retire businesses throughout eternity. The God of all will prosper all people and any legitimate business. All people will be capable of succeeding in life and having a life of prosperity. All poverty will be abolished.

Tithing will be the financial system. Tithing was the system before the law, it was the system under the law, and it has been the system since the law. So no doubt the same system will be used by the government of Christ in the coming ages. There will be plenty of money from such a system to balance the budget and have plenty to spare. There will be no corrupt politics or graft, as Christ and the glorified saints will reign in righteousness and true holiness (Isaiah 32:1-5).

There will be full justice for all. Crime waves will be a thing of the past. The Lord and His glorified saints will judge all men, thus assuring justice to all alike. If a man commits a sin worthy of death, he will be immediately tried and executed. There will not be a 1,001 ways of staying execution or prolonging trial. The law will be enforced to the letter, as it should be under man today (Isaiah 9:6, 7; 11:3-5; 65:20).

Human life will be prolonged. Human life will be prolonged to 1,000 years, and then those who do not rebel against God with Satan at the end of the millennium will be permitted to live on forever and ever (Isaiah 65:20; Zechariah 8:4; Luke 1:33).

There will be an increase of light. Notice that it says an increase of light and not an increase of heat. The light of the sun will be increased seven times and the light of the moon will be as the light of the sun today. No doubt there will be a healing feature in this increased light (Isaiah 30:26; 60:18-22).

There will be changes in the animal kingdom. All animals will have their nature changed. There will be none that will be fierce or poisonous. Things will be as they were in the Garden of Eden before the curse, with the exception of the serpent who will still be cursed (Genesis 3:14; Isaiah 11:6-8; 65:25).

There will be a great restoration. All lands will be restored to a wonderful beauty and fruitfulness with the exception of Babylon and perhaps a few more centers of great rebellion against God, which will be used as object lessons to coming generations of God's wrath on sin. The ugliness and blight that characterizes so much of the world today because of sin and rebellion against God will be done away with and the great restoration will take place (Isaiah 35; Jeremiah 50; 51).

Love and righteousness will prevail. The Gentiles will love the Jews and the Jews will love the Gentiles; and there will be no more animosity, hatred, or jealousy among the races.

THE PURPOSE OF GOD

• To put down all rebellion and all enemies under the feet

of Christ so that God may be all and all as before the rebellion (I Corinthians 15:24-28; Ephesians 1:10; Hebrews 2:7-9).

• To fulfill the everlasting covenants made with Abraham (Genesis 12; 26; 28; 35; II Samuel 7).

• To vindicate and avenge Christ and His saints (Matthew 26:63-66; Romans 12:19; I Peter 1:10, 11).

• To restore Israel and deliver her people from the nations and make them the head of all nations forever (Deuteronomy 28; Isaiah 11:11; Matthew 24:31; Acts 15:13-17).

• To exalt the saints of all ages in some kingly or priestly capacity according to the promises and according to their works (Romans 8:17-21; II Corinthians 5:10; Philippians 3:20; Colossians 3:4; Revelation 1:5).

• To gather together in "one" all things in Christ which are in heaven and in earth and restore all things as before the rebellion (Acts 3:21; I Corinthians 15:24-28; Ephesians 1:10).

• To judge the nations in righteousness and restore the earth to its rightful owners (Isaiah 2:2-4; Daniel 7:9-27; Matthew 25:31-46; I Corinthians 6).

• To restore a righteous and eternal government on earth as originally planned (Isaiah 9:6, 7; Daniel 2:44, 45; Luke 1:32-35; Revelation 11:15; 22:5).

The millennial reign will be the greatest age the world has ever known. Jesus Christ will personally reign supreme from Jerusalem. David will reign over all of Israel under the Lord Jesus Christ. Every saint that has ever lived from the time of Adam to the millennium will be here in his glorified body. The world will then know what it could have had all of these thousands of years that it lived in rebellion against God. It will then know the peace and prosperity that God intended from the beginning. The only way to enter into this great kingdom that is coming is to accept the Lord Jesus Christ as your own personal Saviour (John 3:16; Romans 10:9, 10).

EDUCATION

■ Thousands of Christian schools are being built;
why is this so? Is something wrong with our
public school system?

QUESTION:

THOUSANDS OF CHRISTIAN SCHOOLS ARE BEING BUILT;
WHY IS THIS SO? IS SOMETHING WRONG WITH OUR
PUBLIC SCHOOL SYSTEM?

ANSWER:

Noted newspaper columnist Pat Buchanan said some time ago:
"Millions of parents are fed up with judicial meddling in education, with the scholastic pandering of under-achievers, with a lack of discipline in the schools, with rampant teacher incompetence.

"They are fed up with biology courses that teach evolution as a proven fact, with history courses that fail to highlight American heroes or inculcate patriotic values, with sex education bereft of moral content, with values clarification courses that are nothing but primers in moral decadence.

"They want their children to have the same traditional education they and their parents had."

I say amen!

Not too long ago someone said that two Christian schools are being built every single day in the United States of America. There is a reason — actually, several reasons — for this, as brought out in the above quote. There is a cause for all of this spiritual and scholastic decay, and that cause is secular humanism. You see, the teaching of evolution as fact, the degrading of America's heroes and patriotic values, the sex education courses that have no moral content . . . all of this stems from the onslaught of secular humanism. The public school system is gutted throughout with this amoral, ungodly religion that regards man as a natural object and denies the existence of God.

SATAN'S GREAT EFFORT

Satan's greatest effort to destroy this nation is among the children. Let me explain.

In 1935 Joseph Stalin stated if just one generation in a particular nation could be corrupted, then that nation could be overtaken by Communism. He was right. All it takes is one generation: that generation being the generation of children attending our public schools today. These children are being given an education that has totally excluded

91

God and all of the moral content linked with the teaching of God from the Bible. Consequently, every moral value, every foundation of truth, and every tenet of faith that makes this nation great is being completely destroyed in this present generation by our public schools. It is vital that our children not be exposed six to eight hours a day, five days a week, to this ungodly philosophy. Because our young people will determine the future of this country, I believe that the only hope for the United States of America is Christian education. In fact, it is so important that we must make whatever sacrifices necessary to place our youth under the tutelage of Christian educators whose teaching is totally Christian in content.

THE BATTLE FOR CONTROL

The problem is becoming more pronounced all over this nation as a number of states are endeavoring to close down Christian schools that do not meet with so-called state requirements. I will give you an example that sounds typical of the Soviet Union, but that actually happened here in the United States of America.

Gail and David Carlson, together with their four children, were planning to spend the Thanksgiving Holidays vacationing in Atlanta, Georgia. Instead, Gail became a fugitive running from state to state with her children. David, 32 years old, was put behind bars at the Cass County Jailhouse in Plattsmouth, Nebraska, sharing a cell with six other fathers.

What was their offense? They did not tell a district court whether their children still attended an "unapproved" Christian school at Faith Baptist Church. Is this America? Is it possible that President Reagan should send an ambassador to Nebraska instead of the Vatican?

This battle between state school officials and "unapproved" church schools has moved from crisis to crisis. Pastors and church workers have been attacked to the point of being hauled into court, fined, and even thrown into jail.

Are these Christian teachers giving the students an inferior education? No, they are not. On state-approved tests, almost without exception, the children taught in Christian schools have come out from six months to two years ahead of those educated in public schools. The problem is not *quality* of education — the problem is *control*. The state wants to control the educational process, even when it is church affiliated.

We maintain that freedom of religion is one of the hallmarks of our country's foundation, the very reason why the United States of America was born. We believe that a church has the right to have a school, and that as long as said school maintains educational quality, no state or federal official has the right to tell that school what to do or how to operate.

Listen to this, from our neighboring city of New Orleans.

During a recent season the Word of Faith Church had the number-one basketball team in District 16-C, but the Eagles were grounded for the Louisiana High School Athletic Association play-offs. Why? The school's administration did not subscribe to Darwin's theory of evolution and would not teach science and philosophy courses that suggested anything other than man's creation by God. Because of the school's refusal to meet the state requirements for accreditation, the Athletic Association would not allow Word of Faith to compete for state honors.

I say hallelujah to Word of Faith and to all who take such a stand!

FREEDOM OF RELIGION

If we lose the battle here, freedom of religion will be lost in the United States of America. This is the reason Satan is fighting so hard: the die is cast and the stakes are high. If Satan can shut down the Christian schools in this land, then the generation of which Joseph Stalin spoke will be totally subverted to humanism, atheism, socialism, and Communism. Not only will we lose our freedom, we will lose our nation as well.

We must establish Christian schools wherever and whenever possible. By the term "Christian schools" I do not mean schools that give our children the same education they would receive in the public school plus a course or two in the Bible. We must have a curriculum in which *every course* is taught with Christian convictions, not secular ones. Children must be taught that Christ is Lord over all of life, and that God's Word has implications for every aspect of life and all areas of study. We *must* educate our children within this framework of truth. Our Judeo-Christian base has been largely chipped away through our secular educational institutions, and we must rebuild it by employing the opposite: genuine *Christian education.*

We believe God gave children to parents (Psalm 127:3), not the state. As parents we have a mandate from God: *"Train up a child in the way he should go"* (Proverbs 22:6). It is impossible to fulfill this task with one

hour of Sunday School every Sunday morning. This training must be —
and can only be — accomplished by the provision of a thorough
Christian education. If we can give this generation of children a complete
Christian, biblical education, we will be well on our way to a substantial
healing of all that has gone wrong in this nation.

PUBLIC EDUCATION

One reason the states are screaming over the boom of Christian
schools is that every child who leaves a public school to attend a
Christian school causes the state to lose several thousand dollars of
federal money. One preacher said that probably the greatest thing that
could happen to this nation is for the public school system to go totally
bankrupt. I am beginning to share his viewpoint.

The only thing that is even remotely holding the public school system
together is Christian teachers within the public school system who are
bravely bearing the onslaught of abuse, both physical and verbal, from
their students. In spite of this crass treatment, they continue to do their
best to give these children an education. I applaud these teachers; I pray
for them; but the answer is not Christian teachers teaching a secular
curriculum. The answer is a *thorough Christian education*.

Five years ago I would not have said this, but today I say it loudly.
Any parent who will not sacrifice to the utmost to put his children in a
school where they can receive a well-rounded, Christian education is
tampering with their very soul. Children who attend a school several
hours a day, their pliable mind oftentimes coming under the influence of
atheistic teaching, are apt to believe their parents agree with what is
being taught. Is it possible we could be rearing a generation of atheists? I
will say it again: parents who knowingly and willfully send their children
to a public school are tampering with their eternal destiny by placing
them in a position that can ultimately destroy them. Consequently, even
at great sacrifice, parents ought to do everything in their power to give
their children an education within a Christian school system.

CHRISTIAN EDUCATION

I remember when a battery of reporters asked me, "Aren't Christians
supposed to obey the law?" They were referring to the situation in

Louisville, Nebraska, where the parents had opted for jail instead of forfeiting their religious freedom.

My answer was, "Yes, Christians are the most law-abiding people in the world, *unless* the law violates the Christian conscience." I told them, in addition, "We are admonished by the Word of God to obey the law of the land unless that law violates God's Word; and if it does, the higher law of God's law then must be obeyed."

The Christian school system must maintain the highest quality of education — *and it is* — far above that of the state! It must never, however, allow itself to be brought under the control of the state. Independence from secular regulation is essential to assure the purity and effectiveness of Christian education.

High-caliber academic and moral training is the key to the salvation of this generation. For this and all of the other reasons previously outlined, it may well be said that the hope for this nation is the Christian school system.

EVOLUTION

■ Can an individual believe in creationism and evolution at the same time?

QUESTION:

CAN AN INDIVIDUAL BELIEVE IN CREATIONISM AND EVOLUTION AT THE SAME TIME?

ANSWER:

No, he cannot. If a person says he can, evidently he does not know the meaning of creation and the Bible, nor does he understand evolution. Thomas Henry Huxley (a contemporary of Darwin) said, "It is clear that the doctrine of evolution is directly antagonistic to that of creation . . . . Evolution, if consistently accepted, makes it impossible to believe in the Bible."

Spencer (another teacher) said that evolution is purely mechanical and antisupernatural.

Ernest Haeckel said, 'It entirely excludes the supernatural process — every prearranged and conscious act of a personal character."

Others could be named also, but I think that it is clear that no true evolutionist can be a Christian or a believer in the Bible. There is no place for God in evolution; hence, there is no need of a belief — in sin or a Saviour, heaven or hell. Those in the church who try to harmonize evolution with the Bible rule out God in spite of themselves and are enemies of both God and the church.

Not one single branch of organic evolution has ever been proved, much less the main theory. Actually, evolution is a bankrupt, speculative philosophy — it has never been, and is not now, a scientific fact.

SOME FALLACIES OF EVOLUTION

• Evolution accepts —
. . . heathen and pagan philosophers in preference to God, Christ, the Holy Spirit, and the Bible.
• Evolution nullifies —
. . . the idea of biblical creation by God. Blind force is substituted for the creative power of the personal God who created all things (Genesis 1:1).
• Evolution degrades —
. . . God's image to nothing more than a mere beast.
. . . man from creation by God in the image of God to a monkey ancestry.

99

• Evolution does away with —

. . . the fall of man, for how can a mere beast who has evolved steadily from a molecule to an intelligent being go backward and have a fall?

. . . Bible miracles and the supernatural in all its forms. The only miracle of power in evolution is the inherent force of molecules.

. . . the virgin birth, making it both impossible and unnecessary. It makes Christ a product of evolution in the same sense that it does all other men.

. . . the authority of the Bible as a real revelation from a personal and living God, making it a lie in regard not only to creation but to other doctrine as well.

• Evolution denies —

. . . the bodily resurrection of Christ and declares that it is contrary to the process of evolution.

. . . the atonement; for, according to evolution, there was no fall of man and, therefore, no sin for which to make atonement.

. . . the second advent of Christ and the final restoration and preservation of all things by the personal act of God.

For a person to argue that the Christian can accept evolution on the grounds that the Bible is not to be taken literally is a surrender to the foes of Christ, the Holy Spirit, the Bible, and all Christian teachings. This particular theory is anti-God, anti-Christ, anti-Bible, anti-Christian, and actually anti-intelligence.

WHAT A CHRISTIAN BELIEVES

The Christian must believe —

. . . that the Bible is the Word of God — not that it merely *contains* the Word of God, but that it *is* the Word of God.

. . . that God is a person who creates (brings into existence all material and spiritual substance) and that out of the created material He personally formed the worlds and each creature therein.

. . . that God created man in His own image and likeness in one day, fully mature and highly intelligent, not that he descended from molecules through the lower forms of life to monkey and finally man.

. . . that all angels and spirit-beings were created by God fully mature and intelligent (Psalm 104:4; Ezekiel 28:15; Colossians 1:15-18; Revelation 4:11).

. . . that God created man, animals, fish, fowls, and plants to reproduce themselves after their own kind (Genesis 1:20-31; 2:5-7, 19-25).

. . . that Jesus Christ is the Son of God and, as such, no other man is. The Christian must also believe that Jesus is *the Only Begotten* of the Father, not that He is *a* son of God, in the sense that all men are, but that He is *the* Son of God (I Timothy 3:16, Hebrews 1:1-3; Revelation 1:8-11).

. . . that the Holy Spirit is a person, separate and distinct from both the Father and the Son, and that all three persons of the Godhead have their own personal body, soul, and spirit and make up the divine Trinity (I John 5:7).

. . . that man is a sinner fallen from original righteousness and that he fell from an intelligent and responsible place as head of the present creation.

. . . that except for God's redemptive grace man is lost. Man is *not* the unfortunate victim of environment but, rather, is like he is as a result of the Fall.

. . . that man is justified by faith in the atoning blood of Jesus Christ, resulting in a supernatural regeneration from above (Matthew 1:21; John 3:18; Romans 5:1; II Corinthians 5:17; Ephesians 2:8,9).

. . . that the death of Christ was expiatory, not exemplary. He died for all men. His blood is the only atonement for sin, and by His stripes we are healed.

. . . that Jesus Christ rose bodily from the dead, not spiritually or as a spirit-being. He is alive forevermore in His earthly, resurrected, flesh-and-bone body and represents men before God as their High Priest and Saviour (Luke 24:30; John 10:17, 18; Acts 1:3).

. . . that all men who accept Christ and have conformed to God's plan for man will be saved, will be resurrected from the dead to immortality, and will help God administer the affairs of the universe forever (John 3:16; I Corinthians 6:2; II Timothy 2:12; Revelation 1:6; 22:4, 5).

. . . that all men who reject Christ and do not conform to God's plan will pay the eternal death penalty for sin, will be resurrected to immortality, and will be punished eternally in the lake of fire (Mark 16:15, 16; John 3:16; Revelation 14:9-11; 22:15).

A person cannot know the statements of both the Bible and

evolutionists and believe both, nor can he be neutral. A stand must be taken, either for God and the Bible or for evolution and all that evolution produces — which is only unbelief.

SOME FACTS ABOUT EVOLUTION

• The Bible —

. . . condemns the theory of both cosmic and organic evolution.

. . . declares that God created the heavens and the earth — in fact all things were created by Him (Revelation 4:11).

. . . declares (10 times in the first chapter of Genesis) that everything created by God was given power to reproduce *its own kind.* No one thing could break this law and produce any other kind. Since that law was written, thousands of years ago, it has never been broken. Now, after nearly 6,000 years, the law of reproduction is the same. The sponge is still a sponge and has not become an oyster. No lowly earthworm has ever turned into a spider; and no lizard, a crocodile. No bug or bird has ever been able to reproduce another kind except its own.

• It is a natural law that nothing reproduces anything greater than itself.

• No monkey has ever produced a man, and the missing link is still missing — and actually the link is all the way from "A" to "Z." This is quite remarkable in view of the fact that there are over 2 million species of plant and animal life. Each species proves the law of reproduction (each after its own kind) established by God.

• Science has proved that dead matter cannot generate life.

• Darwin's argument that plants and animals have within themselves tendencies to vary of their own accord in many and all directions to an unlimited degree has been disproved many times.

Some persons have mentioned the cavemen of the past ages as proof of evolution. Actually, there has never been any proof that cavemen existed. Of course, I am certain that men have lived in caves in the past as some live in caves today. But as far as animalistic, crawling primates, uttering some guttural language — half-man, half-monkey — there is not one iota of proof that such ever existed. Those things have been created out of the fertile minds of unbelief and supported by so-called specimens created out of plaster of paris. The movies, television, and much of literature suggest such — but it is only a suggestion.

There is not one scintilla or iota of scientific proof; rather the facts are that such never existed.

Most of the manufactured bones of prehistoric men are fakes. The Piltdown man, for example, was no man at all. It was made from two or three bits of a skull bone, a piece of a jawbone, and a tooth. It was finally acknowledged that these scraps did not belong to the skull and were those of a chimpanzee. The Java man was built in Java from a skull bone, a leg bone, and two molars. The rest was a concoction of plaster of paris. The Peking man of China was made from human skull fragments found in a cave. The Nebraska man was made from a single pig's tooth and said to be 1 million years old.

Such are the hoaxes in the name of science which are being passed upon our innocent boys and girls by many educators.

The theory of evolution is that all forms of life are derived by gradual modification from earlier and simpler forms or from one rudimentary form. It teaches a process in which something complex is developed by itself from a simple beginning. It accepts the existence of the cause or causes of the first substance and the force or forces working successive transformations from a lower to a higher form of matter and life.

Cosmic evolution claims that the vast material suns, moons, planets, and universes were formed by themselves from lower units of matter (atoms and molecules) through random chance, not the intervention of God.

Organic evolution teaches that the vegetable and animal kingdoms evolved from lower forms of life to what they are today. Evolutionists do not say from where the lower forms of life came. Their theory begins with matter or substance already in existence. They do not try to account for how these came to exist or how molecules got their inherent powers or how there came to be definite laws governing them so that they could produce without failure all things as we now have them. These theories do not show why there is such bitter hatred against the God of the Bible as being the Creator of all things.

The evolutionists teach that *hair* is but elongated scales of prehistoric animals. They teach that *legs* of all animals developed from warts on aboriginal amphibians. They teach that *eyes* are but an accidental development of freckles or blind amphibians that responded to the sun. They also teach that *ears* came about by the airwaves calling to spots on early reptiles. They teach that *man* came from monkeys. They teach that the vast *universes* came from a few molecules. They actually teach that *nothing* working on *nothing* by *nothing* through *nothing* for *nothing* begat *everything*!

No, a person cannot believe in evolution and creationism at the same time.

FAITH

■ Do all things work together to our good? For what should we praise the Lord?

■ We have heard it said that Christians today are more knowledgeable in the Word than even Peter, Paul, and the apostles. Is this true?

QUESTION:

*DO ALL THINGS WORK TOGETHER TO OUR GOOD?
FOR WHAT SHOULD WE PRAISE THE LORD?*

ANSWER:

*"We know that all things work together for good to them
that love God, to them who are the called according to his purpose"*
(Romans 8:28).

This is one of the most beautiful Scriptures in the Bible. It has been a
source of strength and consolation to so many Christians.

Since childhood I have heard sermons telling us that no matter what
happened, or how it happened, if we are Christians and love the Lord,
everything must work for our good. Satan has taken advantage of this
teaching and has caused problems for millions of God's children. Satan
causes sickness, so-called accidents, disturbances, and many times
outright chaos. We, as Christians, blunder in our thinking that everything
will turn out all right. However, have you noticed there are many times
when it does not?

I realize some of you will read these words in open-mouthed
astonishment. It is time we ask some questions, and receive some
answers — and quit burying our head in the sand. Satan delights in
ignorance. He can have a field day in this realm.

AUTHORITY OF THE WORD

There is a way that Romans 8:28 can be put into motion and make it
mean exactly what it says — everything working together for our good.

Let us back up a few verses and look at the passage in context:
*"Likewise the Spirit also helpeth our infirmities: for we know not what
we should pray for as we ought: but the Spirit itself maketh intercession
for us with groanings which cannot be uttered. And he that searcheth
the hearts knoweth what is the mind of the Spirit, because he
maketh intercession for the saints according to the will of God"*
(Romans 8:26, 27).

This means that when we, as Christians, face problems, we should
pray those problems through in the Spirit. If we do not know how to pray
about them (and oftentimes we do not), we should pray (about the
problem) in other tongues. The Lord Jesus knows the mind of the Spirit;

and as the Spirit relates to Him our problems (as we pray in other tongues), then intercession can be made for the saints according to the will of God. Our *"infirmities"* (which means, in the Greek, "physical, mental, moral weaknesses, or flaws") are helped and solved. Then, and only then, will everything work together for our good.

Wrong thinking about Romans 8:28 can hinder us severely because we never give effort to resisting the devil, never pray the problem through (in the Spirit), blindly thinking it is working to our good. Consequently, the sick get sicker, the poor get poorer, and the distressed get more distressed. However, when the first attack of Satan comes (in whatever fashion), if we will obey Romans 8:26, 27, then victory can be ours.

A PERSONAL EXPERIENCE

Sometime ago Satan devised a plan to wreck the *Campmeeting Hour.* Evil men made every effort actually to put us off the air or severely cripple us. It was not a small thing. The plan was so well devised and so large that at first it overwhelmed me. I could see no way out. Now what if I had just said, "Well, it will work to my good" and let it go at that? We would have lost over half of our stations, maybe all of them, and the *Campmeeting Hour* would have ceased to work for God. That is what Satan wanted. If I had taken the position that is commonly taught in regard to Romans 8:28, he would have succeeded. However, I went before the Lord, and even though the attack was so gigantic that I did not even know how to start in prayer or what to ask God to do, Jesus knew. I prayed in the Spirit that particular day for about an hour. I could sense the Lord several times as He actually changed the languages. At the end of that hour, a peace filled my heart. I did not know how God would do it, but I knew somehow it must work for my good — and that is exactly what happened. God completely turned the thing around, and instead of Satan's devious device hurting us, it actually helped us (worked together for our good).

Satan does everything he can to twist the Word. If you have been suffering and, it seems, there is no letup — you have consoled yourself with the thought that no matter how bad it is, it will still work to your good — why not first obey the Scripture exactly as it ought to be obeyed? Pray that problem through in the Spirit, then watch the situation change.

ERROR IN PRAISE TEACHING

There have been quite a number of books written in the past few years about giving thanks (praise) to the Lord. Of course, one of the greatest secrets of spiritual strength and victory is praising God. I believe praise and faith linked together is the key to answered prayer — a person cannot praise the Lord enough. We simply should praise Him all of the time. *"Let every thing that hath breath praise the Lord"* (Psalm 150:6).

I read a book sometime ago (there are quite a number of similar ones out) instructing people to praise the Lord for everything — even the bad things. After I read it, I sensed in my spirit that something was wrong. It sounded religious, and to the untrained spiritual eye it appeared to be the right thing to do. (The devil always baits his traps so subtly.) This particular book was derived from Ephesians 5:20 — *"Giving thanks always for all things unto God and the Father in the name of our Lord Jesus Christ."* The book went on to say — and multiple thousands of people have been duped by this — we should thank the Lord for such tragedies as sickness, car wrecks, heart attacks, cancer, et cetera (from verse 20, *"Giving thanks always for all things"*).

Of course, this is actually not what the Scripture means. It means we should give thanks always unto God for the things he has done (not the devil). God is not the author of sickness, pain, accidents, et cetera.

We are to thank Him for all the things, all the times, He has done for us. We know: *"Every good gift and every perfect gift is from above, and cometh down from the Father of lights, with whom is no variableness, neither shadow of turning"* (James 1:17). Now it is permissible when trouble comes to thank God for the opportunity of using His name and His Word to obtain deliverance from that particular trouble. However, to thank Him for the trouble itself is to do so in error. I will attempt to give you the reasons for it.

GOD NOT THE AUTHOR

How must God feel when we falsely lay to His charge such terrible things as cancer, automobile accidents, et cetera? By way of illustration, what do you think the President of the United States of America would do if I started thanking him for the Mafia? After a while a Secret Service agent would knock at my door and would tell me not to link the

President's name anymore with such things. Yet, we have Christians throughout the country thanking God for all kinds of terrible things. To be frank with you, He had nothing to do with them and does not enjoy being linked with them.

How would you feel if someone came to you and thanked you for a car wreck in which you had absolutely no part? You would not be too happy about it, and neither is our Heavenly Father! When will the church realize that God does not put cancer on people or cause them to have car wrecks, heart attacks, divorces, and broken homes and that He does not appreciate it when Christians ignorantly, or otherwise, thank Him for them?

PRAISING GOD FOR THE DEVIL'S WORKS

If you are going to praise God for everything in the way some people believe (and the way the Scripture has been twisted), let us do just that. Let us praise Him for car wrecks, cancer, the devil, murder. Let us go a step farther and praise Him for the people who are in hell and will burn there forever. Let us also praise Him for sin. You see how ridiculous this becomes? If you are going to twist the Scripture and make it mean that we are literally to praise God for everything He does, everything the devil does, and everything anyone else may do, you should include those things I have mentioned. Nowhere in the Bible are we told to thank God, or to praise God, for the works of Satan.

What sense does it make to praise God for sickness and then ask Him to heal you? If you are praising God for it, then the devil knows you will not try to gain victory over it.

A brother wrote me sometime ago after he had read one of the books that tells us to praise God for everything. He was upset because I was telling the people not to praise God for such things. He said he had finally convinced his people to accept everything that came their way and to praise God for it. This is just what the devil wants, because then he can cause all kinds of problems.

I praise my God continually for everything He does, and I hate everything the devil does. I will never insult my Heavenly Father by praising Him for sickness, disease, or car wrecks. I will hate these things with all my strength, and will be so thankful that I can use the name of Jesus to gain victory over them. Praise the Lord!

GIVING THANKS IN EVERYTHING

Now giving thanks *in* everything is vastly different from giving thanks *for* everything that comes along (from the devil or God). No matter what the devil puts on us in the midst of tribulation, we are to continue to give thanks to God (not for the problem, but in worship). A beautiful example of this is, *"Although the fig tree shall not blossom, neither shall fruit be in the vines; the labour of the olive shall fail, and the fields shall yield no meat; the flock shall be cut off from the fold, and there shall be no herd in the stalls: Yet I will rejoice in the Lord, I will joy in the God of my salvation"* (Habakkuk 3:17-19). We are to keep praising God *in* every problem, but not *for* the problem itself.

[Note: For a more in-depth look at this subject you may order our booklet, The Word, the Will, and the Wisdom.*]*

QUESTION:

WE HAVE HEARD IT SAID THAT CHRISTIANS TODAY ARE MORE KNOWLEDGEABLE IN THE WORD THAN EVEN PETER, PAUL, AND THE APOSTLES. IS THIS TRUE?

ANSWER:

Actually, this is the situation. Some persons would advocate the following as documentary evidence of the fact that we are more knowledgeable in the Word today: (1) Mankind has lived through 2,000 years of development that the apostles did not have. (2) The canon of Scripture was not completed when the various apostles wrote their particular books of the New Testament. Of course, this explanation makes no sense, and I will explain.

HOLY SPIRIT INSPIRED

First, the apostles (including the Apostle Paul) did not write of their own knowledge. They wrote as they were inspired of the Holy Spirit, sometimes not even understanding the words they themselves were penning (see I Peter 1:10-12; II Peter 1:20, 21). So, a lack of cultivated knowledge of the (developed) Word was absolutely insignificant.

Neither was it important (regarding what was being written) that the canon of Scripture was incomplete at the time.

TIMELESS

Also, the New Testament (and especially the writings of the Apostle Paul) is the New Covenant and, as such, is timeless. It was applicable when it was written; it was applicable 1,000 years ago; it is still applicable today. If Jesus tarries His coming another 100 years, these Scriptures will still apply just as much as they do at this very moment.

TEACHING ERROR

The basic source for some of this teaching is the hyper-faith movement; naturally it is error.

Sometime ago I wrote an article on "The Balanced Faith Life," taking great care to use the Word of God as my foundation. I attempted to show (from the Word of God) that the Christian life is not always the proverbial bed of roses, that there will be trials and tests. I cited the apostles as examples.

Paul, after having suffered basically every kind of inconvenience, disturbance, and problem possible for a human being to suffer, ultimately was beheaded in Rome. I gave, as an example, the fact that all of the disciples, with the exception of (possibly) John, died the martyr's death. Of course, this is irrefutable truth. The consecration and dedication of these individuals are examples for all peoples of all time.

Individuals who are teaching what we are dealing with in this question have not been able to counter my (balanced faith) message by the Word of God. Their conclusion, rather, is that if Paul, Peter, and others (and some persons even say the Lord Jesus Christ!) had been privileged to have the full revelation that we have today, they would not have had to suffer the trials and problems they encountered.

Not only is this error, it borders on blasphemy! It may be done in ignorance, but it is still irreverent and insulting to the Word and power of Almighty God.

DANGEROUS TEACHING

Terrible and sometimes insurmountable problems are caused when innocent and trusting people absorb this dribble dished out by these hyper-faith teachers.

For example, they suddenly think they have progressed beyond the Word of God; no longer is it necessary that they take the Word of God as an example because they are more developed in knowledge than its writers (such as the Apostle Paul and John the Beloved, to name two).

This is one of Satan's age-old tactics, and is exactly the direction taken by hyper-faith teachings. What started out as a simple ego trip has led to a spiritual superiority which fosters the idea that modern man knows more than the apostles of old and, consequently, does not have to look at their life as an example. What fallacy!

This is how the Christian Scientists, Mormons, Jehovah's Witnesses, Seventh Day Adventists, and other cults were started. You see, when error is propagated as truth, then it must be continually expanded in order to satisfy its adherents and to justify its existence. Truth fades into the background until it is totally hidden in the shadows.

The Old Testament cites difficulties, problems, and even overt sins engaged in by followers of God in the pre-Christian era. *"Now these things were our examples, to the intent we should not lust after evil things, as they also lusted"* (I Corinthians 10:6). Not in the same vein, but most definitely, the New Testament is also our example.

I personally feel this being more knowledgeable in the Word than its writers is some of the most dangerous teaching coming out of this element to date. Its adherents will suffer untold difficulty if they pursue this line of teaching.

"If any man shall take away from the words of the book of this prophecy, God shall take away his part out of the book of life, and out of the holy city, and from the things which are written in this book" (Revelation 22:19). This is speaking not only of the book of Revelation but of the entire Word of God.

QUESTION:

FALL OF MAN

■ What did God mean when He told Adam in Genesis 2:16, 17 that they could eat of every tree of the garden except the tree of the knowledge of good and evil, and in the day that they did eat of that tree, they would surely die? We know that Adam and Eve did not die at that time. What did God mean? . . . The second part of my question is this: Where are the dead? What happens to an individual the moment he dies?

QUESTION:

WHAT DID GOD MEAN WHEN HE TOLD ADAM IN GENESIS 2:16, 17 THAT THEY COULD EAT OF EVERY TREE OF THE GARDEN EXCEPT THE TREE OF THE KNOWLEDGE OF GOOD AND EVIL, AND IN THE DAY THAT THEY DID EAT OF THAT TREE, THEY WOULD SURELY DIE? WE KNOW THAT ADAM AND EVE DID NOT DIE AT THAT TIME. WHAT DID GOD MEAN? . . . THE SECOND PART OF MY QUESTION IS THIS: WHERE ARE THE DEAD? WHAT HAPPENS TO AN INDIVIDUAL THE MOMENT HE DIES?

ANSWER:

I will endeavor to answer your question as you have asked it. It is quite detailed and I will do my best, prayerfully so, to answer it in such a way that you will understand what God was talking about when He spoke to Adam and Eve in Genesis 2. I will also address your question regarding the state of the dead.

DIFFERENT KINDS OF DEATH

There are several different kinds of death in Scripture. There is *physical* death, which means the separation of the inner man from the outer man; in other words, the soul and the spirit become separate from the body. Then, there is *spiritual* death, and that is the kind of death that God was speaking of when He talked with Adam and Eve in Genesis 2. Spiritual death means that man is separated from God because of sin. A person spiritually dead can, at the same time, be physically alive. By the same token, an individual can be dead physically and alive in hell. In other words, he would be conscious in the soul and spirit awaiting the second resurrection of damnation. The third kind of death is referred to in Scripture as the *"second death"* (mentioned in Revelation 2:11 through 20:6). It means eternal death and eternal separation from God in the lake of fire.

Now, when God was talking with Adam and Eve in the Garden of Eden so long, long ago, He did not mean that the moment they partook of that particular tree of the knowledge of good and evil it would be like poison to them and they would fall over and die. He meant that they would be separated from God. Actually, many times in the Bible when the word "death" is used, the word "separation" could be inserted in its place and would give even better meaning to the statement.

So, that is the kind of death God was speaking of when He spoke to Adam that day so long ago. Actually, Adam lived to be 930 years old — which brings us to another great truth. Separation from God (or spiritual death) will cause physical death as well. Adam would never have died physically if he had not first died spiritually. Actually, the moment, the exact instant, he partook of the tree of the knowledge of good and evil, Adam died a spiritual death. In other words, he was separated from God.

The Apostle Paul said, *"[He] that liveth in pleasure is dead while [he] liveth"* (I Timothy 5:6). He meant, of course, spiritual death. In other words, people are separated from God because of their sin.

IMMEDIATELY AFTER DEATH

The second part of your question, which concerns the individual immediately after death, is simple to answer. I will answer it first and then give the scriptural references.

The moment an *unsaved* person dies, that person's soul and spirit instantly go to hell. The body, of course, goes back to the grave where it eventually returns to dust to await the resurrection of damnation, which is called the *"second death."*

The moment a *Christian* dies, his soul and spirit instantly go to be with the Lord Jesus Christ. The body, of course, goes to the grave to await the first resurrection (I Thessalonians 4:16, 17).

Now let us look at the scriptural references. When an individual dies, the body is placed in the grave where it goes back to dust (Genesis 3:19; Ecclesiastes 3:19-21; James 2:26). The body remains dead, which means separated from the inner man, until the future resurrection day when the body will be made immortal (I Corinthians 15:35-54). The soul and spirit continue to be alive (being immortal) whether in heaven or hell, where they also await the resurrection when the body will be reunited with the soul and the spirit.

At physical death, the soul and spirit leave the body (James 2:26). If a person is saved, his soul and spirit go immediately to heaven at death to await the resurrection of the body (Luke 20:38; John 11:25, 26; II Corinthians 5:8; Ephesians 3:15; 4:8-10; Philippians 1:21-24; Hebrews 12:22, 23; Revelation 6:9-11). If the person is a sinner (unsaved), his soul and spirit go to hell at death to await the resurrection of the body (Isaiah 14:9; Luke 16:19-31; II Peter 2:9; Revelation 20:11-15).

FALSE TEACHINGS

Some cults teach that the grave is hell and hell is the grave, but this is untrue. These people change the Bible to suit themselves and gain converts who are always glad to accept any method of escape from the reality of hell. In the Greek language (the language of the New Testament and the Old Testament Septuagint) different words are used for "hell" and the "grave." *Gehenna* means "hell" or "eternal fire"; *mnemeion* means "grave," "sepulchre," or "tomb." Just as in our language these are two separate and distinct subjects.

In the Hebrew language the term *sheol* is used for both "grave" and "hell." A single Hebrew term translates both words. It was the context in which the term was used that expressed whether a person was speaking of "grave" or "hell." *Sheol* is translated "hell" when it refers to a place of punishment for the wicked, but "grave" when it refers to a place of paradise for the saints. We may, but no Jewish Christian would ever, confuse "grave" with "hell," even though the two thoughts are both expressed by the same Hebrew term, *sheol*. There is an impassable gulf between paradise and punishment, because death ends the opportunity to choose. (Read the account in Luke 19:16-31.)

Another word, the Greek *hades*, is variously translated "grave," "hell," or "pit"; it connotes the grim aspect of death. Hell, the place of retribution for the lost, is eternal (Matthew 18:8, 9) and marked by unquenchable fire (Matthew 3:12; Mark 9:44), lake of fire (Revelation 20:14), living death (Mark 9:48), torment (Revelation 14:10), outer darkness, weeping, wailing, and gnashing of teeth (Matthew 8:12; 22:13; 25:30).

Other persons try to tell us there is no such thing as an immortal soul. They say that the term "immortal soul" is not found in the Bible, and of course that part is true. (Neither is the term "rapture" in the Bible, but we believe that a rapture is going to take place.)

We believe the soul and the spirit, called the inner man, are immortal. By "immortal" we mean that they will continue in full consciousness between death and the resurrection of the body, and then in the new resurrected body throughout eternity.

Some people believe in "psychopannychism" or "soul sleep" — a doctrine that teaches the soul will sleep with the body in the earth until the resurrection. Of course, this is contrary to the Scriptures. The Word of God teaches that, instantly, when a person dies, his soul and spirit go to heaven if he is saved (II Corinthians 5:6-8) and to hell if he is unsaved (Luke 16:19-31).

All Scriptures used by cults to prove "soul sleep" refer to death of the body, which knows nothing in the grave (Ecclesiastes 9:5, 10).

I hope that we have answered your question satisfactorily. May God bless you!

QUESTION:

GOSPEL PREACHING

■ What about the hundreds of millions of people on planet earth that have never heard of Jesus Christ? Of course, that would include the billions that have lived before us. Will God send those people to hell even though they never had an opportunity to hear?

■ Is it scriptural for a woman to be a preacher?

■ Why don't you preach more love instead of messages that seem sharply to criticize or condemn?

QUESTION:

*WHAT ABOUT THE HUNDREDS OF MILLIONS OF PEOPLE
ON PLANET EARTH THAT HAVE NEVER HEARD OF JESUS
CHRIST? OF COURSE, THAT WOULD INCLUDE THE
BILLIONS THAT HAVE LIVED BEFORE US. WILL
GOD SEND THOSE PEOPLE TO HELL EVEN THOUGH
THEY NEVER HAD AN OPPORTUNITY TO HEAR?*

ANSWER:

I will do my best to answer your question as you have asked it.

At the present time, there are 4.5 billion people on planet earth, and it has been said that nearly half of these people have never heard the name of Jesus.

There are over 1 billion people in the country of China alone, most of whom have never heard of the Lord Jesus Christ.

I remember standing at the harbor in Shanghai, surrounded by thousands of Chinese, and Frances asked a little 14-year-old boy if he had ever heard of Jesus. He understood English and had taught himself to speak a little English. I will never forget his expression. He did not even know what Frances was talking about. We tried to explain it, and before we left he said, "I want to know more about Jesus." Yet the sad fact is that he had never heard the most beautiful name the world will ever know . . . the name of the Lord Jesus Christ.

When you realize that hundreds of millions of people have never heard, somehow that horrible fact, it seems, crashes in on you with the weight of the world. How tragic it is not to know anything about God, not to enjoy companionship with the Holy Spirit, never to know that precious saving grace of Jesus Christ, and never to understand that He *"daily loadeth us with benefits"* (Psalm 68:19) and *"satisfieth thy mouth with good things"* (Psalm 103:5)!

Actually, I would as soon be dead as to have to live in this world without God, and yet . . . nearly half the population of the world know nothing about the Lord Jesus Christ.

A QUESTION OFTEN ASKED

What will happen to the people who have never heard of Jesus? Is it fair that God would send these people to hell when they know nothing of

God, they know nothing of Jesus Christ, and they know nothing of His power to save? Really, they never even had an opportunity to hear. No preacher was ever sent. They have never heard a Gospel message, never read the words of a Holy Bible, or listened to a preacher proclaim the glad tidings of great joy. They know nothing about heaven, and they know nothing about hell. They know nothing about sin or salvation; they have never heard of regeneration, justification, sanctification, or mercy extended by a Heavenly Father. The statement of Jesus' shed blood cleansing and washing all their sins away would be anathema to them.

What about these people? What will happen to them? Where do they stand in the eyes of God?

Admittedly, this is a question with far-reaching effects, and it is not an easy one to answer or even to understand. However, due to the tremendous eternal value of each soul, we must address ourselves to it.

THE GREAT COMMISSION

Jesus laid down His last command when He said, *"Go ye into all the world, and preach the gospel to every creature"* (Mark 16:15). This command is called the Great Commission. He went on to say, *"He that believeth and is baptized shall be saved; but he that believeth not shall be damned"* (verse 16).

The carrying out of the Great Commission to preach the Gospel to all people on this planet is the mandate dictating the spending of multiple millions of dollars each year by this organization to get the Gospel out by television, radio, the printed page, the building of churches and Bible schools, the sending of missionaries, and the building of schools for the children. It is the same mandate affecting the massive hundreds of millions of dollars spent on all kinds of missionary efforts by virtually every evangelistic church on the face of the earth.

The Gospel is the most important business in the world; it is the biggest business in the world, and one of which every single Christian has a part.

I remember Mark Buntain saying, "As long as the greatest export of the United States (and Canada) is the Gospel of Jesus Christ, the heels of invaders will never walk upon American soil." I have never forgotten that, and I believe it is true. Now, the Great Commission is not delegated to just certain people; everyone must help bear this tremendous responsibility. It is not a burden we bear, but a responsibility we feel. Actually, it is a joy to tell men and women about Jesus Christ. Albeit, the responsibility is great.

We look at many nations of the world today, and they are locked in by the Godless horror of Communism; others are bound by dictatorships that prevent the Gospel of Jesus Christ from being preached. It seems that Satan has effectively locked up hundreds of millions of people with no opportunity to hear the Gospel; and yet, little by little even in these countries — such as the Soviet Union and Communist China — radio programming is being beamed in, and Gospel workers in many cases are finding ways to enter.

Sadly, though, even in countries that are open to the Gospel, there are still millions of people that do not know, and indeed have not heard of Jesus Christ. *"The harvest truly is great, but the labourers are few"* (Luke 10:2).

OUR RESPONSIBILITY

God has already physically accomplished everything that heaven can do. The mission is now up to us; it is our responsibility. We must do all within our power, as quickly as possible, to reach with the Gospel the exact number of people that Jesus mentioned: *"every creature"* (Mark 16:15). It is equally the responsibility of every single, solitary individual, and yet I fear that while some people are privileged to hear it over and over again, others never have the opportunity to hear the first time.

Sometime ago Morris Plotts illustrated this truth so graphically when he was preaching in our church here in Baton Rouge (Family Worship Center). Telling the story of Jesus multiplying the loaves and fishes to feed the thousands that were there before Him, he asked, "What would have happened if the Master had told the disciples to seat all the people in rows of fifties and hundreds — which they did — and then as He multiplied the loaves and fishes and gave them to the disciples to pass out among all the thousands sitting there, if they had gone repeatedly to those in the front rows and given *nothing* to those in the back rows? What do you think would have happened?"

Of course, it did not take place that way. All of the people were equally fed and went away equally filled. Today I am concerned that what Morris Plotts suggested is exactly what *is* happening. Those on the front rows (United States, Canada, South Africa, and other countries we could add) are being fed over and over again while those in the back rows (the Third World countries and many others) receive little or nothing at all. Is this fair? No, it is *not* fair. Still again, the responsibility is ours; we cannot shift it. Yet instead of accepting their share of this responsibility, it seems, so many Christians are unconcerned.

Oh, how I thank God for those who *are* concerned, those who do their best to take this Gospel of Jesus Christ all over the world, to see to it that every individual has at least the opportunity to hear it once! Yet there are so few of these individuals. Now let us look at the answer to your question.

ONLY JESUS

There is only one way to be saved, only one way to get to heaven. No matter where a person lives, no matter who that person may be, there is still only one way to come to God. *"Neither is there salvation in any other: for there is none other name under heaven given among men, whereby we must be saved"* (Acts 4:12). In other words, a person can come to God only through Jesus Christ.

I remember sometime ago a man who heard me preach was somewhat disconcerted when I made a statement to this effect. I had made it crystal clear there was no other way to reach God except through Jesus Christ. He took exception to this. He argued that a person could reach God through Shintoism, Muhammadanism, Buddhism, or any one of 101 ways. Of course, this is not true. Hundreds of millions of people will go to hell simply because they (erroneously) thought they could get to God some way other than through Jesus Christ; but there is *no other way*.

The reason is simple: *Jesus* is the One who came from heaven. It was *Jesus* who died upon the cross of Calvary for our sins. It was *Jesus* who defeated death, hell, and the grave. It was *Jesus* who rose from the dead for our victory. No one else can make that boast. Buddha could not. Confucius could not. Muhammad could not. No other prophet, priest, or proclaimer has been able to say he rose from the grave. Only Jesus!

Jesus made it abundantly clear, *"I am the way, the truth, and the life: no man cometh unto the Father, but by me"* (John 14:6). *"He that entereth not by the door into the sheepfold, but climbeth up some other way, the same is a thief and a robber . . . . I am the door: by me if any man enter in, he shall be saved"* (John 10:1, 9). There is no other way (John 6:66-69)!

Still yet, the question looms large before us: What about those who have never heard of Jesus, those who have had no opportunity to hear?

THE FIRST CHAPTER OF ROMANS

"Because that which may be known of God is manifest in them; for God hath shewed it unto them. For the invisible things of him from the creation of the world are clearly seen, being understood by the things that are made, even his eternal power and Godhead; so that they are without excuse" (Romans 1:19, 20).

The conscience of a person — wherever that person may be and whatever time frame he may have lived in — is either a witness of obedience or of condemnation for disobedience, proving God has not left men without sufficient light to justify or condemn in the judgment. The moral and spiritual nature of men *"shew the work of the law written in their hearts, their conscience also bearing witness"* (Romans 2:15).

Now, what is this telling us? No, it does not at all mean that the heathen who have never heard of Jesus Christ can be saved by following their conscience. We still have to go back to the written law of God, that every person must come through Jesus Christ.

It means that if a person desires to know about God, even though he has not heard by the preaching of the Word about the Lord Jesus Christ, he can look about him and know by this world's system — the sun, the moon, the stars, even this very earth — that there is a God. In other words, that there has to be divine power behind creation, that it did not just happen.

Then the person's conscience will oftentimes lead him in respect to good and evil, although this cannot be a trustworthy guide all the time because a person's *"conscience"* can become *"seared"* (I Timothy 4:2) until he becomes twisted in his thinking. Yet, basically, the conscience and the creation do point toward God.

In many heathen countries there are people who have never heard a Gospel message, and yet their heart has cried out in its own respective way to God. They have cried out for something greater than what they have.

As a result, even though many of these people did not have the opportunity to hear a Gospel message or to be told the way of salvation, they have been led by the Holy Spirit to find a man of God to tell them the beautiful plan of salvation. True, these instances are sometimes few and far between, but this does happen.

I heard A. N. Trotter tell once of a native that came into a church in Cape Palmas, Liberia, West Africa, one Sunday morning. He said that the native lived several hundred miles away, and although he did not know of God, he had tried to pray (to God) as best he could. Then an angel appeared unto him. Of course, he did not know it was an angel, and he described it just as a figure that was glorious and wonderful, that told him to go in a certain direction and he would help him find God.

This man ran most of the way. He ran day and night, stopping only long enough to rest a little; and when he reached Cape Palmas, the angel appeared again and told him this was the town.

He saw what he thought was a church (and actually it was). With his limited knowledge of such things, he (naturally) started to go into the church, but the angel appeared again and said, "No, this is not the place." He then continued running down the streets until he found the church of which Brother Trotter spoke. The angel appeared again and said, "This is the one." The native went in and was gloriously saved. After being saved, he attended Bible school for some two years, then went back and built quite a number of churches for the Lord Jesus Christ and won quite a number of souls to the Lord.

However, for every one who may be saved in this particular manner, millions more will never take the time to seek the truth, and consequently, they will be lost.

So this is not God's ideal way of carrying out the Great Commission.

A MERCIFUL GOD

Someone may ask, "But if the heathen have never heard, wouldn't a merciful God allow them into heaven?" If this would be the case, then we should recall every missionary, we should tear down every church and stop preaching the Gospel, we should not print any more Christian literature, or broadcast any more Gospel radio or television programs.

If keeping people ignorant of the Gospel will guarantee their salvation, then the best thing we could do would be never to preach the Gospel, thereby not allowing anyone to know about Jesus Christ, and thereby guaranteeing their salvation and making heaven their eternal home. Of course, we know this is fallacy. The Lord *"now commandeth all men every where to repent"* (Acts 17:30).

No, ignorance of the Gospel does not give an automatic passport into heaven.

THE GOSPEL OF SALVATION

Let me reiterate: (1) There is only one way to get to heaven and that is through Jesus Christ. (2) God commands *"all men every where to repent"* (Acts 17:30). (3) Even though God deals with man through his conscience and the things He has created, the only way to reach man is to carry out the Great Commission of our Lord and Saviour.

"For whosoever shall call upon the name of the Lord shall be saved. How then shall they call on him in whom they have not believed? and how shall they believe in him of whom they have not heard? and how shall they hear without a preacher? And how shall they preach, except they be sent? . . . So then faith cometh by hearing, and hearing by the word of God" (Romans 10:13-17).

THE JUDGE OF ALL THE EARTH

When Abraham stood on the plains of Mamre and talked with the great God of the heavens, God told him that because of the terrible sin of Sodom and Gomorrah He must destroy these twin cities and all therein. Abraham responded, *"That be far from thee to do after this manner, to slay the righteous with the wicked: and that the righteous should be as the wicked, that be far from thee: Shall not the Judge of all the earth do right?"* (Genesis 18:25).

In closing, I must say this. God is eternally just and fair. He is eternally kind and compassionate. He is the personification of love. *"God is love"* (I John 4:8). He has never done anything that is cruel, inhuman, hurtful, or spiteful. *"As I live, saith the Lord God, I have no pleasure in the death of the wicked; but that the wicked turn from his way and live: turn ye, turn ye from your evil ways; for why will ye die? . . . Have I any pleasure at all that the wicked should die? saith the Lord God: and not that he should return from his ways, and live? . . . Yet ye say, The way of the Lord is not equal. Hear now . . . Is not my way equal? are not your ways unequal?"* (Ezekiel 33:11, 18:23, 25).

So, we are faced with two things here:

First, the obligation of taking this great Gospel message to the whole world is not on God's shoulders; it is on ours. The responsibility belongs to us. What His answer to us at the judgment seat of Christ will be if we have not done our best, only God can tell! It is an awesome and great responsibility. We must do all that we can do. *"Yet if thou warn the wicked, and he turn not from his wickedness, nor from his wicked way, he shall die in his iniquity; but thou hast delivered thy soul . . . but his blood will I require at thine hand"* (Ezekiel 3:19, 20). I have to wonder how many Christians will stand before God at the judgment seat of Christ with the blood of millions of people on their hands.

Second, I cannot answer for the multiple millions of people that never have had the opportunity to hear about Jesus; they know nothing about His saving grace and love. Even though I may be doing everything I can to get the Gospel to them, I cannot reach all of them, and neither can you. So, I will have to leave that to God. I will have to leave it to His mercy and His grace, knowing as Abraham, uttered so long, long ago, *"Shall not the Judge of all the earth do right?"* (Genesis 18:25).

QUESTION:

IS IT SCRIPTURAL FOR A WOMAN TO BE A PREACHER?

ANSWER:

Yes, it is scriptural for a woman (or anyone whom God may call) to be a minister of the Gospel, but there needs to be some clarification on the matter.

First of all, God can call whomever He desires to preach His Gospel. The color of a person's skin, the sex (male or female), background — none of these things matter. Neither does it matter what vocation a person may have been in prior to the time he was saved. Second, God would never violate His Word, and there is nothing in His Word that would hinder anyone with the above-noted characteristics from being used of God in ministry.

AUTHORITY OF THE WORD

Even though it is perfectly proper and scriptural for a woman to be a preacher of the Gospel, certain limitations I feel must be imposed upon this calling.

A woman may be a missionary, a Sunday School teacher, an evangelist, a pastor, or serve in any calling for that matter that God would bestow upon a man. Yet I would be remiss if I did not recognize the limitations that should be adhered to in such cases. To fail to acknowledge those limitations could cause an imbalance in the plan of God with ensuing difficulties and problems within the body of Christ.

It is God's divine order and plan for the man to be the head of the family — and to be the head of God's work on earth. Man was created first and was given dominion over the fish of the sea, the fowl of the air, and so forth (Genesis 1:26). Then God provided man a wife to be a help meet (Genesis 2:18). After the Fall woman was told, *"Thy desire shall be to thy husband, and he shall rule over thee"* (Genesis 3:16), implying perhaps that Eve had learned her lesson and would consider Adam in her future decisions and actions.

If you will notice, even though it was Eve who failed and suffered the terrible consequences (which also included her husband and all future mankind as well), it was Adam, not Eve, whom God called for an accounting (Genesis 3:6-9). God called the person that was in charge, and that was Adam.

THE FEMINIST MOVEMENT

There is a strong push in the United States (and possibly Canada) to circumvent and disavow the laws that God gave in the beginning and that are still valid today. These efforts, fostered by the feminist movement, to put woman in a position that God never intended for her, will cause serious psychological problems for those women lending their support to such actions. Great hurt can be done to the family and to the human race in general.

This is not to say that the woman is not to have rights (just as the man has rights) or to imply that God intended that the woman be a lesser creature. Actually, it has been said that God made Eve from Adam's side (Genesis 2:21-24) for a specific reason — not from man's head to be lorded over or from his feet to be trampled upon, but from his side to be equal with him, from under his arm to be protected by him, and from near his heart to be loved by him. That is a beautiful and appropriate analysis of woman's place with man. No effort to circumvent the plan of God regarding the distinctive roles of men and women today can ever come to a fruitful conclusion. Such will always bring the difficulty, sorrow, and heartache that accompany the opposing of God's plan for the human race.

WOMEN PREACHERS

Paul said, *"I suffer not a woman to teach, nor to usurp authority over the man, but to be in silence"* (I Timothy 2:12). The key to this Scripture are the two words *"usurp authority."* It is not wrong for a woman to teach; if it were, it would be wrong for her to teach even the little children of kindergarten or elementary school age in Sunday School.

It is perfectly proper for a woman to teach children even into the teen years. Qualified women do an excellent job, possibly much of the time even better than men would do. It is also proper for women to teach adult Sunday School classes *providing* there are no men available who are capable of teaching them. Likewise, there is nothing wrong in women evangelizing, pastoring, or performing any of these ministries, and God can certainly call them to do so — once again, *providing* there are no men available capable of occupying the position.

In a local church where there are qualified men to teach adult Sunday School classes attended by men as well as women, the church would be stronger if men filled those positions. Of course, it is proper and acceptable in all churches (or anywhere actually) for a woman to teach a ladies Bible class.

When it comes to pastoring a church, once again in some areas of the country where there is no man available to do the job, a woman could certainly fill that position. However, a man who has the touch of God on his life (in any area of the nation, or anywhere in the world) ought to occupy the position of leadership. This is God's way.

There are some few women serving as evangelists. Actually, the church with which I am ordained has a few women preachers. While I respect and love them, at the same time (I am positive I will receive some criticism for what I am about to say) I feel that it is not God's best order of events for a woman to serve as an evangelist. When a woman puts herself in a position such as this, she is in some way usurping authority over the man. Now in some parts of the world it may well be that God does not have a man to fill the role. In that case a woman may step right in and do the work with tremendous results and, we believe, the blessings of God.

Whenever a woman occupies a position of leadership in the work of God when there are qualified men that could assume the role, it is not wrong, or sinful, or disobedient to God, but the work of God is weakened. (If a person reads I Timothy 2:11-15, he may better understand this.) The ideal situation in the work of God is that the man be the preacher of the Gospel and that his wife help him in the various functions of the church. This is God's way; and when that order is reversed, it does not make for a healthy situation.

Not only is this true in the work of God; but whenever you see a woman that is the strong, dominant personality in the family, you will find a family that is weakened considerably. Admittedly, there are many families where the woman has no choice but to be the leader — simply because her husband chooses not to fill the role. This could be a problem of personality or lack of authority or leadership ability. In cases like this God will help that woman in her effort to provide a Christian home, but this does not negate the ideal situation that God has outlined in His Word.

WOMEN SILENCED IN CHURCH

Now I realize there are many persons who teach it is never correct for a woman to preach, teach, or so forth. Even in the passage we have just discussed (I Timothy 2:11-15), the key is submission to authority. Paul was endeavoring to teach in his letter to Timothy that the woman is to be subject to her husband.

We read, *"Let your women keep silence in the churches: for it is not permitted unto them to speak; but they are commanded to be under obedience, as also saith the law"* (I Corinthians 14:34). Some persons take this to mean it is not even proper for a woman to talk in the church. Of course, such an interpretation would mean that a woman is not permitted to sing, teach the children, lead the choir (or even sing in it), or anything having to do with talking because the Scripture says *"keep silence in the churches."*

Actually, however, what is meant is this: Seating arrangements were somewhat different in the meeting places of the early church than ours are today, where everyone comes in and sits together, many times, in family units. In those days the women were seated on one side of the church and the men on the other. One thing we must remember is that many things were taking place that were totally new to them. The New Covenant, for example, was just coming into force. Actually, everything was basically new and, consequently, much instruction was needed.

In view of all the newness, many things were happening in the services that were not understood by all present, especially the women. (You must remember, women were not afforded the degree of education they are today or the access to the world outside their home and family.) That so few people understood the gifts of the Spirit operating in the church is the basic reason the Apostle Paul wrote I Corinthians.

Oftentimes the women would call out in the service to their husband seated across the building and ask what was meant by certain things that were being done or said. Naturally, this created disturbance and difficulty in the order of the services. So the Apostle Paul was emphasizing here that the women were not to be so bold and take so much liberty, that they were to remember they were under obedience. He continued to admonish them to ask their husband at home if they failed to understand things said or done in the services (verse 35). They were not to disturb the service by asking across the room, but they were to wait until they were home. Paul went on to tell them it was a shame for them to disturb the service in this manner.

Paul's statement did not contradict the fact that women were free to pray and prophesy in the church (Joel 2:28-32; Acts 2:16-21; 21:9; I Corinthians 11:5-13).

GOD'S ORDER OF EVENTS

God has always used women (just as He has men), but He has used them within the order outlined in His Word.

You must remember, too, these instances where God chose men: (1) to head up the twelve tribes of Israel, (2) to be His twelve disciples, (3) to lead the early church.

We also must not forget that it was a woman who first preached the Gospel (Good News) under the New Covenant. Of course, when we speak of this woman telling the Good News, we are not speaking of her pastoring a church or any position of that nature. Rather, we are referring to the fact that Mary Magdalene, when she found that Jesus Christ was no longer dead but had actually risen from the dead, told the news first (Mark 16:10, 11).

Everyone in the world — male, female, red, yellow, black, or white — should be a witness for the Lord Jesus Christ. Everyone should be involved in the work of God. Yet the order of events, with respect to leadership, that God laid down in both the Old and New Testaments should be adhered to. When it is carried forth in this manner, God's work will be healthier, and greater results will be accrued as a result of our collective efforts to do what He desires.

I trust I have answered your question satisfactorily, and may God bless you!

QUESTION:

WHY DON'T YOU PREACH MORE LOVE INSTEAD OF MESSAGES THAT SEEM SHARPLY TO CRITICIZE OR CONDEMN?

ANSWER:

First of all, I consider myself to be one of the greatest preachers of love in the world today; and I will explain. Second, I am called of God: I must preach what I feel He gives me to preach. Paul said to the church at Corinth, *"Woe is unto me, if I preach not the gospel!"* (I Corinthians 9:16). As with Paul, there is a divine calling upon my life.

God told Jeremiah, *"Whatsoever I command thee thou shalt speak"* (Jeremiah 1:7). Jeremiah had to preach much judgment. Because of Israel's great and many sins, the man of God expressed, *"Then I said, I will not make mention of him, nor speak any more in his name. But his word was in mine heart as a burning fire shut up in my bones, and I was weary with forbearing, and I could not stay"* (Jeremiah 20:9). Likewise, John spoke of taking the little book and eating it and observed that it was in his *"mouth sweet as honey"* but in his *"belly bitter"* (Revelation 10:9, 10). Truth is always sweet when it is received by revelation from God, but it becomes bitter when the contents are noted to be woes upon the people to whom it must be proclaimed. The message God gives is not always pleasant. It is His message, and it is tailored to the needs of the hour and must be preached exactly as God gives it.

WHAT IS LOVE?

Any preacher that stands before a congregation of people and does not warn them of the consequences of greed, jealousy, envy, lust, malice, concupiscence, or other such sins does not love his people. These terrible sins plague people constantly. However, the Scripture plainly tells us, *"How shall they believe in him of whom they have not heard? and how shall they hear without a preacher? And how shall they preach, except they be sent?"* (Romans 10:14, 15). How else are people going to understand and know of the terrible temptations that ravish humanity — saved and unsaved alike? People need to know how to overcome sins that attract our modern society such as the movies, dances, drugs, immorality, and a host of other things that could be named. Ministers of the Gospel must warn their people of the dangers that these things pose.

When a nation forgets God and turns her back upon the Bible, someone must cry out against the sin, filth, and profanity — just as the prophets and the apostles in the Bible cried out against it.

It is not pleasant, but I must ask this question: Is love really love that withholds truth from the hearer? that does not warn of catastrophe ahead? If a bridge is out, would it be love for someone knowing the danger not to warn travelers of the consequences?

I think the answers are fairly obvious. As a minister of the Gospel, I have the same obligation. The bridge is out; there is a raging torrent ahead. Certain death looms over the horizon. Likewise, I must warn our nation; I must wake people from their spiritual lethargy.

WHO WILL PREACH LOVE?

It is the man of God that will tell you the truth. The truth may hurt; but the individual that will tell you the truth — irrespective of criticism or what the world may say — that man is your friend. Admittedly, the world does not want that. We are told in God's Word about people in the last days *"heap[ing] to themselves teachers, having itching ears"* (II Timothy 4:3, 4) who tell them things they want to hear; but that man courts the favor of man. He would rather have the applause of the crowd than to reap the results of telling the truth. Let me go a little farther with this.

WHAT HAPPENS TO THOSE WHO TELL THE TRUTH?

Somebody said a long time ago that when a prophet is cursed, reviled, spat upon, and ostracized by the world *and* the church, God can use him; but when he is accepted of men, most of the time, sad to say, God can no longer use him.

The prophets of old were manhandled and some were even killed because they told the truth. Every apostle died a martyr's death, with the exception of John the Beloved. Rivers of blood ran down through the Middle Ages of history because millions of people would not succumb to the rule of the papacy. Yes, there is always a price to pay for truth. Somebody, however, *must* stand up and speak out. To be frank and honest with you, that may be about the only love this poor world will ever realize.

I WILL CLOSE BY SAYING THIS

The man that will stand before you and tell you the truth — irrespective of the cost — the same is your friend.

Jesus was the personification of love, yet few people preached as hard as He did. He stood before the Pharisees and preached harder than I ever have. He called the Pharisees (and that to their face, before great crowds of people) *"serpents"* and *"vipers"* and told them they would not *"escape the damnation of hell"* (Matthew 23:33). These people were leading the nation of Israel down a primrose path of destruction. Jesus knew it. He had to point out those people, and at the same time He had to warn the general population. In other words, He spoke the truth. He did it boldly; and, oh yes, they killed Him for it!

HEAVEN

■ Will we know each other in heaven, and will babies remain babies forever in heaven?

■ Is it possible for a Christian to be happy in heaven if he knows some of his loved ones are in hell?

QUESTION:

WILL WE KNOW EACH OTHER IN HEAVEN, AND WILL BABIES REMAIN BABIES FOREVER IN HEAVEN?

ANSWER:

Oh, yes, we will know each other in heaven. The Apostle Paul said we will know, and we will be known (I Corinthians 13:12). There is implication in this Scripture that not only will we know each other and rejoice together in the love and grace of our Lord, but also we will know the mind and thoughts of everyone there. Likewise, everyone there will know our mind and thoughts. Jesus said, *"Nothing is secret, that shall not be made manifest"* (Luke 8:17). This is one of the reasons heaven will be such a wonderful place: there will be no secrets. Secrets make for confusion and cause people to interject their own feelings and verbalizations into what they do not know (or what is secret to them). Oftentimes this causes feelings to be hurt and friendships lost; misunderstandings occur and a thing is totally misinterpreted. Thank God, there will be none of this in heaven!

MEMORY

Someone may ask, "Will we remember all the past mistakes we made?" The Bible does say, *"The former things [shall pass] away"* (Revelation 21:4). Of course, it is speaking primarily of hurts, disease, and so forth; but it could include things in the past that were not good. However, I believe this will especially include past sins, because the Bible tells us that God Himself *"will not remember [our] sins"* (Isaiah 43:25). If He forgets them, it stands to reason that we will forget them too. I do know this: there will be nothing that will bring any kind of unhappiness in the portals of glory.

BABIES

Concerning the second part of the question: yes, there will be babies in heaven. However, I do not believe babies will remain in the infant state throughout eternity. This would be totally unlike God. God always develops what He creates. For a baby to remain an infant (or even a small child) forever and forever would not at all be in keeping with the Word of God.

Whenever babies die and go to heaven (and all babies do go to heaven when they die), they arrive in heaven as infants or small children, but from that moment they develop and mature until they arrive at the complete stature God desires. Even though the Bible does not specifically state this, the spirit of it is there.

QUESTION:

IS IT POSSIBLE FOR A CHRISTIAN TO BE HAPPY IN HEAVEN IF HE KNOWS SOME OF HIS LOVED ONES ARE IN HELL?

ANSWER:

This question was raised one time at one of our camp meetings, and, of course, it is a question that is probably on the mind of a lot of people. A person loves the husband or wife or daughter (or whomever it may be) so much that it is like a hand squeezing his very heart to think that he himself will live throughout eternity in bliss in the portals of glory, while there is the possibility a certain loved one may be suffering the tortures of an eternity in hell. That is a sobering thought. How could anyone be happy under such circumstances?

HAPPINESS IN HEAVEN

The first thing I would call to your attention is this: The Lord Jesus Christ is in heaven and He is happy. Surely He knows all things — not only there in glory but also on earth. Also, He loves us (*and* the sinners) more than we could ever love our loved ones. Yet, Christ is happy. He even related in Luke 16 that He looked into hell and heard the cries of the rich man tormented in flames. He notes every time one little sparrow falls; He counts the number of hairs on our head (Matthew 10:29, 30). He also takes notice of all of the rebellion and bitterness in the heart and life of the unsaved, remembering that He *died* for these people. Even though He paid such a tremendous price for their salvation, they continue to rebel in their stubbornness. How it must grieve Him! How it must hurt Him! Yet He is happy in heaven.

You see, we have one major problem: We are trying to gauge the thoughts and feelings we will have in heaven by the way we understand and know things on this present earth, but it is not possible to do that. We will be changed into His likeness (I John 3:2). Not one single thing will be able to fasten itself to our mind in heaven (in eternity) that is capable of bringing grief or sorrow. The Bible tells us, *"The former things are passed away"* (Revelation 21:4). Now that is a tremendous statement and one on which we can comfortably and logically dwell.

THE JUSTNESS AND MERCY OF GOD

It is difficult to comprehend how any mother (especially a Godly mother) could say amen to the Lord Jesus Christ as her child is taken away to hell, but it will be possible because she will have full knowledge of the justness of God as well as His mercy. Everything reasonable was done to bring that soul to repentance, but the consequences were rejection and rebellion. Every single Christian who has to watch helplessly as his loved ones are eternally lost will do so, certainly not with gladness, but with full knowledge and realization that the great God of glory was totally fair, *was* totally honest, and *was* totally merciful in all His dealings. The eternal consequences of the rebellion of the unsaved loved one will have been an individual choice, certainly not God's.

This may sound somewhat harsh, but you must remember, Christianity is not a new provision. It has been in effect from the fall of Adam until now (see Genesis 3:15). It shall, of course, continue. So much has already been done to bring sinners to the Lord Jesus Christ, and the quest will ever continue; but we must not spend valuable time (that we could spend winning these loved ones) worrying that Christians will be grieving in heaven because of them. That just will not be the case. The Bible tells us, *"God shall wipe away all tears . . . and there shall be no more death, neither sorrow, nor crying, neither shall there be any more pain: for the former things are passed away"* (Revelation 21:4).

HELL

■ There is a teaching becoming quite prominent today which says that not only did Jesus Christ die physically, but He died spiritually as well. In other words, He became sin and went to hell and suffered, just as a sinner would die and go to hell. Is this scripturally correct?

■ When the Bible speaks of hell and the fire of hell as mentioned in Luke 16, is this particular fire literal or is it just a figure of speech?

QUESTION:

THERE IS A TEACHING BECOMING QUITE PROMINENT TODAY WHICH SAYS THAT NOT ONLY DID JESUS CHRIST DIE PHYSICALLY, BUT HE DIED SPIRITUALLY AS WELL. IN OTHER WORDS, HE BECAME SIN AND WENT TO HELL AND SUFFERED, JUST AS A SINNER WOULD DIE AND GO TO HELL. IS THIS SCRIPTURALLY CORRECT?

ANSWER:

The question being asked is, Did Jesus become sin at Calvary and experience spiritual death? Did He become sin on the cross, as this particular doctrine teaches, or was He a sin offering?

We teach and believe that Jesus was a sin offering. We also teach that He was holy and pure just as the Old Testament foreshadowed.

Jesus did not go to hell for three days to redeem mankind from the terrible ravages of sin. Rather, He went to be with His Heavenly Father, because He Himself said, *"Father, into thy hands I commend my spirit"* (Luke 23:46).

Just before Jesus died on Calvary, He uttered the words, *"It is finished"* (John 19:30). What was finished? The work Christ came to do. As of that moment, man's salvation was complete. Nothing else was needed. Nothing else could be done that would aid or abet the finished work at Calvary. So these three words stand as a permanent rebuke to the doctrine that Jesus had to go to hell and die spiritually to redeem man, and whatever else this spurious doctrine claims.

This particular false doctrine also teaches that the sinless Son of God became unregenerate and died as a lost sinner at Calvary, and that He had to be born again and justified from sin. The pitiful thing about this whole line of thinking is that He was somehow born again in, of all places, hell!

Now if perchance this were true, it would have been necessary for someone to die for the Lord Jesus Christ to redeem Him from His unregenerate state and provide for His justification. Of course, we know this is all utter foolishness, because Jesus did not become unregenerate and He did not die a lost sinner.

Sometime ago one of the leading proponents of this heresy stated, "When His blood poured out, it did not atone. It did away with the handwriting of the ordinances that were against us." He went on to say that Jesus redeemed man, not on the cross but in hell. Hopefully, the proponents of this doctrine do not know what they are doing, for they are actually denying the blood atonement of Jesus Christ. It seems they do not understand that they have negated the power of Jesus' blood to cleanse from sin by their teaching that Jesus became an *unholy* sacrifice on the cross. This is heresy, and it is dangerous.

IDENTIFICATION OR SUBSTITUTION?

This heresy appears to teach that Jesus identified with the sinner on the cross, while it seems to ignore the fact that Jesus became a substitute for sinners — confusing the identification of Jesus with the human race at His birth with His substitution for sinners on the cross.

If Jesus had become literal sin and had become lost and unregenerate while He hung on the cross of Calvary, then He would have been an unacceptable sacrificial offering to God for the sins of others. Whereas if He indeed remained pure and holy as the Scriptures prove, then God could accept Him as a substitute on behalf of sinners. It was only in this way that He could fulfill the Old Testament type whereby the animal for the sin offering had to be spotless and *"without blemish"* (Leviticus 4:2, 3). If you remember, the sin offering was regarded as most holy even *after* its death.

Someone may ask, "What difference does that make?" It makes all the difference in the world because according to the Word of God our eternal salvation rests upon what we personally believe concerning the blood atonement of Jesus Christ. It is here, at the cross, that a person's salvation either stands or falls. The doctrine of Jesus dying spiritually on the cross and going to hell, and His having to be born again as a sinner, is heresy of the most serious kind — its seriousness stemming from the fact that if a person believes this perverted doctrine, he will find that in the end he has been robbed of the blood atonement on his behalf.

The Bible is emphatic on this matter: one sinner cannot redeem another sinner. Only one who is guiltless could ever act as a substitute and suffer the punishment for the guilty party, thereby saving the guilty party. Even Jesus could not have done this if He had become guilty Himself, as this particular doctrine contends. The central thrust of the entire Old Testament sacrificial system is that Jesus was the guiltless substitute who, like the Old Testament type, remained pure and holy both on the cross and after His death.

THE BASIC TEACHING

This doctrine generally follows something like this:

Jesus became sin on the cross when He yielded Himself to Satan. He swallowed up the evil nature of Satan, thus becoming one in nature with the adversary, taking upon Himself the diabolical nature of Satan. At that time He became a lost man crying, *"My God, my God, why hast thou forsaken me?"* (Matthew 27:46; Psalm 22:1). He had now died spiritually (according to this spurious teaching, that is).

Jesus was then taken to the pit of hell where He was chained with the fetters of sin, wickedness, disease, and all other evils of Satan. The devil stood before the darkness crying, "We have conquered the Son of God." There followed a gala celebration down in the pit. Satan believed he had finally triumphed over God.

Jesus consequently suffered agonies beyond description in the pit for three days as all the hosts of hell were upon Him. Then suddenly Jesus was justified. From His throne in heaven Almighty God arose and put His hands to His mouth and screamed, "It is finished; it is enough." Jesus was now born again and made spiritually alive once more.

Hell itself was shaken. Jesus shook off His chains of sin, sickness, and evil. He walked over to the devil, grabbed him, and threw him to the ground. As the devil cowered and trembled on the floor of the pit, Jesus put His foot on top of him and took the keys of death, hell, and the grave from Satan.

At this time the Holy Spirit kicked open the gates of hell and raised Jesus from death. He then ascended to the Father and announced, "I have paid the price. The prison is now open." He was now a born again man who had defeated Satan. Jesus was the firstborn from the spiritually dead. Thus it was at the time Jesus was made alive down in the pit that the believer was also made alive. The church had its origin in the pit of hell when Jesus was begotten from the dead as the *"firstborn among many brethren"* (Romans 8:29).

At first glance it appears to be cause for rejoicing. However, if you think about it, you have never read anything of this nature in the pages of your Bible — because it is not in the Bible! It is fictitious from beginning to end.

The truth is, *"[He] blott[ed] out the handwriting of ordinances that was against us, which was contrary to us, and took it out of* the way, nailing it to his cross; And having spoiled principalities and powers, he made a shew of them openly, triumphing over them in it" (Colossians 2:14, 15). *"Nailing it to his cross . . . triumphing over them in it"* means that Jesus' great victory was won on the cross.

THE OLD TESTAMENT SACRIFICES

The Old Testament animal type (a type of Jesus), which was to die as a substitute for the sinner, had to be without spot or blemish (Leviticus 4:3, 27-30; 9:3, 4; Deuteronomy 15:21) to teach Israel (and the church) that a substitute acceptable to God had to be holy and guiltless in order to bear the punishment for the guilt of the sinner.

This ritual, carried out again and again in the Old Testament, was realized in Jesus Christ as the Lamb of God, who *"offered himself without spot to God"* (Hebrews 9:14).

When these teachers teach that Jesus literally became sin with the inherent need to become born again, they expose the basic flaw in their doctrine, which stems from apparent ignorance of the nature of the Old Testament sacrifices, especially the sin offering. They conveniently forget (if indeed they ever knew) that the Old Testament clearly teaches that at no point does the sin offering become an unholy sacrifice, either before or after its death.

SIN OR SIN OFFERING?

The Apostle Paul said, *"For he hath made him to be sin for us, who knew no sin"* (II Corinthians 5:21).

In the Hebrew language the term *chetta't* is the same word used for "sin" and "sin offering." A single Hebrew term translates both words. "Sin" and "sin offering," then, are one and the same. It was the context in which the term was used that expressed whether a person was speaking of "sin offering" or "sin."

For example, if it was a matter concerning sacrifices, *chetta't* was understood to mean a sin offering. If the matter was one of offense, the same word would be used; but the people involved would understand the meaning by the usage, the tenor of it.

We may, but no Jewish Christian would ever, confuse "sin" with the "sin offering," even though the two thoughts are both expressed by the same Hebrew term. It is the same with the terms "trespass" and "trespass offering." The same Hebrew word is used, *asham,* meaning that Jesus' death on the cross is to be regarded as a trespass offering for sinners and not that He Himself became a "trespass" or "sin."

THE SERPENT (SATAN) AND CHRIST

This erroneous doctrine contends on the basis of Numbers 21 (which presents the account of the lifting up of the brazen serpent in the wilderness for the healing of those bitten) that Jesus was also lifted up as a serpent when He was made sin on the cross, and at that time took on the evil nature of Satan. They quote, *"And as Moses lifted up the serpent in the wilderness, even so must the Son of man be lifted up"* (John 3:14). From this they take it that Jesus became one with the serpent, Satan, and died spiritually.

However, the account in Numbers 21 does not support this fantasy. God did send fiery serpents as punishment against the rebellious Israelites. As a result of the intercession of Moses, God directed him to make a figure of a serpent in brass, to be elevated on a pole so that it could be seen from all quarters in the camp. All who looked in faith in its direction were healed. Naturally, we understand that the brazen serpent did not produce healing; it was merely an emblem of their sin and signified the nature of divine judgment. Their faith in God's promise to heal brought deliverance through their obedience. To look upon an inanimate object (in this case, a serpent of brass) in itself could never produce healing.

By analogy, if Jesus became a serpent in nature as this erroneous teaching contends, then healing was provided by Satan, the serpent (Numbers 21:4-9), not God.

What was being spoken of here was the manner in which Jesus would die, not a change in His nature. As that serpent was lifted up on a pole, Jesus would also be lifted up on a pole — the cross.

JESUS, A SINNER?

First of all, we know that all men are the children of wrath (Romans 3:9; 5:12; Ephesians 2:3). But we also know that Jesus lived without committing any act of sin (John 14:30; II Corinthians 5:21; Hebrews 4:15).

The "Jesus died spiritually" teachers say that Jesus did not personally sin, but He was made by God to be sin, that He took upon Himself the sinfulness of the human race and became evil with Satan's nature.

Of course, this is impossible. Sin is a personal act of disobedience to the will of God, and Jesus never once disobeyed His Father, and certainly not while He hung on the cross.

Sin is not something tangible like a coat of black paint that God could drape over His Son, nor is it some type of inoculation of germs that scientists could inject into the bloodstream as the Nazis did to some of their victims in World War II. Sin is an act (whether deed, word, or thought) that a person must personally commit. This fact alone rules out any possibility that Jesus could be made sin.

In the study of biblical theology, the scriptural doctrine of imputation shows that sin or righteousness can be imputed or charged to another's account in a legal sense. Applied to Jesus and His sacrifice as a sin offering, this indicates that He did not become sin, but remained sinless that He might be able to bear the punishment for our guilt that was imputed to Him. In other words, Jesus did not bear the wickedness and the filth of our sinful nature, but He did bear the terrible punishment that should have been poured out on us.

Our punishment was imputed to Him. Our sins, in regard to their moral character, are our own. They could not by imputation become someone else's. However, Jesus Christ could take upon Himself the punishment for the guilt of our sins, which has reference to the legal liabilities that Christ assumed on our behalf.

So the transfer of our sins to Jesus Christ was not a transfer of the actual *transgressions* themselves — that is not possible — but Christ made Himself liable to endure the *penalty* for our sins. On that cross and in His death, Christ was a holy, spotless sin offering. To have been anything otherwise would have violated the Old Testament type and would have disqualified Him as an acceptable substitute to God.

JESUS, JUSTIFIED IN HELL?

These teachers conclude from the phrase *"justified in the Spirit"* (I Timothy 3:16) that Jesus Himself had to be justified, that He had to be made sin and possess an evil, satanic nature. Thus, it is said, He had to be made righteous once more, justified and born again; but according to the

Greek "to justify" is "to declare righteous" or "to show to be righteous." Jesus was "evinced to be righteous as to His spiritual nature."

The Bible, in this passage, was not saying that Jesus was being made righteous but that His righteousness was being announced. Jesus never ceased to be righteous, He never ceased to be just.

Without any scriptural support whatsoever, these teachers declare, "Suddenly God justified Jesus in the pit (hell) and He was born again."

God did not arbitrarily wave His hand over Christ and say, "Be thou cleansed," and suddenly Jesus was justified (made righteous), born again, and restored to Sonship with the Father. There is no scriptural basis for this doctrine.

JESUS, ABANDONED BY GOD?

Was Jesus abandoned by God at Calvary? No! Jesus was God's own sacrifice, chosen by Him (Isaiah 53; John 1:29; 3:16), and never out of divine favor for one moment. He was called *"an offering and a sacrifice to God for a sweetsmelling savour"* (Ephesians 5:2). This is in perfect harmony with the Old Testament teaching that the sin offering was most holy to God (Leviticus 6).

First of all, it is impossible to separate the Godhead — Father, Son, and Holy Spirit. *"For in him dwelleth all the fulness of the* Godhead *bodily"* (Colossians 2:9). If Jesus had died spiritually, then at the cross — by His being lost — He would have divided the Godhead, or at the least have made the entire Godhead sinful and in need of the new birth. The idea of dividing up the Godhead for three days by sending the Son of God to hell as a lost sinner, totally abandoned by God the Father and God the Holy Spirit, is totally ridiculous. This spurious teaching even goes so far as to say that God was no longer the Father of Jesus while He was in hell.

When Jesus uttered the words on the cross, *"My God, my God, why hast thou forsaken me?"* Jesus was quoting from a prophetic passage, Psalm 22:1. He also said, *"I thirst"* (John 19:28), an utterance based upon another Old Testament prophecy, Psalm 69:21. When He uttered these words, *"My God, my God,"* the religious leaders and the people of His day misinterpreted them saying, *"This man calleth for [Elijah]"* (Matthew 27:47).

With these words Jesus consciously identified Himself as the One of whom the Old Testament prophecies spoke. Someone has even supposed that Jesus recited all of Psalm 22 as well as other prophecies concerning Him while He hung on the cross for several hours. We do know, of course, that not everything Jesus did was recorded. Only a small portion was recorded (John 21:25).

Was Jesus forsaken by God? No, He was not. God had temporarily "turned a deaf ear," in that instead of delivering His Son from death, which He did do on several occasions (compare John 7:30, for example), the Father delivered Him up unto death when He became a sin offering for others; but this was not abandonment. Jesus Himself said, *"Behold, the hour cometh, yea, is now come, that ye shall be scattered, every man to his own, and shall leave me alone: and yet I am not alone, because the Father is with me"* (John 16:32). He could say this because *"God was in Christ, reconciling the world unto himself"* (II Corinthians 5:19).

JESUS, PHYSICAL OR SPIRITUAL DEATH?

The Bible states again and again that Jesus offered up His *body* as a sacrifice for our sins, that He was put to death *in the flesh*. In other words, Jesus died physically but not spiritually. Nowhere in the Word of God does it tell us that Jesus died in His spirit. It does say however that . . .

"Christ . . . his own self bare our sins in his own body on the tree" (I Peter 2:21-24).

"Christ . . . [was] put to death in the flesh, but quickened by the Spirit" (I Peter 3:18).

"Christ hath suffered for us in the flesh" (I Peter 4:1).

"He reconciled [us] in the body of his flesh through death" (Colossians 1:21, 22).

"We are sanctified through the offering of the body of Jesus Christ once for all" (Hebrews 10:10).

"[He] abolished in his flesh the enmity, even the law of commandments" (Ephesians 2:15).

So while the Scriptures repeatedly stress that Jesus offered up His body and His flesh as a sacrifice for sin, not once do they say He died in His spirit.

God could not die spiritually. Else why would the Son of God need a body of flesh? He took on flesh so that He could die physically on behalf of sinners, as had the Old Testament type.

The erroneous teaching, it seems, is that the shedding of Jesus' blood was insignificant. The following are some of the ridiculous theories of this doctrine:

• When His blood was poured out, it did not atone. (How silly can we get?)

• Jesus bled only a few drops, and when people sing about the blood of Jesus, they do not know what they are talking about.

• Jesus died by an act of His own will, when He wanted to (with respect to His physical death).

To comment on these would be a foolish waste of time. The efficacy of the atonement did not depend on how much blood was shed on the cross, or how much time was involved in the process of dying. The atonement's validity depended on the fact that the Son of God shed His spotless blood and died on our behalf.

JESUS, BORN AGAIN?

This false teaching claims that:

• Jesus was born again in the pit of hell as the first man to be born again under the New Covenant. The proponents of this doctrine apparently are referring to the verse that says, *"God . . . hath raised up Jesus again; as it is also written in the second psalm, Thou art my Son, this day have I begotten thee"* (Acts 13:33).

• He was the first begotten from spiritual death, citing, *"Jesus Christ, who is the faithful witness, and the first begotten of the dead"* (Revelation 1:5).

• Jesus started the church in hell when He was born again in the pit, citing, *"[Jesus became] the firstborn among many brethren"* (Romans 8:29).

• He was righteous while on earth, on the cross became unrighteous, went to hell, then in the pit was made righteous once more. That seems strange when the Bible says that He is unchangeable (Malachi 3:6; Hebrews 13:8).

The first thing we must make clear is that two different English terms were used by the King James translators to translate the same Greek word. "Firstborn" and "first begotten" both translate *prototokos*. "First begotten" (Hebrews 1:6; Revelation 1:5) is "firstborn." "Begotten" (Acts 13:33), a different Greek word altogether, refers to the physical resurrection of Jesus and completely rules out the fanciful notion that Jesus was born again in hell.

In the preceding verses (Acts 13:16-32) Paul spoke of Christ's physical death and the burial of His body in a sepulcher. Verses 30-33 speak of His physical resurrection from the dead. The resurrection of Jesus in the Bible always has reference to the resurrection of His body and not of His spirit, since His spirit did not die (Luke 24:36-46; I Corinthians 15:20-23).

The term "firstborn" in Scripture is used not only to refer to the physical birth of the first child into a family, but also to speak of position and inheritance rights. So the term refers not merely to birth, but also to birthright as well as to position or status. The firstborn always held a special position in God's sight, possessing special rights and privileges. In this same sense Jesus Christ is called the "firstborn" (Romans 8:29; Colossians 1:15; Hebrews 1:6). The term in such passages speaks of position, rank, legal rights, and special privileges. It never has any reference to the new birth (being born again).

JESUS, IN HELL?

Jesus did go down into paradise, which was a part of hell, where the righteous souls — such as Abraham, Isaac, Jacob, David, and other Old Testament saints — were kept against their will. These souls were not in the burning part of the pit, but rather in the place commonly referred to as "Abraham's bosom" or "paradise." This is the place to which Jesus was referring when He said to the dying thief, *"To day shalt thou be with me in paradise"* (Luke 23:43). He was speaking of that place in the heart of the earth where He would go. The other thief would go to the punishment side of hell where the rich man was.

After Jesus died on the cross, He went down into paradise. Then, the Bible says, *"When he ascended up on high, he led captivity captive"* (Ephesians 4:8). In other words, those righteous souls who were kept against their will in the side of hell called paradise were led by Jesus to heaven (like an earthly conqueror). That is what Scripture means when it says Christ descended first into hell, the lower parts of the earth (Psalm 16:10; Acts 2:27; Ephesians 4:8-10). He captured the righteous souls from Satan, leading them captive to heaven when He ascended on high. This fulfills Psalm 68:18.

Prior to this, all righteous souls went into *hades* or *sheol*, along with the souls of the wicked who went to another compartment. These two compartments had a great gulf between them (Luke 16:19-31). Now the souls of the righteous no longer go into the heart of the earth to be held captive against their will. They go immediately into heaven at physical death to await the resurrection of the body (II Corinthians 5:8; Philippians 1:21-24; Hebrews 12:23; Revelation 6:9-11).

The wicked will continue to go into the torment compartment of *hades* or *sheol* until the end of the millennium. Then death and *hades* will deliver up the wicked souls, which will be reunited with their body and resurrected to be sentenced to the lake of fire (Revelation 20:11-15).

In this context a person could say that Jesus went to hell, but it in no way means that He went down into the burning flames of the pit as a sinner. Nor was He molested by Satan, triumphed over by the powers of darkness, and then suddenly justified by God and born again as the *"firstborn among many brethren"* (Romans 8:29). This is an erroneous teaching that does not understand the scriptural sense of the atonement and the vicarious sacrifice paid by Jesus Christ at Calvary's cross as a sin offering.

No, Jesus did not die spiritually on the cross. He did not go to the burning (punishment) side of hell. He was not placed under Satan's domain. He was not subject to the evil one. He was the perfect sacrifice as our substitute, given up as a sin offering. He died physically, not spiritually.

QUESTION:

WHEN THE BIBLE SPEAKS OF HELL AND THE FIRE OF HELL AS MENTIONED IN LUKE 16, IS THIS PARTICULAR FIRE LITERAL OR IS IT JUST A FIGURE OF SPEECH?

ANSWER:

Hell (and the fire of hell) is literal, and I will attempt to explain.

"For I am tormented in this flame" (Luke 16:24). This Scripture must be taken literally. God said what He meant and meant what He said. We do not have the prerogative of taking a literal statement from

Scripture and making it into a figure of speech. It would do extreme violence to the Word of God.

If we had this right, we would take the description of the New Jerusalem in Revelation 21:10 as a figure of speech as well. In my years of living for God, I have never heard that John's description of the New Jerusalem was only a figure of speech; but I have heard it said that Jesus' description of hell in Luke 16 was a figure of speech. Let us look closer.

A LITERAL PLACE

We believe the place called hell exists exactly as stated in the Word of God (Matthew 16:18; Luke 16:19-31). It is the torment compartment of *sheol* or *hades* where wicked souls have gone, or will go, until the end of the millennium. The wicked will be brought out of this place to be reunited with their resurrected, immortal body and be cast into the lake of fire for eternity (Revelation 20:11-15).

We further believe that death and hell will be cast into the eternal lake of fire prepared for the devil and his angels and the wicked (Matthew 25:41, 46; II Peter 2:4; Revelation 14:9-11; 20:6-15; 21:8).

We believe that hell is . . .

• A place of sorrow (Genesis 42:38; II Samuel 22:6; Isaiah 14:9, 15).

• A place of fire (Deuteronomy 32:22; Luke 16:19-31).

• A place of full consciousness (Isaiah 14:9-15; Ezekiel 32:27-31; Luke 16:19-31).

• A place of torment (Luke 16:23-25, 28).

• A place of regret (Luke 16:25-31).

• A place so terrible that those who are there plead for a means of warning others not to come there (Luke 16:27-31).

• A place where fire is literal and yet souls are not consumed (Mark 9:43-48; Luke 16:22-31).

AN ETERNAL FIRE

The word "fire" is found in Scripture 542 times but is used figuratively in only a few instances. It is always clear whether it is used figuratively or literally, however.

If language means anything in the Bible, the torments of hell are eternal. The Word of God gives us the following:

- Danger of eternal damnation (Mark 3:29)
- Eternal judgment (Hebrews 6:2)
- Vengeance of eternal fire (Jude 7)
- Shame and everlasting contempt (Daniel 12:2; John 5:28, 29)
- Everlasting fire (Matthew 18:8)
- Everlasting punishment (Matthew 25:46)
- Torment day and night forever and ever (Revelation 14:9-11; 20:10)

The same words translated "eternal," "everlasting," and "forever and ever" are also used to declare the eternity of God, Christ, and the Holy Spirit. Therefore, if these statements are eternal, then "hell" and "punishment" are eternal as well. The Hebrew word *olam* and the Greek word *aionios* used to describe "eternal" means "eternity, always, forever, everlasting, perpetual, without end."

Some cults interpret *"The day that cometh shall burn them up"* (Malachi 4:1) to say that hellfire is not eternal. However, this statement refers not to hell but to the Battle of Armageddon.

It is taught that the wicked will be annihilated and, consequently, that the fire of hell is not literal. However, Scripture does not teach the annihilation of any part of creation. All passages in the Word of God teach that the soul is immortal and that the body will be immortal in the resurrection. Others state that men will suffer absolute destruction in hell. However, the Greek word for "destruction" in II Thessalonians 1:9 means ruin, not extinction. Still others state that the wicked will die and be extinct. However, spiritual death means separation, not annihilation.

SUMMARY

We believe the Bible teaches that hell is a literal place. The endeavor is made to construe the story of the rich man in hell as a mere parable. However, a parable illustrates certain points and names are not used. To the contrary, in Luke 16 no point is illustrated, and at least one person is identified by name. The story is the literal one of two beggars — one begged in this life, the other in the next life.

We further teach that the soul is immortal. As a consequence, the punishment of hell must be eternal. Jesus declared in plain terms that the immortality of the soul and consciousness of the soul after leaving the body are a reality.

As stated above, we believe that hell is eternal. We teach that the fire of hell is literal and that the human soul and spirit cannot be burned up. Even when the body is reunited with the soul and spirit in the second resurrection of damnation, the body itself cannot be destroyed. Pain and punishment are literal, real, and eternal.

Men continue to rebel against the teachings of the Word of God, but this opposition does not negate the truthfulness of what God has stated. A terrible price was paid at Calvary's cross for man's redemption. Man does not have to go to hell; he chooses to go there by his unbelief. What the Bible says about hell is literal, factual, and eternal.

QUESTION:

HOLY
COMMUNION

■ Do the ordinances of the Lord's Supper and water baptism have anything to do with a person's salvation?

QUESTION:

DO THE ORDINANCES OF THE LORD'S SUPPER AND WATER BAPTISM HAVE ANYTHING TO DO WITH A PERSON'S SALVATION?

ANSWER:

No, and we have always to be absolutely clear respecting salvation: *"For by grace are ye saved through faith; and that not of yourselves: it is the gift of God: Not of works, lest any man should boast"* (Ephesians 2:8, 9).

There is an inherent nature within mankind that wants to earn salvation; in other words, man's logic tends toward doing, working, and involving himself in receiving his salvation experience. Of course, that kind of thinking is erroneous. There is absolutely nothing that a person can do to save himself or to help Jesus Christ in the great salvation plan. Always salvation is a gift of God — it has never been more and it will never be less. While there is much that a person can do to aid and maintain in the salvation experience that may be helpful, strengthening, encouraging, instructive, and informative, still these things contribute nothing toward the salvation of his soul.

To answer your question further: no, as meaningful as the Lord's Supper is, and as significant as water baptism is, neither of these precious and wonderful ordinances will save anyone; however, they do have spiritually beautiful and symbolic meanings. We will address ourselves to those meanings.

THE LORD'S SUPPER

Three of the Gospel writers give an account of the Lord's Supper (Matthew 26:26; Mark 14:22; Luke 22:19). The Apostle Paul wrote, *"When he had given thanks, he brake it, and said, Take, eat: this is my body, which is broken for you: this do in remembrance of me. After the same manner also he took the cup, when he had supped, saying, This cup is the new testament in my blood: this do ye, as oft as ye drink it, in remembrance of me"* (I Corinthians 11:24, 25).

Paul here was admonishing the church in Corinth that partaking of the Lord's Supper was not just eating and drinking to satisfy their natural hunger. *"If any man hunger, let him eat at home"* (I Corinthians 11:34).

163

The Lord's Supper was special; it was spiritual. It was a memorial to observe and partake of until the Lord Jesus Christ returned (I Corinthians 11:26).

From the accounts in Matthew and Luke, it seems that this ordinance will continue to be observed in the new kingdom (Matthew 26:29; Luke 22:16, 18, 20). The Lord's Supper is a memorial, but it is more; it is a symbol of what Jesus Christ has done for us. Still, we must not confuse the symbol with the fact of salvation or even the cause of salvation. The type is never to be confused with the anti-type, nor the symbol with what is real.

If you will notice, in our Scripture reading, it was Jesus who said, *"This do in remembrance of me"* (Luke 22:19). That word as given by the Holy Spirit to the Apostle Paul was quoted in I Corinthians 11:24, 25. Jesus did not say, "This is my body which is broken for you, this do in order that you might be saved." What He did say was, *"This do in remembrance of me."* The Holy Spirit was exact and perfect in what He said. That is all that is to be read into it.

There was no instruction given as to the frequency of which the Lord's Supper should be observed. The Bible just uses the term *"as oft"* (I Corinthians 11:25).

UNWORTHY PARTICIPATION

Paul even went on to say in I Corinthians 11:27, 28 that a Christian should not partake of the Lord's Supper unworthily. In other words, if there are spiritual problems within a person's life, that person should refrain from partaking until those spiritual problems are repented of and resolved. Verse 28 says it clearly and simply: *"let a man examine himself."* To partake of the Lord's Supper as a matter of habit or custom (as it is done in many churches today) is to eat and drink unworthily and to take upon oneself damnation. *"For he that eateth and drinketh unworthily, eateth and drinketh damnation to himself, not discerning the Lord's body. For this cause many are weak and sickly among you, and many sleep"* (I Corinthians 11:29, 30).

Herein is the major problem: *"not discerning the Lord's body"* (verse 29). Paul felt so strongly concerning this that he went on to warn that this would cause physical and spiritual weakness even to the degree that some Christians could die prematurely. This is a tremendous and fearsome statement made here, and I am concerned the Lord's Supper is not being entered into with proper seriousness and thought in Christendom today.

ONLY A SACRAMENT

Many people are being taught in error that the Lord's Supper is a sacrament of salvation (helping earn their salvation and consequently making them saved). However, remember, this is a sacrament, not a sacrifice. We must reject out of hand the teaching of those who regard the bread and the cup in the Lord's Supper as a sacrifice — be it the so-called sacrifice of the mass of the Catholic church or the offering up of the bread and the cup converted into the flesh and blood of Christ. You see, the Catholics (and I speak of the doctrine and not of the people personally) teach transubstantiation, which states that the bread is converted into the flesh of the Lord Jesus Christ, and the (real, fermented) wine is converted into the blood of Christ as both are consumed by the participant. We believe nothing could be more contradictory to the Word of God.

TRANSUBSTANTIATION

This doctrine of the Catholic church was first formulated by the Abbot of Corbey, Paschasius Radbert, in the beginning of the ninth century. It was first denominated "transubstantiation" by Hildebert of Tours in the beginning of the twelfth century and made an article of faith by the Lateran Council in the beginning of the thirteenth century.

Again, we state that we must, out of all knowledge of the Word of God, repudiate this dogma as (1) opposed to Scripture and (2) contradicted by the evidence of the senses. For when a person *handles* (touches) the elements, they remain the same; when a person *tastes* them, they are the same; and when a person *smells* them, there is no difference in odor. They are still bread and juice with all their original qualities; they are unchanged and will ever remain unchanged. They are merely, as blessed and wonderful as they are, a memorial to our Saviour's serving as a sinner in our stead. We reject this doctrine of transubstantiation because of the superstitions connected with it and the idolatrous practices ingrafted therein.

CONSUBSTANTIATION

We must also reject the doctrine perpetrated by the Lutherans called consubstantiation. This teaching says that though the substances of the elements are not changed, yet the body and blood of Christ are mysteriously but corporeally present in, with, and under the elements and are received corporeally with the mouth by communicants along with the symbols. In other words, by partaking of this sacrament a person is saved. Of course, this too is untrue.

MEMORIALS FOREVER

Memorials have always been a part of the church and they always will be. I speak primarily of the church in the wilderness after the children of Israel were released from Egyptian bondage, on up to this present day and throughout eternity (as we related from the accounts in Matthew and Luke).

First, the Passover Feast was similar to the Lord's Supper. The children of Israel were commemorating what had already taken place — their deliverance from Egyptian bondage. It was something they were never to forget. Second, we are commemorating what is past — our Lord's death — and we are to do so until He returns.

Third, as I mentioned earlier, the Word of God infers that the commemoration of the Lord's Supper will be carried on even in the Kingdom Age and, consequently, forever — as, once again, a symbol and memorial of the tremendous price paid by the Lord on Calvary for the redemption of man.

WATER BAPTISM

To answer your second question: no, water baptism cannot save anyone. Water baptism is the answer of a clean conscience toward God and a symbol of the birth, death, and resurrection of our Lord. In essence, it is a type of our birth (born again experience), death (dead to the world), and resurrection (risen in His likeness and His image).

THE LIKE FIGURE

Some people misunderstand when they read, *"The like figure whereunto even baptism doth also now save us (not the putting away of the filth of the flesh, but the answer of a good conscience toward God,) by the resurrection of Jesus Christ"* (I Peter 3:21). Many people focus in on the passage *"baptism doth also now save us,"* but they miss the point of what is being said when it says, the "like figure" whereunto even baptism saves us. Is it the water that saves or the "like figure" that saves? Water baptism has never saved any soul. It is a person's faith in the death, burial, and resurrection of Jesus Christ that saves the soul. In other words, it is the "like figure," or that of which baptism is a figure, that saves the soul.

Water baptism is a type or figure of what has already happened in the heart and the life of an individual. A mere figure has no power to save but the reality of the figure can, and that real figure is Jesus. Lest anyone should trust in water baptism to save his soul, Peter made it clear that baptism does not save a person from the filth or moral depravity of the flesh. Water baptism is the answer of a good conscience toward God — a conscience that has been made clean by faith in the resurrection of Jesus Christ.

It is not possible for a person who trusts in the Lord Jesus Christ to be only partially saved until he is baptized in water, and then be completely saved. The moment an individual trusts Jesus Christ as his Saviour, that person is saved — instantly, totally, and completely. He can never be more saved no matter what else he may or may not do.

Now we come back to the works syndrome. I heard a preacher say once, "The water saves." I wondered what kind of water he was talking about — river water, flowing water, deep water, shallow water, water from the River Jordan? What kind of water?

Water baptism is a sacred, holy, and precious symbol that a person should by all means follow after, but he should partake of it for the reasons given, and not for salvation. Water baptism does not save; it is a public confession of faith in the Lord Jesus Christ.

CONCLUSION

Remember: many people are interested in tacking some kind of works onto salvation. They will say you have to join their particular church or be baptized in the manner of their church or take the Lord's Supper in their particular fashion. However, this is nothing short of adding to the great price that Jesus Christ paid. Of course that is not possible, much less needful. As wonderful as these symbols and sacraments are, they only represent the reality; they are not the reality. The reality is Jesus. The Scripture still says, *"Looking unto Jesus the author and finisher of our faith"* (Hebrews 12:2), not water baptism, not the Lord's Supper, not church membership, not religious traditions, but Jesus!

HOLY SPIRIT

■ How can a person know that the Spirit of the Lord is speaking to him? Does God tell people to tell other people to do certain things?

■ I suppose my question should be considered in separate parts, so I will pose it that way: (1) Does God speak to people today? (2) How does God speak to people? (3) If a person says that the Lord has spoken to him, does this mean that we are automatically to follow him?

■ If you believe and teach that every recipient of the Holy Spirit speaks in other tongues, why not teach the tongues of fire on the head and the sound of the mighty rushing wind?

■ Some preachers have said there is no such thing as Holy Spirit conviction, that what people are really feeling is condemnation. Consequently, it is not of God but of Satan. What about this?

■ Just exactly what is a Charismatic, and should Charismatics leave their old-line churches?

■ What does it mean to "walk in the Spirit"?

QUESTION:

HOW CAN A PERSON KNOW THAT THE SPIRIT OF THE LORD IS SPEAKING TO HIM? DOES GOD TELL PEOPLE TO TELL OTHER PEOPLE TO DO CERTAIN THINGS?

ANSWER:

I will have to answer your question in several different ways so that (prayerfully) we can come to a correct conclusion in the matter.

There is no exact pattern, per se, that a person can go by that would guarantee an easy answer in all respects for every person. If it were so, you would not be asking the question. There are as many answers as there are people, but I will do my best to help you, and I believe with the help of God I can.

First, I will address myself to some things that you may observe in others that will tell you whether or not they are being led by the Lord. Then, we will discuss how you yourself can tell if God is speaking to you.

GOD'S WORD

God's Word will never be violated. If an individual says God told him to do something or that God is speaking to him, it must *never* contradict the Word of God. If what that person is doing (or not doing) is a violation of God's Word, you may be sure it is not God speaking to him. Either he is doing this out of his own spirit or else it is Satan guiding and directing him. I could go into a long dissertation as to what the Word of God is, but I think it is obvious. You must consider the following criterion: no matter who a person is, no matter what that person has done in the past or how good and wonderful his works may be, if a course of action is taken with God presumed to be the guide and director, and yet it violates the Word of God, you may know that that person is *not* being directed and led by the Lord. In other words, God is not speaking to him, and it is not the Holy Spirit doing it.

THE HOLY SPIRIT

If an individual were to go up to someone in a crowded place and shout loud enough for everyone to hear, "If you don't get saved, you are going to hell," that would not be the Lord; that would be an embarrassment to the work of God and to the individuals involved, and the Holy Spirit will never embarrass Himself or anyone else in His directions to people.

Now it may be true that a certain person is lost; and if he does not change his ways, he will die and go to hell. All of that could be correct, but in dealing with that person, God would not approach him in this way. So, if someone said, "Well, I did this because God told me to do it," then that person would be in error because the Holy Spirit never embarrasses Himself or other people.

You can always mark this down and use it as a criterion and guideline: The Holy Spirit is always a gentleman; He is always gentle. He always moves lovingly, with kindness and tenderness, never placing a person in a position of hostility or embarrassment that would result in driving that person away from God instead of bringing him to God. The Holy Spirit is the only agent that can bring a person to the Lord Jesus Christ; so, consequently, He uses all tender means to do so.

THE SPIRIT-FILLED LIFE

The individual's life must reflect what he is saying God has told him. If the person is living a spotted, careless life that lacks consecration, I would view with skepticism anything that person construes as being God's voice. The two just simply cannot go together. Many individuals think they can live any way they want to live and God will still speak to them. God does not work that way. Admittedly, none of us is perfect. All of us need forgiveness, seemingly oftentimes. However, the matter of the heart is a matter of grave concern. If a person is honest and earnest before God and strives with all his heart, even though he is imperfect and at times flawed and inconsistent, God certainly honors that person because most of us are in this category as far as inconsistency is concerned; but if a person's motives are wrong and that person's life is not what it ought to be and he is, in essence, making only a halfhearted attempt (if that) to live for God, I would hold with great suspicion whatever he says is from God.

AIR OF SELF-IMPORTANCE

Many people use certain "code words" to indicate that God has spoken to them, simply to draw attention to themselves. It makes them feel spiritual. For instance, a great deal of people in this great

Charismatic renewal have a habit of going up to people and saying, "I have a word for you from the Lord." Now that sounds very high and very holy, and I admit there are times when God has spoken to people in this very way.

I was in South Africa once undergoing a tremendous burden concerning the work. I had spoken to a group of preachers and their wives that morning; there must have been several hundred people there. Immediately after the message and the service, a lady came up to me (I did not know her) and said, "Brother Swaggart, I believe the Lord would have me speak something to you that I think He has given me." Immediately, the manner in which she said this indicated a sense of seriousness and humility. It was not some great, thundering "thus saith the Lord." She then went on to give me the message that she said God had given her. I definitely believe it *was* from God. The presence of God was so real that I broke down and began to weep, and it was a strength to my heart; it was an encouragement; it was edifying and uplifting. On the other hand, I have known people to come up to me and say, "I have a word for you from the Lord," when most of the time it was not from God. I am concerned that, even though the people were not of Satan, they were speaking out of their own spirit.

So, individuals who have a habit of calling attention to themselves by relating messages from the Lord to others ought to be looked at closely before we adhere to their words.

GUIDANCE FROM OTHERS

In these last few years, many people have prophesied over others, telling them to give certain amounts of money, to move to certain places, or not to do this, or to do that, and saying it was from God, and the Spirit of God had spoken to them.

Here is something I want you to read carefully. This is never from God unless, first of all, God has spoken to the person being addressed. In other words, God may confirm something He has already told you, but He will never use anyone else to guide and direct your life. He is capable of speaking to you yourself if He wants you to do something.

Sometime ago, a brother told me that he had moved from one city to another city, and he stood there with head bowed and said, "Brother Swaggart, my life has been a shambles ever since I moved. I left a good job, but somebody prophesied over me and said I was to leave that city and move to this one because God wanted me here. I have been unable to find work, my family has suffered greatly, and I have lost almost everything I had." I stood there looking at the man, and I asked him, "Sir, did God tell you personally to move to this city?"

He said, "No, Brother Swaggart, God did not tell me anything. I had never heard anything from the Lord concerning this; but I considered the person who told me this to be spiritual, and I felt he had heard from God."

Now this is where he made his mistake. If God had wanted him to move, He would have told him without going through someone else. That person who was doing the telling was trying to order, guide, and direct someone else's life. The Holy Spirit never works that way, and you can chalk this kind of thing up as coming from someone who is *not* in the mind and will of God. I would turn a deaf ear to anything of this nature, no matter who said it, unless God had spoken to me first and it was simply a confirmation of what He had already said to me by speaking to someone else also. This happens many times, but, in the opposite order, it just cannot be presumed to be a message from God.

THE VOICE OF GOD

All the things I have said about observing other people holds true for the individual in question. God will never contradict Himself. Neither will He embarrass others or Himself. Neither will He draw attention to you to puff you up by making you seem superspiritual. He will never use you, likewise, to guide the life of other people by what you think God has spoken to you. So, if any of these things, plus others that could be named, come to your heart and mind, it is out of your own spirit or from Satan. It is not of God.

Whenever the Lord speaks to a person, it is always gently. It is never cruel or caustic even though at times it may be urgent.

I remember when God spoke to my heart to go on television. (I could use this same expression about hundreds of other things He has spoken to my heart.) First of all, I started sensing a burden for the television ministry. (We must always remember that God is not in a hurry — most of the time. We should try the spirits. We should not only make sure it is God speaking to us but make sure we have the timing right as well.) The burden became heavier and heavier. I could not get away from it. I did not exactly want to do it. I had no desire to go on television.

Now something must be said here. Many people have a strong desire to do something and then they try to look for signs saying that God is giving these signs and consequently wanting them to do certain things; but God never works this way. I am not saying that every single thing He wants us to do, we will have the opposite feeling, but I am saying that this has little or nothing to do with our desires.

I continued to sense this burden. It grew heavier and heavier, and it would not go. I started finding myself waking up in the night thinking about it. I would pray about it, and every time I would pray the burden would grow heavier. I would weep. I could not shake it; I could not get away from it.

That was the Holy Spirit speaking to me. I heard no voice. I saw no outward sign, but, at the same time, that on my heart was urgent; and of course it was God, and God has used the television ministry in a tremendous way to bless untold thousands of people.

"But," you may ask, "can we always be absolutely certain that it is God speaking to us?" This is not an easy question to answer. Even the great Apostle Paul was going to go to a certain place and no doubt he and his co-workers had prayed about it and *thought* they had the mind of God on the matter (Acts 16:7). A person could even say they thought God had told them to go there; but then after their starting out on this journey, *"the Spirit suffered them not"* (verse 7). He stopped them. Then, they had the vision where the man appeared to them and told them to *"come over into Macedonia, and help us"* (verses 9, 10).

So, it is not always easy; however, if a person will be humble before God, seeking and desiring the full will of God in all matters, God will not allow him to go wrong. Admittedly, it is not always easy to ascertain if it is God speaking to you or not, but if you will be sincere before Him, He will make Himself real. He will not allow Satan to lead an honest, dedicated Christian astray if that person will stay humble before God and seek to do God's will.

Jesus said, *"If a son shall ask bread of any of you that is a father, will he give him a stone? or if he ask a fish, will he for a fish give him a serpent? Or if he shall ask an egg, will he offer him a scorpion? If ye then, being evil, know how to give good gifts unto your children: how much more shall your heavenly Father give the Holy Spirit to them that ask him?''* (Luke 11:11-13).

This has a great meaning. It is speaking of God answering prayer. It is speaking of the Lord giving the Holy Spirit to them that ask Him and being assured that they will not receive a wrong or false spirit. It is also saying that if a person is totally dedicated to God, the Holy Spirit will guide him and direct him.

QUESTION:

I SUPPOSE MY QUESTION SHOULD BE CONSIDERED IN SEPARATE PARTS, SO I WILL POSE IT THAT WAY: (1) DOES GOD SPEAK TO PEOPLE TODAY? (2) HOW DOES GOD SPEAK TO PEOPLE? (3) IF A PERSON SAYS THAT THE LORD HAS SPOKEN TO HIM, DOES THIS MEAN THAT WE ARE AUTOMATICALLY TO FOLLOW HIM?

ANSWER:

I will attempt to answer your question in the manner and order that you have asked it.

You asked, "Does God speak to people today?"

Yes, God does speak to people today. The Apostle Paul wrote, *"God, who at sundry times and in divers manners spake in time past unto the fathers by the prophets, Hath in these last days spoken unto us by his Son, whom he hath appointed heir of all things, by whom also he made the worlds"* (Hebrews 1:1, 2). Paul went on to say, *"Jesus Christ the same yesterday, and to day, and for ever"* (Hebrews 13:8).

These two passages are proof enough that God does speak. Now, for the second part of your question.

DISCERNING THE VOICE OF GOD

You asked, "How does God speak to people?"

God is a communicator. He has many and varied ways of speaking to people, and I think it would be profitable for us to go back to the beginning and give a little synopsis of the many ways God can use to speak to individuals.

Audible Voice. Adam and Eve *"heard the voice of the Lord God walking in the garden in the cool of the day"* (Genesis 3:8). The following verses go on to relate God's conversation with Adam and Eve. I think that God spoke to Adam and Eve just as men speak to each other today — in an audible voice. We read, *"Now the Lord had told Samuel in his ear a day before Saul came, saying . . ."* (I Samuel 9:15). Then the Bible goes on to give what God actually told Samuel.

God can speak to people with an audible voice or a whisper in the ear, just as the Scriptures describe here. The Prophet Samuel heard the voice of the Lord in the same way he heard any other voice. There is a possibility that many of the other prophets received revelation from God in the same manner.

Personal Appearance. Second, the Lord can speak to men by appearing directly to them. A person may say He did this with Adam and Eve, as I have already discussed. Another example is the time when Abraham actually saw, talked with, and had lunch with God (Genesis 18:8). It was here that God told Abraham what He was going to do about Sodom and Gomorrah and even announced that Sarah would conceive a son, Isaac.

Saul (Paul) *"heard a voice saying unto him . . ."* (Acts 9:4). He asked, *"Who art thou, Lord?"*

The Lord replied, *"I am Jesus."*

"The men which journeyed with him stood speechless, hearing a voice, but seeing no man" (verse 7). However, Paul later reported, *"And last of all he was seen of me also, as of one born out of due time"* (I Corinthians 15:8). So it is obvious that God appeared to men in Old and New Testament times, and even spoke in an audible voice. He can do so today if He so desires.

Angels. Third, not only can God speak in an audible voice, but He can also speak through angels. The Angel Gabriel came to the Virgin Mary and told her of the coming birth of the Lord Jesus Christ (Luke 1:26-38). The Apostle John heard the voice of many angels as they were crying with a loud voice, *"Worthy is the Lamb"* (Revelation 5:12). Many other incidents of angels speaking could be given, but these will suffice. So even today there is nothing in the Word of God that forbids angels from speaking to mankind.

Dreams and Visions. Fourth, God can speak in dreams and visions. The Bible gives an illustration of an *"angel of the Lord [appearing] to Joseph in a dream"* (Matthew 2:13). Not all dreams are from God, of course, but a few are.

Impressions. Fifth, God can speak by impressions on a person's spirit. It is like the Holy Spirit speaking to a person's heart. This was the way the Holy Spirit spoke to Peter concerning Ananias and Sapphira (Acts 5:3, 8, 9). In this same manner, God speaks to many people today.

Circumstances. Sixth, God can also speak through events. He did so when He sent an earthquake to Philippi when Paul and Silas were wrongly beaten and held captive (Acts 16:25, 26). That earthquake, incidentally, did not kill anybody. It actually resulted in the saving of many souls. At times, like this one, God does speak through catastrophe, but still we know God is a *constructive* God rather than a *destructive* God. At times in the past He has had to resort to destructive methods because of the terrible wickedness of man, but God's basic attribute is constructive.

Scriptures. Then, last of all, God speaks to us through His Word. This is probably the greatest method He employs to communicate to us. You can find references to this in John 1. Of course, many other incidents and Scriptures could be given.

I hasten to add that God could use many means of communication with man, not only the basic methods I have listed here. Any means He used in the Old Testament, God could have and did use in the New Testament. Anything He used in Bible times, be it old or new, could certainly be used today, simply because *"Jesus Christ [is] the same yesterday, to day, and for ever"* (Hebrews 13:8). God chooses certain methods of communication because of man's lack of spiritual or mental development or perhaps even through circumstances that are brought to pass. We are living today in a spiritually enlightened age; consequently, God, most of the time, speaks to us through His Word or through the Holy Spirit bearing witness with our spirit, or through an impression on the heart, and so forth. This does not negate the fact, however, that God can speak to us in an audible voice or any other way that He chooses to do so.

DISCERNING THE VOICE OF MAN

You asked, "If a person says that the Lord has spoken to him, does this mean that we are automatically to follow him?"

Now, this is the heart of the answer to your question — *no!* Just because an individual says that God has spoken to him does not mean that we are automatically to follow him. There are certain things that must be proved.

We are told that every prophet (and his prophecy) should be judged (I Corinthians 14). Everything revealed to a person is not necessarily divine revelation. This is the reason everything must be judged. We are also told, *"Beloved, believe not every spirit, but try the spirits whether they are of God: because many false prophets are gone out into the world"* (I John 4:1).

In other words, John was saying here that any spirit inspiring preachers, teachers, or whoever to deny the incarnation, Jesus' passion, His death, bodily resurrection, and bodily ascension into heaven is not of God and is anti-Christ.

Word of God. First, if a person says that God has told him to do something, it must line up with the Word of God; it must never contradict the Word.

Life-style. Second, the individual's life must be looked at. What kind of personal character does he have? Does he live for God? Is his life holy, clean, and pure? These things have to be addressed. God does not use people in the sense that many persons claim when, in reality, they live a spotted life.

Fruit of the Spirit. Third, what kind of attitude does the person have? Is it belligerent, unteachable, or intractable? Is the person humble, teachable, and desirous of flowing in the mind and Spirit of God? These things have to be considered.

Church Government. Fourth, does the individual care for his statement (what he claims God told him to say or to do) to be judged by other brethren? As I mentioned above, the Scripture tells us that we should not mind if something we say or do is judged. In fact, every child of God is admonished to judge anything that people profess to be of God.

REVERENCING THE VOICE OF GOD

More people today than ever before are claiming that God told them things. Oftentimes, this is a come-on designed to influence people to do what they desire them to do — to follow them. It is an easy thing to fling around the statement, "God told me to do this, or that, or the other." It sounds holy, high, and mighty. It sounds like the individual has close contact with God, but on closer look it also rings of ego and pride.

I learned a long time ago seldom to say, "God told me to do thus and so." It is only after years of retrospective action that I use the term. In other words, it is only after I can look back and see that what I thought God told me proved out to be exactly that way. Then, and only then, am I willing to say God told me. I also use the terminology, "Now, I *believe* that God has spoken to me," or "I *trust* that the Holy Spirit has desired me to do thus and so." For you see, I am human, and so is everyone else. We are all prone to mistakes. Sometimes we may think God told us to do something, when He did not. Maybe it was just uncurbed zeal or enthusiasm for the thing that we wanted to do. At other times, He may have told us to do a thing, but the timing was unclear. He did not mean for us to act at that very moment as we thought He did.

So, you see, it is easy for us to make mistakes and unwise to state dogmatically that God told us to do something. Admittedly, there are some persons who have been spoken to by God, and they may be right in saying God spoke to them; but I seriously doubt that God speaks to people several times a day (or even a month, for that matter) as some preachers or other individuals claim. These people would be much wiser to say, "I believe God told me," or "I think God told me." Then that leaves the door open to inspection. They are admitting, by their statement, "I am human; I could make a mistake; I am not infallible."

You can come much closer to trusting an individual whose attitude is that of humility, as I have just described, than someone who carelessly flaunts God's (supposed) guidance. Most of the time, God has not spoken to these people; they are only speaking out of their own spirit.

The older a person becomes in the Lord, the more he learns. First of all, we eventually learn we are not nearly as close to God as we think we are. Second, we learn that even though we may feel close to Him, we are still actually so far away. We also learn that we are fallible; we make mistakes. God never does; but, sad to say, we do.

The fact is, God does still speak to His choice creation — man. Thank the Lord for this. He is the great communicator. Whether He speaks to our heart or in other ways of His choosing, it is a high and holy thing for the great God of glory to speak to a human being. We should always treat this communication with humility, respect, and a tremendous awe that should accompany any visitation by the Holy Spirit — whether it be by an impression upon our spirit or in a more graphic form.

I trust that I have been able to answer your question. I have tried to do so as completely and accurately as possible. May the Lord use what I have written to the enlightenment of your heart.

QUESTION:

IF YOU BELIEVE AND TEACH THAT EVERY RECIPIENT OF THE HOLY SPIRIT SPEAKS IN OTHER TONGUES, WHY NOT TEACH THE TONGUES OF FIRE ON THE HEAD AND THE SOUND OF THE MIGHTY RUSHING WIND?

ANSWER:

"When the day of Pentecost was fully come, they were all with one accord in one place. And suddenly there came a sound from heaven as of a rushing mighty wind, and it filled all the house where they were sitting. And there appeared unto them cloven tongues like as of fire, and it sat upon each of them. And they were all filled with the Holy Ghost, and began to speak with other tongues, as the Spirit gave them utterance" (Acts 2:1-4).

THE FULFILLMENT OF PROPHECY

The sound of the rushing, mighty wind, tongues of fire, and speaking in tongues are mentioned collectively only in this one single passage; however, tongues are mentioned and discussed some 22 times in the Word of God.

When Peter preached to Cornelius and his household, the Holy Spirit fell on them and they spoke with tongues (Acts 10:44-46). There was no mention made of a rushing mighty wind or tongues of fire. In Ephesus

Paul asked John's disciples, *"Have ye received the Holy Ghost since ye believed?"* (Acts 19:2). They answered him in the negative. He laid hands on them, and *"they spake with tongues, and prophesied"* (verse 6). No mention was made of tongues of fire or of a rushing mighty wind.

Paul, guided by the Holy Spirit, designated the proper use of tongues (I Corinthians 12 through 14); but he never mentioned the tongues of fire and the rushing mighty wind. Of course, there is a reason that these two experiences are not mentioned after the Day of Pentecost.

Acts 2:2, in talking about a rushing mighty wind filling all the house where the people were sitting, reveals the coming of the Holy Spirit according to the promise of the Master. The Holy Spirit came on that day. He has not left; He has remained. If He came and went, then possibly there might be reason to hear the sound of the rushing mighty wind again; but praise the Lord, He does not come and go! He came to abide forever; consequently, it is not physically or spiritually possible to hear that particular sound anymore.

On the Day of Pentecost *"there appeared unto them cloven tongues like as of fire, and it sat upon each of them"* (Acts 2:3). This fulfilled John's prophecy that Jesus would baptize us *"with the Holy Ghost and with fire"* (Luke 3:16; Acts 1:5).

THE ESTABLISHMENT OF THE WORD

It is unscriptural to build a doctrine on any statement in Scripture that is made only one time. The Bible says, *"In the mouth of two or three witnesses every word may be established"* (Matthew 18:16; Deuteronomy 19:15). If the tongues of fire and the rushing mighty wind had been mentioned in other passages, along with speaking in tongues regarding the infilling of the Holy Spirit, then it would be proper for us to expect that too; but as it was not mentioned again (and rightfully so for the above reasons), it is not proper for us to expect these two experiences.

However, as I said, speaking in tongues is mentioned some 22 times in the Word of God, and every believer should rightfully and scripturally expect to speak in other tongues as the Spirit of God gives utterance when he is baptized in the Holy Spirit.

QUESTION:

SOME PREACHERS HAVE SAID THERE IS NO SUCH THING AS HOLY SPIRIT CONVICTION, THAT WHAT PEOPLE ARE REALLY FEELING IS CONDEMNATION. CONSEQUENTLY, IT IS NOT OF GOD BUT OF SATAN. WHAT ABOUT THIS?

ANSWER:

I have heard some people make this statement, but I do not think they know what they are talking about. Condemnation and conviction are two different things. Condemnation is being declared reprehensible, wrong, or evil. Conviction is being convinced of error and being compelled to admit the truth. We are told, *"There is therefore now no condemnation to them which are in Christ Jesus"* (Romans 8:1).

THE JUSTIFIED CHRISTIAN

In Romans 8:1 Paul was speaking of the new life the new Christian has in Christ Jesus. He has been justified, and the word "justification" means all the sins of the past have been totally erased as though the individual in question never committed them. The person is justified — made right with God. Consequently, the Christian should never allow Satan to bring up to him sins that were committed in his unconverted state. They are gone. They do not exist anymore. The Christian cannot legally be condemned by them.

Then there is a second meaning to condemnation, which refers to Christians who make a mistake and sin. If they do such a thing, of course they should ask God immediately to forgive them, resolve by God's help and grace not to commit that sin again, put it behind them, and accept God's mercy and forgiveness. It, too, is washed away and cleansed and the Christian is once again justified as far as that act is concerned.

SATAN AND CONDEMNATION

However, Satan will not let it stop there. He will immediately seize the Christian with condemnation. A bad feeling accompanies the experience even though he has already asked God's forgiveness. That is condemnation. The Christian should not listen to it. He should rebuke Satan; and even though he is so sorry for the sin he committed, he should rejoice in God's mercy and grace and not allow Satan to weigh him down with condemnation (I John 1:9).

THE HOLY SPIRIT AND CONVICTION

Now, conviction is something that is totally different. The Holy Spirit works in many ways. Actually, everything on this earth that is done by God is done through the Holy Spirit (who is also God). Conviction is one of those qualities that works in the heart of both the unsaved and the saved alike. Paul spoke of it in his first letter to the church of Corinth. Although he was speaking here of prophecy and the results of prophecy, it applies also to tongues and interpretation of tongues, and also to the preaching of the Word. He said, *"And thus are the secrets of his heart made manifest; and so falling down on his face he will worship God, and report that God is in you of a truth"* (I Corinthians 14:25). You see, the reason this individual reacts in this manner is that things of truth are felt in his own heart that no one knows about. He is convicted by the Holy Spirit. It is Holy Spirit conviction. As the Holy Spirit brings to attention the need in the individual's heart, he is made to realize that certain things need to be accomplished. Then the Bible says he will fall down on his face, which means humility, and he will worship God.

In my praying, I am continuously asking God that Holy Spirit conviction will settle upon hearts as I minister. This is the moving of the Spirit that accomplishes the same thing I have mentioned above. People are stricken by it. That is what happened to the Philippian jailer when he fell down before Paul and said, *"What must I do to be saved?"* (Acts 16:30). He had seen what had happened through the life of Paul and Silas. An earthquake had come, and yet the prisoners did not leave. The Holy Spirit used this incident to strike him with conviction.

Peter preached on the Day of Pentecost and told the assembled multitude how they had crucified the Lord Jesus Christ. *"Now when they heard this, they were pricked in their heart, and said unto Peter and to the rest of the apostles, Men and brethren, what shall we do?"* (Acts 2:37). That was the Holy Spirit convicting them, and of course it resulted in 3,000 men being saved.

So, there is a vast difference in Holy Spirit conviction and condemnation. Conviction is of God; condemnation is of Satan.

EMOTIONALISM AND THE MOVING OF THE HOLY SPIRIT

A lady wrote me the other day and said, "Why do you Pentecostals resort to emotionalism to get people to cry or something of this nature when appealing to them?" Of course, what the lady did not understand was that this has nothing to do with emotions. She was referring to my making appeals for people to be saved, or whatever the situation was, and what was happening was this: the Holy Spirit was moving on what I was saying and it caused people to weep and some people became extremely uncomfortable. This was the Holy Spirit striking the individuals with conviction; in other words, they were being told that they needed to do something about what I was saying (whatever it was).

Years ago one good brother wrote me (the owner of a radio station) and upbraided me because of my program. He said he did not like the *Campmeeting Hour* because at times it made people cry. Of course, what the dear brother did not understand was that it was not Jimmy Swaggart making them cry; it was the convicting power of the Holy Spirit. You see, many churches, even entire denominations, know absolutely nothing about the convicting power of the Holy Spirit, and religion becomes a liturgical, cold formality that deals basically in the letter and ignores the Spirit; hence, no conviction. There is little heart response from its adherents, simply because the Holy Spirit is not there. Actually, Holy Spirit conviction is what we desperately need in our churches, in our preaching, and in our teaching. It demands results, and God give us more of it!

I hope I have answered your question and explained this matter satisfactorily.

QUESTION:

JUST EXACTLY WHAT IS A CHARISMATIC, AND SHOULD CHARISMATICS LEAVE THEIR OLD-LINE CHURCHES?

ANSWER:

You have actually asked two questions, and I will attempt to answer them in the order in which you asked them.

The dictionary gives this word in several different forms — "charismatic," "charisma," "charism[s]," "charismata." Basically the term means (1) "an extraordinary power given a Christian by the Holy Spirit for the good of the church" and (2) "a personal magic of leadership arousing special, popular loyalty or enthusiasm for a public figure such as a political leader or military commander." This could also include the special, magnetic charm or appeal of a popular actor or entertainer, et cetera.

However, the term as it has come to be used by the religious community does not exactly fit either of these categories. For most Christians the word "Charismatic" means (1) "a person who has received the baptism in the Holy Spirit with the evidence of speaking with other tongues, and who is a member of one of the old-line churches such as the Baptist, Methodist, Presbyterian, Episcopalian, Catholic, et cetera" or (2) "a Spirit-filled person who has elected to stay in his old-line church."

This, I think, as the religious community understands it, aptly describes a Charismatic. It is a person who has been baptized in the Holy Spirit with the evidence of speaking with other tongues. And even though his new experience is Pentecostal (and there are many Pentecostal churches that major, along with salvation, in the infilling of the Holy Spirit), the individual elects to stay in a church that has not taught and does not now teach the Acts 2:4 experience; hence, he is called a Charismatic.

If an individual receives the Acts 2:4 experience, being a member of one of the old-line churches and electing to leave that church and associate himself with one of the Pentecostal movements (such as the Assemblies of God, the Church of God, the Pentecostal Church of God, the Foursquare, or an independent Pentecostal church), that person is not a Charismatic. Neither is an individual a Charismatic that has been reared in one of the classic Pentecostal churches and has received the Holy Spirit. For instance, my family started attending an Assemblies of God church when I was about five years old. It is the only church to which I have ever belonged; consequently, I do not consider myself a Charismatic. This also pertains to any other individual that has been involved in a Pentecostal church all his life or who has switched from one of the old-line churches to a Pentecostal church. Neither of the two is considered a Charismatic. He is simply considered Pentecostal, as I am considered Pentecostal. I suppose an abbreviated answer is that "a Charismatic is an individual who is Pentecostal and yet practices a denominational belief."

Now, of course, that is an abbreviated statement, but possibly with the explanations we have given it will be easier to understand.

OLD-LINE CHURCHES

First of all, I cannot tell anyone where to go to church. I can give guidelines according to the Scripture, but still that decision has to be determined by an individual according to what he believes is the leading of the Holy Spirit.

It is certainly conceivable that God might tell people to stay in certain churches for specific reasons known only to Him, and naturally He must be obeyed at all costs. At the same time, a person must also be sure that it is God telling him to do this and that he is not staying there for personal, family, social, or material reasons.

After an individual has been baptized in the Holy Spirit, if God does not distinctly tell him to stay in his particular church he has been in for quite some time, he should seek out a church that preaches and practices in its doctrine the Pentecostal experience (Acts 2:4). Of course, this includes many other great basics of the faith as well. What a lot of people need to realize is the following.

Most Pentecostal churches have the same general tenets of faith (with some exceptions) as the so-called mainline denominations. Of course, I am using generalized statements now and not going into detail, but I will give this example.

The doctrine of the Assemblies of God is similar to the Baptist doctrine, with the exception of unconditional eternal security and the evidence of the baptism in the Holy Spirit. You may be sure that these two doctrines cover a wide range of biblical instruction, but these are basically the only differences. The teaching of salvation in the Assemblies of God (as well as other Pentecostal organizations), as far as I know, is identical with the Baptists. Of course, the same could be said for the tenets of faith concerning the Methodists and other mainline denominations. So, you see, there is not much difference in doctrine, yet the small difference is gigantic when it comes to a person's walk with God.

For years the notion was perpetrated that Pentecostals believed weird things, and I agree, there *are* some weird beliefs in Pentecostal doctrine. I am constantly speaking out against them! For example, some Pentecostals teach that a person must speak in tongues to be saved. We do not believe this (and, by far, the greater number of Pentecostals do not believe it either). Still other Pentecostals, it seems, lean more toward baptism with regeneration; we do not accept this teaching, as the main body of Pentecostal believers do not.

The mighty baptism in the Holy Spirit produces a tremendous difference in the heart and life of the believer. For this reason, I believe — unless God specifically states otherwise — an individual (after he has received the Holy Spirit) should seek out a church that preaches and practices not only the great tenets of the faith including the salvation experience, but the mighty baptism in the Holy Spirit as well. The difference is unbelievable! And there are several reasons why I believe this.

Many Charismatics have been told to remain in their particular mainline churches and to do missionary work; in other words, to help other people to be baptized in the Holy Spirit, et cetera. The intention and the motive may be good, but I feel there is dishonesty involved in the effort and I will explain.

If a person belongs to a particular church, he, in essence, has agreed to abide by the tenets of faith of that particular church. Even though those tenets of faith may be right or wrong, the person has pledged to abide by them; and if the person is to remain in that church, he should abide by them. That is one reason I believe — unless God states otherwise — that a person should leave. In this instance, whenever a Charismatic makes efforts to indoctrinate other members of his particular church, this can cause confusion. What he is saying is biblical and true, and he feels people ought to hear it. However, once again, he is being dishonest in not abiding by the tenets of faith of the church he has pledged to keep. So the correct, honest, and Christian thing to do is this: if a person can no longer abide by the teachings of his church, he should leave that church, continuing to work with friends and family involved in the church he has left. He will be doing so not as a member of the church whose bylaws he has pledged to uphold and keep, but as a member of another church. Consequently, he then has the right to witness as he so desires.

If the pastor of the church actively seeks the involvement of a Charismatic, this is a different thing altogether. The individual then has "permission" and can do a great work for God; but to indoctrinate behind the pastor's back, even though the pastor may be wrong in his doctrine, is not correct. My mother used to tell me two wrongs do not make a right.

It is difficult for a person to be spiritually fed in an environment that is not conducive to Spirit-filled worship. To be frank and honest with you, there is precious little there to draw the person to God, and the individual will be consistently seeking out Pentecostal meetings of a particular nature where he can get his soul fed, and that is the way it should be. The better arrangement, in my opinion, is for him to find a church that teaches and preaches the Full Gospel to attend and associate with its members.

The Spirit-filled believer needs fellowship with other Spirit-filled believers. He will suddenly find that he has little in common with the individuals whom he has associated with for years. They no longer believe as he does, there is no agreement, and, consequently, there is no basis for fellowship. Every Christian needs fellowship; it is a vital part of us. We are commanded to forsake not the assembling of ourselves together (Hebrews 10:25). The Spirit-filled believer needs fellowship with like-minded Christians, and the only way he can receive that fellowship is by associating himself with individuals who have experienced what he has.

CATHOLIC CHARISMATICS

Catholic Charismatics fall under the same category, with some exceptions. Let me explain.

First of all, the Catholic individual should, of course, obey God. There may be some specific reason for God wanting him to stay in a specific place for a specific purpose. Naturally, God is perfectly capable of running His own business. At the same time, it must be understood that God will never violate His Word. For me to say that a Catholic should never remain in the Catholic church, I feel, is carrying it too far. However, it is important that a person make doubly sure that God is telling him to stay and that he is not doing it for social or family reasons, because there is the danger that if he does stay, he could lose his soul or, at the least, cause himself severe spiritual difficulties.

Some Catholic doctrine is absolutely scriptural. The Catholic's confirmation of the deity of Christ is right on target scripturally. The Catholic's admonition to faithfulness is certainly commendable. The Catholic's contention that the Bible is the Word of God is biblical and scriptural. The Catholic contention that Jesus was born of the Virgin Mary is, once again, totally biblical and scriptural. While there are some Catholic doctrinal teachings that are scriptural, there are more doctrinal teachings in the Catholic church that are totally unscriptural than any other particular church in Christendom. This makes it difficult for a person, after having come to Jesus and having been filled with the Holy Spirit, to continue in erroneous practices.

For instance, how can a person who has been saved and filled with the Spirit continue to pray to Mary when it is absolutely unscriptural? How can a Spirit-filled person confess to a priest when the Word of God is adamantly opposed to such and we are directly bidden to come to God through Jesus Christ (I Timothy 2:5)? How can a Spirit-filled Christian pray to saints in heaven when there is no scriptural reference for doing such a thing? How can a Spirit-filled Christian obey church tradition that is opposed to the Word of God and continue in this vein? How can these things be?

There is one thing we must remember: we have to walk in the light as He gives that light (Ephesians 5:8-14; I Peter 2:9; I John 1:5-7). If we do not progress, we digress; it is that simple. There is no standing still in God. Now let me add one last thing.

Anytime a person takes a stand and makes statements that are diametrically opposed to the teaching of other people, the automatic assumption is that the one taking the stand does not love these people. To be frank and honest with you, this person is the one that *really* loves the others. It is not pleasant to take the abuse that I have received from some of my Catholic brothers and sisters — simply because they do not believe what I tell them — though what they believe could cause them to be eternally lost. It would be much more pleasant for me to avoid the issue, but I cannot. I am an evangelist; I have to do what God has told me to do. I do it with love, with compassion, and with concern. I do it knowing that lies will be told about me and abuse will be heaped upon me; but I must not be disobedient unto the heavenly vision (Acts 26:19, 20).

FINALLY

I must conclude by saying these words. It is not my business to judge people; it *is* my business to preach the Gospel; it is my business to outline the Word of God as I believe God deals with my heart; but the final judgment is always up to God. I can never say and will never say who is saved and who is not saved. Once again, that prerogative belongs to our Heavenly Father, and thankfully so.

There are perhaps many Catholic people who indulge and engage in unscriptural practices that I have mentioned, and yet their heart is right with God. I will leave that in the hands of God. I have absolutely no animosity toward anyone, anywhere. It is only my desire that all men come to the Lord Jesus Christ. I care not whether they are Catholic, Pentecostal, Baptist, Methodist, or whatever; I just want them to make heaven their eternal home. I will close with the words the Lord said to Samuel so long, long ago: *"The Lord seeth not as man seeth; for man looketh on the outward appearance, but the Lord looketh on the heart"* (I Samuel 16:7).

QUESTION:

WHAT DOES IT MEAN TO "WALK IN THE SPIRIT"?

ANSWER:

I believe your question refers to the passage, *"This I say then, Walk in the Spirit, and ye shall not fulfill the lust of the flesh. For the flesh lusteth against the Spirit, and the Spirit against the flesh: and these are contrary the one to the other: so that ye cannot do the things that ye would. But if ye be led of the Spirit, ye are not under the law"* (Galatians 5:16-18).

These Scriptures are often misinterpreted to mean that a constant warfare is going on between the flesh and the Spirit with the Christian being a helpless victim. Of course, this is not the case at all. These verses, quite simply, describe the condition of the Galatians addressed in this epistle — or anyone else, for that matter — who attempts to seek perfection through the flesh and self-effort. It is not speaking of the Christian living under grace and walking, to the best of his ability, in the Spirit.

Actually, Paul was telling the Galatians, who had left the grace of God to go back under the law, that if they would once again receive the Gospel of the grace of God, and once again permit the working of the Spirit in their life, they would not experience the kind of struggle outlined in verse 17. Renouncing the law would free them from its bondage. Thus the flesh with its affections and lusts would be crucified, and they could live the Christian life once more.

WALKING IN THE LIGHT

To answer your question more fully, to walk in the Spirit means to walk in the light. *"If we walk in the light, as he is in the light, we have fellowship one with another, and the blood of Jesus Christ his Son cleanseth us from all sin"* (I John 1:7). The two terms (light and Spirit) actually are, or should be, interchangeable.

After we are saved, God begins to give us the light of His glorious truth. And according to the extent that we walk in this light, we will progress or we will digress in our spiritual walk with Him. Let me elaborate on this a little bit.

Multiple thousands of Christians have been baptized in the Holy Spirit and yet are not walking in all the light God has given them — while, on the other hand, there are thousands who have not been baptized in the Holy Spirit who are walking in all the light they know.

Now I must ask the question, "Which one is really walking in the Spirit?" I think the answer is obvious: the one who is walking in all the light he knows is the one really walking in the Spirit.

This leads us to ask, "What happens to a person who does not walk in all the light that he knows?" Jesus Himself gave the answer: *"I know thy works, that thou art neither cold nor hot: I would thou wert cold or hot. So then because thou art lukewarm, and neither cold nor hot, I will spue thee out of my mouth"* (Revelation 3:15, 16).

Jesus was speaking here to Christians. The Laodiceans had "cooled off" spiritually. They were not living a totally backslidden life, nor were they on fire for the Lord. They were tepid; they were lukewarm. In other words, they were not walking in the light that God had given them, and because of this Jesus said He would spew them out of His mouth.

REFUSING THE LIGHT

If any Christian is given the light on a particular work of God and he does not walk in it, he is simply refusing to walk in the Spirit. Consequently, he will start to walk in the flesh and to fulfill the lusts thereof. We were created spiritual beings, and, particularly in Christian America, we cannot remain neutral on a particular thing or situation once God sheds His light on it (whatever it may be) and we understand what He wants of us. Neither can we walk in the flesh and in the Spirit at the same time. When a person ceases to walk in the light, he also ceases to walk in the Spirit. At that time he actually begins to walk in the flesh.

THE BLIGHT OF CHRISTENDOM

When my mother was a new Christian so many years ago, she did not feel it was wrong to go to movie theaters, and she made the statement that she would continue to go. But, little by little, the Holy Spirit opened up the light to her on this matter, and through *His* illumination (light) she saw that it was wrong. She never went again.

What would have happened if my mother had refused to follow the leading of the Spirit because she liked to go to movies? To be frank with you, knowing my mother as I did, she would have lost out with God. Of course, the Holy Spirit would have continued to deal with her in all patience. But spiritually she would have started to digress. I cannot say exactly when the line would have been crossed, marking the point where God would have "spewed her out of his mouth"; but that time would surely have come if she had chosen that course. Again, I cannot know for a certainty, but I strongly suspect that our whole family might also have gotten off course. Jimmy Swaggart might not be preaching this great Gospel that God has seen fit to spread around this world through this unworthy vessel.

Do you see what I am getting at? The consequences of my mother's actions could well have charted the course for untold thousands, perhaps even millions, of persons who have found Jesus Christ through this Ministry.

How many Christians have been told by God that it is wrong to engage in social drinking or to go to dances? Or that they should be faithful to their church and pay their tithe? On and on it goes. Thank the Lord many persons respond as they ought to and walk in the light as God gives it. These individuals go on to prosper and grow in Him. Other persons, however, fall back and eventually lose out with God. They cease to walk in the Spirit because they refuse to walk in the light as God gives it.

THE MIGHTY BAPTISM IN THE HOLY SPIRIT

In the last few years God has poured out His Spirit in an unprecedented manner all over this nation and around the world. The light of the Holy Spirit has been given to many persons that heretofore had not known it. Multiple thousands of persons have accepted and received this light and gone on to grow in the Lord. Other persons — even preachers — have fought it and refuse to accept and receive it and walk in the light that God has given. What will happen to these preachers?

I do not know, of course; God will be the final judge. But, at the same time, whenever anyone — especially a minister of the Gospel, I believe — rejects spiritual light as it is given to him, he then starts to rebel against that light, and he begins digressing instead of progressing. Yet God continues to deal with him. To listen is to become victorious; to continue fighting is to become lukewarm. Eventually (again I emphasize that God will have to be the judge) God will push him aside and he will lose his way — or maybe even his soul.

A GREAT CHURCH

Years ago Frances accompanied me to a great church in a particular Western city for a revival. The church had been purchased a short time before from a large non-Pentecostal group, and the pastor had been tremendously influential in this nation and in other parts of the world. However, something happened in his life that eventually destroyed him. I will relate to you the story.

Back in the late 1940s and early 1950s, God began to move in a great way in the divine healing revivals. Multiple thousands of persons were gathering under the great tents to worship the Lord Jesus Christ. Thousands of persons were saved, thousands were healed, and many were baptized in the Holy Spirit. God used those mighty healing meetings to awaken America from her spiritual lethargy and to introduce her people to a God of might and power.

(Now, by all means, that does not mean every single one of the preachers involved in this great move of God was perfect or even that all of them did everything just exactly right; some preachers were quite the opposite, in fact. But even though the vessel sometimes might have been impure and unclean, the oil that was poured into that vessel was perfect, and, of course, I speak of the oil of the Holy Spirit.)

At any rate, this world-renowned preacher fought against these meetings. And as I stood there in the midst of that church, looking at the big building that had once belonged to this pastor and his congregation, the present pastor told me this: "Brother Swaggart, this man made the statement from this pulpit that if divine healing and the baptism in the Holy Spirit with the evidence of speaking with other tongues were real, then he was crazy and did not have any sense at all."

Sure enough, one of those meetings came to his city, and God worked in great ways. This man fought it, tremendously so, even to the point of buying ads in the newspapers to warn people not to attend. He made a lot of other rash statements along with the one I just mentioned.

From that moment this man started to digress; he started to lose his way. His friends noticed something happening to him. His mind literally went from him. He spent the last two years of his life walking around his church, his mind totally gone, muttering and mumbling to himself. He would walk for hours circling the church, day after day.

He refused to walk in the light as God gave him the light. He refused to walk in the Spirit. The bold statement he had made about being "crazy" if things such as divine healing and the power of the Holy Spirit were real came to pass exactly as he had said it. Now this church was owned and filled with the very people he had criticized so vehemently; and the congregation he once had, which at one time was one of the largest in America, was scattered and no more.

What happened to this brother? Did he go to heaven or hell? I will be frank with you, I do not know; I have to leave that with God (who, as I have said, is the final judge). But I will say this: I would not be in his shoes for anything in the world. I hope and pray that God had mercy on him. But through refusing to walk in the light and thereby in the Spirit, he placed himself in a perilous situation.

We must walk in the Spirit, and we can only walk in the Spirit as we walk in the light that God has given us. I will say it again: if we do not walk in the light that God has given us, we will start to digress spiritually, and the terrible words of Jesus will come back to haunt us: *"I will spue thee out of my mouth."*

HOLY TRINITY

■ Would you please explain to me the meaning of the Trinity?

■ Is it possible to prove there is a God?

QUESTION:

WOULD YOU PLEASE EXPLAIN TO ME THE MEANING OF THE TRINITY?

ANSWER:

The word *Trinity* as such is not found in the Bible; however, in its simplest form *trinity* means three (I John 5:7).

To answer your question: (1) I believe the Trinity can be understood. (2) I believe there is one God manifested in three persons. (3) I believe that each member of the Godhead has His own personal spirit body. I will explain.

Many Bible scholars today say that the Trinity cannot be understood. They have gone so far as to say that the reason they believe this is that they themselves cannot understand it — yet they believe in the Trinity! I think that is somewhat ludicrous. I do not want to believe something I cannot understand. The Word teaches there is a divine Trinity, and I believe that in this divine Godhead there are three separate and distinct persons — each one having His own personal spirit *body*, personal *soul*, and personal *spirit*. Yet, there is only one God. There are not three Gods, only *one*.

Many people conclude that the Father, the Son, and the Holy Spirit are all one and the same. Actually, they are not. These people take I John 5:7 (*"For there are three that bear record in heaven . . . and these three are one"*) to mean one in number, when this is not what is meant at all. They evidently have not studied this in the original Greek language to get its actual meaning. The word "one" in this passage means one in *unity*. Jesus prayed, *"Holy Father, keep through thine own name those whom thou hast given me, that they may be one, as we are"* (John 17:11).

Jesus did not mean here that every member of the body of Christ would physically inhabit one body. What He did pray was that we would be one in unity, one in desire, one in purpose, one in design. He used the term again when He said, *"that they may be one, even as we are one"* (John 17:22). If we read this casually without effort of study, it seems to be contradictory because Jesus used the plural pronoun "they," then asked that "they" may be "one." It is only possible to make several people into one when you speak of unity, and of course this is what is meant here.

The Father, the Son, and the Holy Spirit are spoken of individually

199

and separately in Scripture. There is *one* God the Father, *one* Lord Jesus Christ, and *one* Holy Spirit (I Corinthians 8:6; Ephesians 4:3-6). There are three separate persons in divine plurality and divine individuality. The Father is called God, the Son is called God, and the Holy Spirit is called God. Individually they are each God, and collectively they are *one* God *because of their perfect unity.*

There are things said of each person of the Deity as to position, office, and work that could not be said of the other members of the Godhead. For example, the Father is the head of Christ (I Corinthians 11:3), the Son is the Only Begotten of the Father (II John 3), and the Holy Spirit proceeds from both the Father and the Son (John 14:16; Acts 2:33, 34).

God said, *"Man is become as one of us"* (Genesis 3:22), the pronoun "us" proving plurality of persons. Two Lords are spoken of in Genesis 19:24 — one on earth and one in heaven. In Mark 1 *three* are represented at Jesus' baptism. God the Holy Spirit descended on God the Son like a dove, and then God the Father spoke from heaven. We read (Jesus speaking), *"For David himself said by the Holy Ghost, The Lord said to my Lord, Sit thou on my right hand, till I make thine enemies thy footstool"* (Mark 12:36). Three are referred to here.

THE MYSTERY

The mystery of the Trinity comes about by people trying to force three separate personalities into one person, because they do not care to recognize the true meaning of the word "one" as referring to unity in the Scriptures pertaining to the Trinity. Mankind itself would be just as great a mystery if we endeavored to relegate "all men" to refer to just one person.

You can think of God the Father, God the Son, and God the Holy Spirit as three different persons exactly as you would think of any three other people — their "oneness" pertaining strictly to their being *one* in purpose, design, and desire. There is *"no variableness, neither shadow of turning"* (James 1:17) from the design purpose of the Godhead.

IN HEAVEN

In heaven we will see all three members of the Godhead: God the Father, God the Son, and God the Holy Spirit.

We are told of the great vision the mighty prophet Daniel had when he saw God the Father *and* God the Son (Daniel 7:13, 14).

Jesus again and again used the pronoun "He" when referring to the Holy Spirit, denoting that the Holy Spirit is a person (John 16).

Even though men have seen symbols of the Holy Spirit (Mark 1; Revelation 5:6), but never the Holy Spirit Himself, I believe when we get to heaven, we will see God the Holy Spirit as well as God the Father and God the Son.

There is a word used by some theologians called "anthropomorphic." This word basically means the effort of God to portray Himself to mankind in ways that man can understand and not in one actual form. This would mean that statements such as we read in Daniel 7 would not be the way that God is. I do not believe this. I believe God told us the truth in His Word exactly as it is and exactly as He meant for us to believe it. Consequently, when Moses said He saw God, I believe Moses actually saw God and not some "body" that God took for Himself just so He might appear to Moses. I believe the way Moses saw God is the way God looks.

When Genesis says that God made man in His own image, I am convinced that it meant not only in the spiritual image but also in the physical image. I realize many Bible scholars would chuckle at this statement, but this is the way I see it. I believe that God has a spirit body. I believe He is *omnipresent* (meaning "everywhere"), but I do not believe His body is *omnipresent*. I believe His body is in one place at one time, wherever that may be.

I feel strongly that when we get to heaven, we will see a real figure encased in light, sitting upon a real throne. I believe His Son, Jesus Christ, our Redeemer, will be sitting by His side in the same human body (albeit in a glorified state) that He had while on this earth. I believe the nail scars in the Master's hands will be there forever and forever. I also believe, as previously mentioned, that we will see the Holy Spirit.

TO CLOSE

I believe the books of the Bible, from Genesis to Revelation, as written by the prophets and apostles of old, were given to mankind by God Almighty. I believe the Bible is *the* Word of God, and I believe God said exactly what He meant and meant exactly what He said. When

Genesis says (17:1; 18:1; compare Exodus 6:3) that God appeared to Abraham, I believe God appeared to Abraham and that Abraham saw Him and talked with Him.

When the Bible said that God appeared to Moses (Exodus 3; 4; 32; 33; Leviticus 9; Deuteronomy 31:15), I believe that God appeared to Moses and that Moses saw Him and talked with Him.

When Daniel (chapter 10), Ezekiel (chapters 1, 8), and others (for example, Isaiah 6; Revelation 1) described God, I believe that they described Him precisely as they looked upon Him with actual physical vision; and I believe God looks just the way they said. I do not believe God changes form at will.

I believe the understanding of the Trinity is basically simple, if we will only choose to believe what the Bible reveals concerning it. To believe the Word of God totally and without reservation concerning the eternal Godhead will illumine a person's understanding of the matter and alleviate all mystery. For a certainty, in heaven all will be understood, if not now. *"For now we see through a glass, darkly; but then face to face: now I know in part; but then shall I know even as also I am known"* (Paul the Apostle in I Corinthians 13:12).

QUESTION:

IS IT POSSIBLE TO PROVE THERE IS A GOD?

ANSWER:

Yes, I definitely believe that it is, and I trust the following will qualify my statement.

CREATION

That the cosmic worlds had a beginning not only is declared by Scripture but is confirmed by geology, astronomy, and other sciences. Everything in existence owes that existence to a source greater than its production. A person cannot think of the vast and orderly creation of the cosmos (the extraterrestrial vastness of the universe as compared to the earth alone) with its suns, solar systems, and worlds — complete with the inhabitance of intelligent beings — without concluding that some intelligent being planned, designed, and brought them into existence. To think otherwise would be blind and willful unbelief. The Bible says, *"The heavens declare the glory of God; and the firmament sheweth his handywork"* (Psalm 19:1; also see Psalm 8:3).

DESIGN

That the world has a design cannot be questioned. The changing of the seasons, the flowers, the rotation of the earth on its axis — plus myriad other things that could be named — all show design. In back of all design must be a designer.

For instance, take the snowflake. Out of 5,300 pictures of snow crystals cataloged, no two are exactly alike. Yet, each has six points crossing at a 60-degree angle, and each flake has three distinct triangles. (The Hebrew word for "snow" equals 333. Could it not be that God has set His symbol of the triune God in each flake?) Considering that the average snowstorm produces about 1,000 billion crystals, could not only an intelligent being design so many forms? This same infinite design is carried out with every detail of creation, proving an infinite mind — thus proving God.

INTUITION

All men have an intuitive belief in God. (Intuition is an immediate apprehension, a faculty of attaining to direct knowledge, a conviction without evident rational thought and inference, quick or ready insight.) Admittedly, some people have blindly ignored and blocked out this natural faith by unnatural and destructive efforts until it is not recognized by them; but in the face of sudden danger and/or other hard-core realities of adversity, they automatically call upon God for help. Even the Communists, who proclaim themselves to be self-avowed atheists, at times invoke the name of God.

No creation has to be school-trained in behavior peculiar to its nature. So man does not have to *learn* that there is a God. He knows intuitively that there is a God and that *"in him we live, and move, and have our being"* (Acts 17:22-28).

NATURE

Man's very nature (moral and spiritual) knows there is a God who approves or condemns all acts of right or wrong. Conscience is the voice of God in man. His moral nature makes man a responsible creature and requires him to consecrate himself to the highest good of being and of the universe.

If there were no God, then moral nature would be a lie. Man's native moral obligation to moral law implies a moral lawgiver and moral governor of the universe; thus, man's moral and intellectual being proves the existence of a God to whom he is responsible.

UNIVERSAL BELIEF

The vast majority of men of all ages and places have acknowledged the existence of God. The lowest tribes in the most destitute of religions, as well as the most highly civilized and religious, have equally believed in a Supreme Being. Such is manifested in the manners, customs, literature, religion, and conduct of all men (Romans 1:21-32).

Napoleon, when asked if he believed Jesus Christ was really the Son of God and actually rose from the dead, said, "You can go from the Indians of North America to the crowned heads of Europe and when you mention the name, 'Jesus,' millions would gladly die for Him. Yes," he said, "I believe He was and is God and did rise from the dead."

No dead man could command that kind of respect.

UNIVERSAL HUNGER

The heart of every man hungers for God, for satisfaction of soul, and longs for a Saviour and a Deliverer from all the ills and curses of life. Man may not understand what the hunger is, but it is apparent in his efforts to satisfy it — even though he attempts to satisfy it in all the wrong ways most of the time.

DEPENDENCE A NECESSITY

All men of all ages and places not only recognize the existence of a Supreme Being, but at times recognize their dependence upon Him.

They also recognize an absolute necessity for His blessings to sustain life. They realize their own helplessness, and they long for and call upon God for help in time of need — even those who profess not to believe that He exists (Psalm 107:1-43; Jonah 1:5-16).

HARMONY

To believe in the existence of God is the only natural, normal, practical, beneficial, satisfying, factual, necessary, and scriptural way to believe. When a person has the key that will unlock a door, he knows he has the right key. Atheism does not hold the answer to one single problem; it makes lies of nature, creation, the Bible, and God, and leaves helpless, floundering man a victim of misery and despair. Only God has all the answers.

HISTORY

The record of events in all of history gives overwhelming evidence of the existence and providence of God — in the rise and fall of nations, in the preservation of races, in the government of peoples, and in enumerable events that could have had no natural or possible explanation other than being the act of a Supernatural Being. The nation of Israel is an excellent example.

This nation, brought into being by God and kept by God, is a perfect example of the existence of God. The promises given to the Israelites thousands of years ago are an ever-present testimony that God exists.

To deny the existence of God is as foolish as denying the existence of creation, electricity, heat, light, cold, and myriad other things, seen and unseen. Multitudes of people today can testify of a changed life through faith in God. Multiple millions of people the world over can also testify of various other personal spiritual experiences, such as answers to prayer for healing, for example. While this is true of Christians, not one infidel, agnostic, or atheist can boast of any benefit whatsoever from his unbelief. For the acid test of both Christianity and atheism, consider the actual benefits of their converts.

SCRIPTURES

The Bible begins by assuming the existence of God and His creation of all things (Genesis 1:1). In over 20,000 statements about God in Scripture, we come to know all that we need to know about the subject.

[Notes taken, in part, from Dake's Annotated Reference Bible.*]*

QUESTION:

HOMOSEXUALITY

■ Are homosexuals born that way?

■ Some persons have stated that David's relationship with Jonathan was a homosexual affair. Is there any truth in this?

QUESTION:

ARE HOMOSEXUALS BORN THAT WAY?

ANSWER:

One of the gross sins of this or any age is the sin of homosexuality. It has become so prevalent in American society that we are told one out of every 10 American men is either homosexual or has homosexual tendencies. This is a staggering proportion. Homosexuality is a sin against society, against nature, against the human body (which should be a temple of the Holy Spirit), and against God. *"For this cause God gave them up unto vile affections: for even their women did change the natural use into that which is against nature: And likewise also the men, leaving the natural use of the woman, burned in their lust one toward another; men with men working that which is unseemly, and receiving in themselves that recompence of their error which was meet"* (Romans 1:26, 27).

WORST SIN IN THE WORLD?

I heard a preacher say once that the sins of homosexuality and lesbianism are the most terrible sins known to man. I do not know whether that is true. I know that murder, adultery, and kidnapping are vile and terrible sins; but the sin of homosexuality does carry with it a penalty that no other sin, to my knowledge, has ever carried. *"The Lord said . . . the cry of Sodom and Gomorrah is great, and . . . their sin is very grievous"* (Genesis 18:20). *"Then the Lord rained upon Sodom and upon Gomorrah brimstone and fire from the Lord out of heaven"* (Genesis 19:24). The only record in Bible history of God personally destroying a place was the destruction of the twin cities of Sodom and Gomorrah, and this because of the terrible sin of homosexuality. God's intervention and destruction had always been indirect, but this time the sin was so grievous and so terrible that He personally took a hand and rained fire and brimstone upon these twin cities and destroyed them from the face of the earth until there is left no record of their former position and place.

The sins of homosexualilty and lesbianism are Satan's diabolical thrusts against God's choice creation; namely, man. Satan hates man because man is created in God's image. The breath of God is actually

209

in him. His body should be the temple of the Holy Spirit. God has chosen man to rule and reign under Christ Jesus, over His creation, forever and forever. God deemed man's salvation so important that He paid a price so staggering it is impossible for our imagination to conceive of its significance.

The sin of homosexuality is Satan's strongest and most conscientious effort to destroy the human race; and since man is favored by God, this would be a great victory for the forces of evil. If this terrible sin became pandemic, Satan's end would be fastly achieved, for humanity would cease to exist; but Satan has not succeeded, and he never will. Still, that does not make the gross sin of homosexuality any less grievous. I am not sure whether, in the theological catalog of horrible sins, homosexuality is the worst sin in the eyes of God, but it is certainly possible because of its destructive power.

CAUSE

Although many people want to think and believe that a person is born this way, I do not believe that is the case. *"Let no man say when he is tempted, I am tempted of God: for God cannot be tempted with evil, neither tempteth he any man: But every man is tempted, when he is drawn away of his own lust, and enticed. Then when lust hath conceived, it bringeth forth sin: and sin, when it is finished, bringeth forth death. Do not err, my beloved brethren"* (James 1:13-16). From this Scripture we see that a person becomes a homosexual because he is tempted by Satan and yields to that temptation. Finally then, he becomes snared and bound by the horrible thing.

What makes this terrible sin so dangerous is that homosexuals recruit other people. Now, the Scripture mentions enticement; and with this sin multiple thousands of young boys are enticed into this web of deceit and this malignity of darkness because of promises, gullibility, or whatever. Many of those enticed eventually become homosexuals themselves. I repeat, I do not believe a person is born a homosexual; he becomes that way when he yields to the temptation.

THE RECOMPENSE OF THEIR ERROR

The Scripture tells us that those who walk in this deception of darkness will receive in themselves the *"recompence of their error"* (Romans 1:27). The Greek word for "error" means "wandering, wrong action, wickedness." Now, this means that their body is weakened and debilitated so that they receive in themselves the penalty of their wickedness. You can almost tell homosexuals by their mannerisms, actions, personality, and even their facial expression. The sordid life-style actually changes the individual's personality. I realize that in this wicked age someone may refer to professional athletes who are homosexuals and are not changed in this manner. However, if they continue in this dreadful path of darkness, it will change them just as surely as the Scripture says it will.

SATAN'S DIABOLICAL SCHEME

Under the label of freedom, there is a movement afoot today in America publicly to educate our society that the homosexual is normal, if a bit different. Every effort is being made to take from the books the laws that guard our children (and the rest of society, for that matter) from this scourge of Satan. A news commentator on the *CBS Morning News* stated sometime ago, "You cannot legislate morality." He was quite lengthy in his dissertation, but the gist of his subject was this: he felt that the homosexual should be treated as anyone else. He opposed all efforts to keep America free from the sin of homosexuality. As I listened to this particular broadcast, I felt it was a blatant abuse of the airwaves. Of course, the statement was made in educated and suave terms. He was a capable commentator. He made it seem as if homosexuality was not so bad after all, and anyone who opposed the life-style of these individuals had to have something wrong with him. Yet, this man was dead wrong in his summation of the legislation of morality.

Naturally, laws cannot force a person to do good. The problem is more than moral, it is spiritual. At the same time, stealing is a spiritual problem, and we have laws to protect us from thieves (as much as laws can). We do not force banks or other places of employment to hire ex-convicts or convicted felons just so we will not violate their rights; and we would not want to be forced to hire a person known to be a child molester to baby-sit our children. No, you cannot legislate morality when it comes to forcing people to do right. They have to *want* to do right; but even though you cannot force morality, people can be made to wish they had not sinned and that they had done right. A nation without laws is a nation without government, without a standard, and without direction. If a person wants to be a homosexual — as deceiving, vile, and degrading as this is — he has that right. Even God gives him that choice. He will go to hell for it, to be sure, but he is a free moral agent and has that choice. At the same time, I do not feel that government can legislate that such people can teach our children in public schools or that they can hold places of position and trust in employment that demand Christian concepts and morality. Many of these poor individuals are filled with guilt and condemnation, and there are those who are so deep into this power of darkness that they have turned into reprobates. These individuals would like to be in a position where they could recruit young men and boys (or girls) into their life of debauchery and filth. Yes, we must have laws on the books that protect society and our innocent children from becoming victims of this scourge of darkness.

CURE

Thank God there is hope. There is not a power of darkness that the power of Almighty God cannot break. There is not a darkened stain of sin that His blood cannot cleanse. The Bible speaks of *"abusers of themselves with mankind"* (I Corinthians 6:9). The Greek word for "abusers" is *arsenoloites*. It means "a person guilty of unnatural offenses: a sodomite, a homosexual, a sexual pervert." *"Such were some of you: but ye are washed, but ye are sanctified, but ye are justified in the name of the Lord Jesus, and by the Spirit of our God"* (verse 11). In other words, the Lord Jesus Christ can deliver a person from this dreadful sin of homosexuality. Of course it takes the blood of Jesus to cleanse any sin, but there are some sins that are so strong (and I believe homosexuality is one of them), so deeply empowered by Satan, that it takes a direct act of the power of God (a miracle) to break the terrible bondage that besets humanity.

The devil will try to make an individual bound by this terrible sin to believe there is no hope. He will first try to make him believe this is normal. If that does not work, he will tell him that he cannot be free, that he cannot be normal; but Satan is a liar and the father of lies. There is absolutely no sin that the blood of Jesus Christ cannot cover and cleanse.

Scripture plainly says that those who do these things *"shall [not] inherit the kingdom of God"* (I Corinthians 6:9, 10). It is impossible to be a homosexual and a child of God at the same time; but if homosexuals will come to the Lord Jesus Christ, He can cleanse them, wash them, sanctify them, and justify them in the name of the Lord Jesus. America's only hope is God. Man's only hope is God. Trying to normalize sin to make it acceptable will not work — it only makes it worse. Turning from that sin to the Lord Jesus Christ is the only answer.

> *"What can wash away my sin?*
> *Nothing but the blood of Jesus.*
> *What can make me whole again?*
> *Nothing but the blood of Jesus."*

QUESTION:

SOME PERSONS HAVE STATED THAT DAVID'S RELATIONSHIP WITH JONATHAN WAS A HOMOSEXUAL AFFAIR. IS THERE ANY TRUTH IN THIS?

ANSWER:

God forbid! No!

There have been some homosexuals who have tried to make it appear this way; but actually there was not even the hint of such a relationship, and I can give biblical proof to support my statement.

There are two basic scriptural references to the friendship of David and Jonathan.

The first one is as follows: *"And it came to pass, when he had made an end of speaking unto Saul, that the soul of Jonathan was knit with the soul of David, and Jonathan loved him as his own soul. And Saul took him that day, and would let him go no more home to his father's house. Then Jonathan and David made a covenant, because he loved him as his own soul. And Jonathan stripped himself of the robe that was upon him, and gave it to David, and his garments, even to his sword, and to his bow, and to his girdle"* (I Samuel 18:1-4).

The other reference, in part, states: *"I am distressed for thee, my brother Jonathan: very pleasant hast thou been unto me: thy love to me was wonderful, passing the love of women"* (II Samuel 1:26).

Now, let us look and see what all of this means.

JONATHAN AND DAVID

When David killed Goliath, he was probably somewhere between 16 and 18 years old. Scripture refers to him as a *"stripling"* (I Samuel 17:56). This word, in the Hebrew, is *elem,* which means "a lad not grown up enough to enter public life." This further emphasizes David's youth.

When David accomplished this mighty feat by the help and grace of God, he aroused the excitement of the entire nation of Israel. The effect was so great, in fact, that the Bible tells us the people shouted, *"Saul hath slain his thousands, and David his ten thousands"* (I Samuel 18:7).

Jonathan was about 40 years old at this time. He took David under his wing, and it appears that he taught him how to use the sword and the bow (I Samuel 18:4). You see, Jonathan was also a mighty warrior in his own right. Their relationship was similar to father and son.

A DIFFERENT CULTURE

In Old Testament days it was a common practice — even a normal and desired one — for an older man to take a younger man under his wing and teach him a particular trade. Although our American culture does not operate in this vein much today, this is still the case in many countries of the world. Considering this, we can see that such is what Jonathan did for David. He taught him all that he knew, training him greatly in the art of war. Their friendship was indestructible — it remained unto the end (compare John 13:1).

Truly, Jonathan must have been a Godly man. He was actually heir to the throne, being the oldest son of King Saul, and yet he knew that God had laid His hand on David. He knew that David had been anointed king over Israel. The normal and expected procedure would have been for him to hate David, even to try to kill him, but not Jonathan. He knew that God's hand was on this boy, and he would not oppose him; rather, he endeavored to help David. This demonstrates that he was a man of extraordinary courage and character.

Jonathan realized that his father, Saul, was an ungodly man. He also realized that the doom of the kingly lineage through Saul had been pronounced because of Saul's jealousy, pride, and disobedience to God. As far as we know, Jonathan himself was faithful to God. David was fortunate to have a friend such as Jonathan.

It is easy to see how such a friendship could develop during this period when Saul was endeavoring to kill David and had actually made every effort to do so. Then Jonathan proved himself a true friend, doing all within his power to save David and being used by God to this end. He was a tremendous blessing to Israel and the work of God, as well as to David. This kind of atmosphere lended itself to such a friendship — a bond even closer than that of brothers.

THE ODE TO SAUL AND JONATHAN

The latter part of I Samuel records the death of Saul and Jonathan. They were both fighting in a battle against the Philistines. Jonathan was killed, and Saul, being severely wounded, *"took a sword, and fell upon it"* (I Samuel 31:4). David sang an "ode" or "lamentation" respecting the death of Saul and Jonathan (II Samuel 1:17-27). Verse 26 talks about Jonathan's love for David *"passing the love of women."*

In older times the ode, lamentation, or song was the common manner used to express exaltation — that is, strong feeling — over a tremendous experience or happening. The title of this ode in Hebrew is called *Kesheth*, meaning, "the bow." It was customary in the East to give quaint and even farfetched titles to odes and treatises and to use such language in these works. In other words, things would be *written* in these Oriental odes or songs that would not normally be *said*, in order to intensify the message. Actually, this same technique is still used often today. Expressive statements are made in songs that we sing constantly, yet we would not speak this way in a direct conversation.

So we must remember that II Samuel 1:17-27 was not a statement made *to* somebody, but an ode or a song sung by David concerning the death of Saul and Jonathan.

DAVID AND BATHSHEBA

Note the weakness David exhibited toward the opposite sex respecting his affair with Bathsheba and the terrible extent of his passion for her (II Samuel 11). This, I think, should lay to rest all accusations made respecting the relationship between David and Jonathan.

No, David was not perfect, but he was a *Godly* man. Anyone who takes these Scriptures and twists them to mean some homosexual liaison is, in my opinion, bordering on blasphemy.

The sin of homosexuality is a grievous one, and, as somebody said, it may be the worst sin on the face of the earth. It is recorded, among other places, that *"for this cause God gave them up unto vile affections: for even their women did change the natural use into that which is against nature: And likewise also the men, leaving the natural use of the woman, burned in their lust one toward another; men with men working that which is unseemly, and receiving in themselves that recompence of their error which was meet. And even as they did not like to retain God in their knowledge, God gave them over to a reprobate mind, to do those things which are not convenient"* (Romans 1:26-28).

This clearly states that individuals who have gone into homosexuality have been turned over to a reprobate, or perverted, mind; but, yes, they can be saved if they will come back to the Lord Jesus Christ and ask His mercy and His forgiveness. The blood of Jesus Christ still *"cleanseth . . . from all sin"* (I John 1:7).

QUESTION:

INFANTICIDE

■ If parents had a terribly deformed baby born to them, should they let the baby expire without medical help, or should they use every available means to keep their baby alive, even though the child would be little more than a vegetable?

QUESTION:

IF PARENTS HAD A TERRIBLY DEFORMED BABY BORN TO THEM, SHOULD THEY LET THE BABY EXPIRE WITHOUT MEDICAL HELP, OR SHOULD THEY USE EVERY AVAILABLE MEANS TO KEEP THEIR BABY ALIVE, EVEN THOUGH THE CHILD WOULD BE LITTLE MORE THAN A VEGETABLE?

ANSWER:

This is a difficult question. To be honest, I have prepared my thoughts several times, unsatisfied with each answer, because I suspect this question would tax the very wisdom of Solomon.

Sometime ago a well-known evangelist sat in my office. He and his wife had experienced a tragedy when a little boy was born to them, terribly deranged due to difficulties in birth. The situation had been a heartrending ordeal that, it seemed, would never end — a pain that would never stop hurting. This minister of the Gospel, who had had great success in winning thousands of souls to the Lord Jesus Christ, sat there with tears rolling down his cheeks as he relived this painful scene for me to partially understand. Of course, the couple had believed God for a miracle over and over, but as of yet no miracle had occurred. They watched their little boy who was, at that time, nearly four years old — yet his mind was that of about a six-month-old baby. It would never improve — unless, of course, God ordained differently. He told me something that possibly cost him more than words could ever begin to express (and many of you will not agree with it); but before criticism is made, possibly you should walk in his shoes awhile.

He said, "Brother Swaggart, my wife and I have sought God earnestly for our little boy to be healed. We have done everything we know to do, apparently to no avail. He has not progressed; he has, instead, remained static with no sign of improvement. The brain damage is extensive; it would take more than divine healing — it would take a miracle!"

He went on to say, "Of course, we know that God is able to do all things. He is a God of miracles; but, at the same time, we have not seen it. I will tell you something that maybe I've never told anyone else." He said (if I remember his statement correctly), "If God does not perform a miracle in the physical body and mind of our little boy, I pray that He will take him home to glory."

I saw what this was costing our brother. I saw the tears roll down his cheeks. I personally have never had to face anything like this. Some people may criticize this brother severely, but I have no criticism or condemnation for him whatsoever. I think I understand his feelings — even if only a little bit. There *are* some things worse than death.

He went on to tell me that he knew his son would be with the Lord Jesus Christ — and, I might add, *without* the terrible deformity that will forever keep him from developing in any form or fashion in this present world.

THE JUDEO-CHRISTIAN CONCEPT

In the last few years there has been a deluge of information in the news concerning babies born with severe deformities; and the argument rages now in the media and in legal circles, "What posture should the government take? the people? the parents?" There is no easy solution! Many persons will read the account that I have just related to you and decide that death would be better in this case; hence, some young folk (or elderly ones) ought to be allowed to die — even encouraged to do so. This is not correct. The terrible pain these young parents are suffering because of the son (and the many parents who are faced with the same decision in this nation and throughout the world) has nothing to do with the decision at hand.

The Judeo-Christian concept places a high value on life. It stems from man's belief in God. We are told, *"And God said, Let us make man in our image, after our likeness . . . . So God created man in his own image, in the image of God created he him; male and female created he them"* (Genesis 1:26, 27).

Whenever the Judeo-Christian concept is adhered to, tremendous worth or value is placed on human life. When the Judeo-Christian concept is replaced by a humanistic philosophy, the worth of human life gradually decreases. Today terrifying things are unfolding before our very eyes. Our schoolchildren are taught that God did not create man — that he is a product of evolutionary processes. Consequently, man has no soul and there is no such thing as a God, heaven, hell, eternity, or judgment. When man dies, the humanists tell us, there is nothing left. If this is the case, then *this* is the only life that matters; and human life becomes worth less and less.

However, when man takes the position that God created man in His own image, that man possesses an eternal soul and spirit, and that man will live forever and ever, then man takes on a completely different posture. He becomes tremendously valuable, and his worth increases dramatically — simply because he *is* made in the image of God.

SACREDNESS OF LIFE

Human life, in view of the foregoing, must be held sacred. Little babies must be protected all the way from conception to old age. Human life must never be sacrificed needlessly or taken by anyone — man or state — unless a particular individual sets himself up to eradicate life by cold-blooded murder, et cetera. *Then,* according to the Word of God and because of the sacredness of human life, that individual should be stopped and his life must be taken by the state — as a warning to others that human life is most valuable and must not be squandered or wasted. This is what we mean by capital punishment for capital crimes. *"Whoso sheddeth man's blood, by man shall his blood be shed: for in the image of God made he man"* (Genesis 9:6).

In any country where the Judeo-Christian concept is not adhered to, life becomes cheaper and cheaper as time goes on, for the simple reason that an individual is not looked on as a person made in the image of God or else there is a warped concept of God.

Abortion, infanticide, suicide, and euthanasia are tremendously abhorrent. *Yet,* all four of these terrible derangements of evil are being subtly promoted in the press, through television, and through the educational process. Now we have *abortion-on-demand* . . . to the tune of 1.5 to 2.0 million babies being murdered a year. We are talking in this question and answer about killing little babies who have already been born and yet have some kind of defect (*infanticide*). And running like a thread through a needle in all of this is the word *suicide*. Suicide is becoming more and more acceptable and is being promoted by humanistic philosophy.

"Death education" is starting to be taught in a cunning way, even to children in many schools today. The groundwork is being laid to do away with useless members of society who can no longer contribute to society because of old age, sickness, or deformities. Encouragement is given to these people to commit suicide quietly or else treatment will be withheld from them so that they can quietly pass from the scene (*euthanasia*).

In other words, whenever the Christian concept of life is done away with, an individual is seen as just a part of a mass; and if he does not produce for the state, then he must be eliminated.

INFANTICIDE

So the question you have asked is one that falls on all segments of society. The cheapening of human life brought about by abortion-on-demand has, like falling dominoes, made other impacts on our society as well. The first is infanticide, and this is what we are discussing in this answer. By infanticide we mean the killing of a newborn by active or passive means as the child is considered to have a "life not worth living." Media coverage in the United States today clearly indicates that some doctors *are* practicing infanticide. When physicians are willing to counsel the parents of a newborn child with a congenital defect to allow the child to starve to death, we should examine the motive. Yet the law of the land has apparently turned its back. Infanticide, in reality, is *homicide* (murder).

EUTHANASIA

The next problem is *euthanasia* or "mercy killing." This means the termination of a life, allegedly for the benefit of the individual. Today there are reports about elderly people in approved nursing homes who are not having their infections and fever symptoms treated. It has nothing to do with the limitation of medicine; rather, a decision has been made by staff personnel based on social problems of the patient in question.

At the Nuremberg Trials, when the horror of the Holocaust was examined, Leo Alexander, the American psychiatric representative, said, "It all began with the concept that there was such a thing as human life not worthy to be lived." In Germany, in the 1930s, 276,000 people were destined for destruction. Who were these people? They were the aged, infirmed, retarded, senile — otherwise described as "useless eaters." These people were eliminated. This probably paved the way for the horrible Holocaust that developed with the murder of some 6 million Jews. If the doctors in Germany had maintained the "right to life of every individual," the Holocaust, at the least, would have been slowed down or minimized. Right now in America, we have children with congenital defects; we have old folk who have become a cramping nuisance to our society or to their family. Gradually the idea is being promoted to do away with these useless individuals.

You see, our nation has prided itself on its lack of discrimination on any grounds, but it has succumbed to discrimination against the unborn because they cannot speak for themselves, against the newborn because they have a life not worthy to be lived, and against the elderly because they are social and economic burdens.

Not long ago a Nobel laureate suggested that children not be declared alive until they are three days old and that each family be given the right to reject the child if it so wishes. In other words, if some kind of defect is seen, the child may be eliminated even up to three days after birth.

THE RIGHT TO LIFE

What we are discussing here is not the pain and agony of a particular family. My heart breaks for every individual that has to face this, as I outlined at the beginning; but what we are facing is a program of death that is being fostered by satanic forces, which could destroy society as we know it today, when carried out to its illogical conclusion. Life must be protected at all costs. It is sacred. We must do all within our power to save life — even the life of those with congenital defects, even those that others may look at as useless, for these individuals are made in the image of God.

What I have been discussing is so-called mercy killing. Any way that this is labeled or any way that it is carried out, it is murder in the eyes of God. However, we are faced with another problem of mammoth difficulties. This is one at the very heart of your question: What does a parent or person do when he realizes that a child or a loved one can be kept alive only through artificial means of support? This is definitely a difficult question to answer.

I was talking with a minister of the Gospel the other day when he spoke of the demise of his father. He said his dad requested that he be taken out of the hospital so he could go home and die with dignity. It has to be a demoralizing thing for a family to watch a loved one hooked up to and kept alive by a life support system for an indefinite period of time.

The answer I am going to give is not an easy one. It does not solve all the problems, but it is the only answer that is scriptural and practical considering the difficulties involved.

Every effort must be made, even in these trying circumstances, to keep the individual alive. Whenever the floodgates are opened, there is no end to the difficulties involved. If the medical profession states that "when a certain point is reached, then the individual should be pulled off the life support system," then that step is shortened just a little more. Finally we will come to what we call "mercy killings," which are being practiced today to some degree. The sacredness of life takes on a totally different meaning; it becomes cheaper and cheaper; hence, "death education."

THE PERSONAL LEVEL

Even after I have said all of these things and taken a stand for what I believe, the answers that I have given have to be reaffirmed considering the problems involved. Yet at the same time, I cannot find it in my heart whatsoever to condemn a parent or any individual who has had to watch his loved one exist as a vegetable, kept alive only by mechanical devices, if such a person should desire that life support systems be removed in order for the loved one to die with dignity. Each case would have to stand on its own merit. I cannot play God and judge an individual in these matters.

Still, once again, the final conclusion of the matter must be stated. When we try to address ourselves to these problems, we are not speaking of individual problems as much as we would like to think. We are speaking of a national deterioration; and if this deterioration is allowed to continue, the result will be another holocaust, with human life becoming more and more depreciated. This must be stopped at all costs.

MARRIAGE

■ In light of Ephesians 5:22-24, should a Christian wife do things that are unlawful, unscriptural, and even sin, if commanded by her husband to do so?

■ Is oral-genital sex scripturally permissible between husband and wife?

■ Would it be scripturally or morally wrong for a woman to undergo artificial insemination in order to have a baby if she and her husband were unable to conceive?

QUESTION:

IN LIGHT OF EPHESIANS 5:22-24, SHOULD A CHRISTIAN WIFE DO THINGS THAT ARE UNLAWFUL, UNSCRIPTURAL, AND EVEN SIN, IF COMMANDED BY HER HUSBAND TO DO SO?

ANSWER:

The teaching that Christian wives should submit to their husband in everything, as indicated in the last two words of verse 24, has caused many problems between husband and wife and much controversy within religious circles, but it is easily explained. This is an old argument that surfaces every once in a while when Satan can persuade a few people to believe error; thus, the difficulty.

OBEYING THE SCRIPTURES

The teaching has been that a Christian wife should obey her husband no matter what he asks her to do. In other words, if he asks her to go to a nightclub with him, she should go. If he asks her to drink alcoholic beverages with him, she should drink. If he asks her to lie or bear false witness, she should do that, too, because in doing this, the teaching bears out, she is obeying the Scriptures. However, this is blatantly and obviously erroneous teaching.

In the first place, God never contradicts His own Word. The God that said, *"Thou shalt not bear false witness"* (Exodus 20:16), does not command a Christian woman (or anyone, for that matter) to break that law by obeying an ungodly husband.

OBEYING THE HIGHER LAW

Second, any law that is given by a husband (or even the state, for that matter) is subject to a higher law; namely, the law of God. We are also told to *"render . . . unto Caesar the things which are Caesar's"* (Matthew 22:21; Mark 12:17; Luke 20:25) and to *"obey them that have the rule over [us]"* (Hebrews 13:17). However, the majority in the early church died before they would obey those in rulership, yet they were not breaking God's laws or contradicting them. The Roman Caesar simply stated that they (the early Christians) had to do obeisance to him,

227

and to recant their faith in the Lord Jesus Christ and declare him (Caesar) as god. The early Christians died rather than do this, and rightly so. They would have lost their soul if they had obeyed.

Likewise, millions of Christians have died on the line of march from the Day of Pentecost until now simply because they would not obey those who had the rule over them; because those who had the legal rule over them were often ungodly, satanic, and adamant in their demand that the Christians recant their faith in the Lord Jesus Christ. Were they breaking the laws of God by not yielding to the demands of these ungodly leaders? Certainly not! These commands given by the Lord Jesus Christ and the Apostle Paul were not, and are not, to be taken out of context. The Lord was speaking of money (taxes) that was owed Caesar. He was simply telling the Jews that they should pay their taxes because they received certain benefits from the state and consequently owed something to it in return.

The Apostle Paul meant that just because a person is a Christian does not mean he is above the law. Christians have to obey the rightful law as well as anyone else.

The same application may be made to Christian wives obeying ungodly husbands.

However, what Paul meant here in Ephesians was this (and he was speaking to Christian wives and Christian husbands): a wife's obedience to the husband in all things is based upon the husband loving his wife as Christ loved the church. No husband who is an imitator of the Lord Jesus Christ will demand that his wife do anything unscriptural, unholy, or ungodly. Any husband who is Christlike in conduct and attitude, which he should be, should be reverenced by his wife; and she should submit to him as unto the Lord. She should submit in everything, knowing that everything will be scriptural, Godly, and Christlike.

QUESTION:

IS ORAL-GENITAL SEX SCRIPTURALLY PERMISSIBLE BETWEEN HUSBAND AND WIFE?

ANSWER:

No, I do not think so. The Bible says the *"marriage . . . bed [is] undefiled"* (Hebrews 13:4), but the Holy Spirit certainly did not mean uncleanness or perversion.

The Apostle Paul spoke of couples *"dishonour[ing] their own bodies between themselves"* (Romans 1:24). He used the term *"without natural affection"* (Romans 1:31) and spoke of an unholy desire for unnatural experiences between husband and wife or between partners in a homosexual or other sexually deviant situation.

This more or less says it all. We must always remember that Satan, since the Fall, has endeavored to debase the human body. He has sought to pervert the sex drives God placed originally in mankind. Those sex desires run the gamut from unnatural and excitable sex acts to sex acts that include murder. As children of God, we must always remember our body is a temple of the Holy Spirit and we are never to desire perversion or uncleanness.

I also feel masturbation is wrong. For this act to be carried out to the satisfaction of the individual concerned, male or female, the imagery of the mind has to dwell on that which is sordid and filthy. Masturbation is one of the reasons pornography is so successful. Magazines filled with hard-core sex acts provide a picturesque setting for the completion of the masturbation act. The scenario becomes worse and (always) worse.

I repeat, the Christian's body is *"the temple of God"* , *"the temple of the Holy Ghost"* (I Corinthians 3:16, 17; 6:19, 20). We must never forget this. Anything that tends to debase the human body or pervert it is wrong, sinful, and wicked.

QUESTION:

WOULD IT BE SCRIPTURALLY OR MORALLY WRONG FOR A WOMAN TO UNDERGO ARTIFICIAL INSEMINATION IN ORDER TO HAVE A BABY IF SHE AND HER HUSBAND WERE UNABLE TO CONCEIVE?

ANSWER:

The question of artificial insemination is becoming quite pronounced at this particular time. Right or wrong, I think, given time, it will become progressively more common. I have thought about it quite a lot, and it is not an easy question to answer. The Bible does not say anything about it per se. So, consequently, I can only answer it in two ways. I pray my answer will be of help to you.

ADOPTION BETTER

A woman would not be committing adultery if she had artificial insemination in a doctor's office. She would not be violating any Scripture. However, at the same time, it would not be a wise thing to do. Adoption would be more in order and more in keeping with the Word of God.

If a woman should decide to have a baby by artificial insemination, here are some important factors to consider:

• It must be the decision of the woman and her husband, and must have *his* absolute approval.

• The sperm used must be that of a man unknown to the two of them, and they should never know the identity of the donor.

• The donor, likewise, should never know what woman was given his sperm.

• The biological father should never be revealed to the child, and it would probably be best that the child not know that conception was not by natural means.

EMOTIONAL PROBLEMS

Because of the many emotional problems and dangers involved, it would be extremely unwise for anyone to follow such a course. Naturally, the husband should have the final word in it, and again I emphasize the wisdom of using adoption in such cases. Even though the woman may strongly desire to bear a baby of her own, artificial insemination would only partially be able to fulfill that desire because it would not be brought about through the act of love with her husband. Besides, it could bring about a host of emotional problems. Of course, there are problems with adoption, but they are more or less cut-and-dried.

I have given the answer I consider correct. There is no easy answer to such a question. Nevertheless, what I have said may be of some help.

QUESTION:

MONEY

■ Does Romans 13:8 ("owe no man any thing") mean
that it is wrong to purchase anything on time
payments?

■ Why do the wicked prosper?

■ Why don't you quit asking for money over television
and trust God for the finances? Second, doesn't Gospel
television weaken and draw money away from the local
church?

■ Should a Christian expect God to give back to him
when he gives to the Lord?

■ In giving my money to spread the Gospel all over the world, I want to make sure that it accomplishes its intended purpose. How can I be sure that this is done?

■ Do you think it is scripturally permissible for a Christian to participate in state lotteries, which are seemingly gambling?

QUESTION:

*DOES ROMANS 13:8 ("OWE NO MAN ANY THING")
MEAN THAT IT IS WRONG TO PURCHASE ANYTHING
ON TIME PAYMENTS?*

ANSWER:

The Holy Spirit instructed Paul to tell the body of Christ that every soul (and that includes Christians) must be subject to the government — *unless* it violates his Christian conscience (Romans 13:1-7). Paul went on to explain that government as a whole is ordained of God and Christians must submit to it. (Of course we know God did not ordain bad government.) For this reason we must pay taxes or tribute, dues, or what-have-you (verse 6).

CHRISTIAN RESPONSIBILITIES

"Owe no man any thing" (verse 8) simply means that being Christian does not exempt us from paying our due debts, taxes, and other legitimate responsibilities. We should *"render therefore to all their dues: tribute to whom tribute is due; custom to whom custom; fear to whom fear; honour to whom honour"* (verse 7). Even though Christ is our King, we must still pay what is justly due to government officials, and even to pastors and ministers (or anyone of this nature) that God has called. We must not fail to pay honor, or whatever; hence, the reason for the statement, *"Owe no man any thing."*

This is not to refer to a just debt of money and other material things. Rather, it simply expresses the idea that Christians owe to each other mutual love. We are not bound to obey our brethren as we obey civil rulers and laws, but we are bound to them by love.

TIME PAYMENTS

Some persons have taught in the last few years, from this Scripture, that it is wrong to purchase anything on a time-payment plan. Admittedly, many Christians do go deeper into debt than they should and bring upon themselves much difficulty. However, if that Scripture is interpreted to mean what some persons say it means, most people in the United States could not ever buy a house, a car, or anything of that nature.

233

But, of course, it does not mean that. It would be virtually impossible for the majority of the public (including Christians) to come up with enough cash to purchase a house. Whenever a person signs a contract to pay for a house or a car or whatever, he agrees to pay so much (interest plus principal) over a period of time, and he actually does not owe anything until that note is due each month (or whenever).

BUDGET

I hope I have explained this satisfactorily. However, all of us should be careful about going into debt further than we are able to handle simply because the Scriptures also state, *"The borrower is servant to the lender"* (Proverbs 22:7). Many Christians have caused themselves undue difficulty by overextending themselves, and this is wrong too. We are to be examples of integrity, honesty, and righteousness in the midst of this world. Christians who buy more than can be afforded on their budget are doing a disservice to Christ.

CASH ONLY

I do not recall that Frances and I have ever purchased anything on a time-payment plan (except a house and car). When we were first married, we saved our nickels and dimes until we were able to pay cash for whatever we needed — living room suite, stereo, and so forth. We simply did not go into debt to buy. Admittedly, we did without some things other people had, but it taught me fiscal responsibility, and I think God desires that. Of course, we could not come up with a large enough amount of money to buy a house or a car, even though our house was humble and our car was a third- or fourth-hand used one. However, everything else was paid for with cash or we did not buy it. I still think this is good advice to follow.

QUESTION:

WHY DO THE WICKED PROSPER?

ANSWER:

"As for me, my feet were almost gone; my steps had well nigh

slipped. For I was envious at the foolish, when I saw the prosperity of the wicked" (Psalm 73:2, 3).

Satan is *"the god of this [present] world [system]"* (II Corinthians 4:4). Consequently, he will help some people get rich to further his kingdom. He wants people to believe that sin and following evil pays in the so-called good things of life. This is the reason millions today are blinded. They look at wicked people who have land, houses, fame, and popularity. Deceived by this, millions of young people think it is smart to learn how to drink, smoke, gamble, and engage in the things that God has forbidden. Many of the so-called famous people of this world are heralded far and wide for doing these things. Young and old alike are led to believe that emulating these individuals will bring happiness; but Jesus said, *"A man's life consisteth not in the abundance of the things which he possesseth"* (Luke 12:15). Proportionately, there are more up-and-outers than down-and-outers who commit suicide. A man who sets his heart to seek only riches is in for a rude awakening.

I remember years ago a co-worker I knew and respected so much made the statement that when he was living for the devil it seemed that everything he touched turned to money. Now, it seems, he could not make ends meet. The devil had allowed him to prosper. In so doing, Satan can keep millions of people in bondage. They think they are doing well when they are actually selling their soul for a few baubles and trinkets. When people trust in riches and walk in wickedness, *"How are they brought into desolation, as in a moment! they are utterly consumed with terrors"* (Psalm 73:19). I read some time ago that the heir of one of the great fortunes of America died of an overdose of sleeping pills; actually it was suicide. Having everything money could buy did not bring him peace and satisfaction.

Christians must remember if they will believe God and use their faith, they can be prosperous in the Lord Jesus Christ. One of the great myths that Satan has perpetrated is that to be Godly, a person has to be poverty-stricken. Those who allow Satan to persuade them that living an evil life brings prosperity are living in a fool's paradise. The only true way to enjoy prosperity and use it for the benefit of others is through the Lord Jesus Christ.

MONEY AND HAPPINESS

Why does it seem that those who deal treacherously are happy? The answer is simple: their enjoyment comes from the wickedness in which they are involved. Naturally, they are happy. However, happiness has to do with our present surroundings. Lasting temporarily, it has nothing to do with real and everlasting joy. Joy comes from within. Consequently, one of the big stumbling blocks for the child of God is seeing people who consistently live an evil life yet, it seems, are so happy and carefree. Satan allows this, but again, Psalm 73:19 applies here too. *"How are they brought into desolation, as in a moment! they are utterly consumed with terrors."*

If Christians obey the Word of God, they are the happiest people in the world. Some time ago, a survey of the different strata of life in the United States was taken to find the happiest people. Much to the pollsters' amazement, it was found that born again Christians who believe entirely in the Word of God and do their best to live for the Lord Jesus Christ are the most contented, joyful, and happy people in America. Of course, I did not have to read the article to know this to be a fact. Overcoming Christians *are* the happiest people in the whole world. Jesus said, *"The thief cometh not, but for to steal, and to kill, and to destroy: I am come that they might have life, and that they might have it more abundantly"* (John 10:10). Living for God now and for eternity is still the happiest life man has ever known.

THE ENEMIES OF GOD

I know some Christians have thought and probably even vocalized their feelings that God should clear the earth of all rebels, He should annihilate every person who is living in wickedness and evil. At times they wonder why He does not do it. There are reasons:

First of all, God is merciful. *"His mercy endureth for ever"* (Psalm 106:1) and *"is from everlasting to everlasting"* (Psalm 103:17). We have all lived in sin and ungodliness, but God's mercy spared us, and we came to the saving knowledge of the Lord Jesus Christ. We ceased to be enemies of the Gospel and became born again Christians.

Sometimes enemies of God change. It would have been easy for God to have stricken a man by the name of Saul. He made havoc of the church, dragging Christians from their homes and throwing them in jail. He stood by while other enemies of God stoned Stephen, one of the greatest men of God that ever lived. Actually, *"the witnesses laid down their clothes at a young man's feet, whose name was Saul"* (Acts 7:58). He was probably the most notorious enemy of the church of the Lord Jesus Christ of that day; but at high noon outside the city walls of Damascus, Saul met the Lord Jesus Christ. A great light shown about him and Saul fell to the ground as one stricken dead. He was actually blinded by the brilliant light. The Lord Jesus Christ spoke to him and changed his name to Paul. This apostle of hate became the greatest apostle of love the world ever knew. (Read Acts 26.)

Second, we do not have to worry about the enemies that are against God today. The Russian bear may roar, but her bones will bleach on the sands one day.

I stood in Rome, Italy, sometime ago and looked at the great Coliseum where the blood of multiple thousands of Christians had stained its floor. Rome, with all of its power, had done everything within its grasp to eliminate the memory of the Lord Jesus Christ. Yet for every one Christian who was snatched from the ranks, his body torn to pieces by wild beasts in the Roman arena, 10 stepped in and took his place. I stood there looking at it. What is Rome today? She is nothing but a drowsy beggar watching the hands of a broken clock. Her caesars are peanut vendors; her mighty military generals are organ grinders. On the other hand, where is Christianity today? She is greater than ever!

We must also remember that one day every enemy will be defeated. After sufficient mercy has been expended and God has given every opportunity to every enemy to kneel at the foot of the cross, then (I shout, "Thank God!") Satan will be *"cast into the lake of fire and brimstone"* along with *"the beast and the false prophet"* (Revelation 20:10). Every enemy will be done away with. Victory, power, glory, honor, and above all love will reign when Jesus Christ comes back.

THE GRACE OF GOD

Ours is the day of grace. God does not pour out fire and brimstone or issue execution for millions of people, simply because He is striving for the salvation of all men. He is *"not willing that any should perish, but that all should come to repentance"* (II Peter 3:9). It is not His desire to see one single person lost. There is no joy in heaven over the death of a sinner (compare Luke 15:7).

Another factor that must be reckoned with is this: man has a free moral will. God does not force His will on anyone; neither does He force anyone to be evil. Man has the power of free choice. He can choose to curse God or to praise Him. He can choose to disobey God or to obey Him. He can choose to follow the Lord's commandments, or he can break those commandments. He has all the powers of a free moral agent. Actually, this is the primary cause of all the problems in this world today. God is not at fault; man is. We realize Satan is the originator of evil, but man does not have to make Satan his choice. He can make God his choice.

THE STORY OF ASAPH

Psalm 73 is the story of Asaph, David's song leader in Israel. It is one of the great chapters and examples of the child of God who gets his eyes on the wicked, begins to ask questions that Satan places there, and consequently causes himself difficulties. Asaph said, *"My feet were almost gone; my steps had well nigh slipped"* (Psalm 73:2). The reason for this was that Asaph was envious of the prosperity of the wicked. Satan had made him believe they did not have trouble as does the child of God, neither were they *"plagued like other men"* (verse 5). Asaph thought the wicked had more than their heart could ever wish. Yet they were corrupt, and they continually spoke evil. They set their mouth against the heavens and spoke great railing things against God. *"And they say, How doth God know? and is there knowledge in the most High?"* (verse 11).

Yet for all this, Asaph said, evil men prosper and increase in riches. He went on to say that when he looked at this, it seemed he had cleansed his heart in vain because he had suffered nothing but plagues and chastening. However, when he returned to the sanctuary, *"then understood I their end"* (verse 17). We are people of worship. Our life does not consist in the abundance of baubles, trinkets, and gadgets of this present world. We are *in* the world but not *of* the world. We must understand our life is not temporal, but eternal. He went on to say, *"For a day in thy courts is better than a thousand. I had rather be a doorkeeper in the house of my God, than to dwell in the tents of wickedness. For the Lord God is a sun and shield: the Lord will give grace and glory: no good thing will he withhold from them that walk uprightly. O Lord of hosts, blessed is the man that trusteth in thee"* (Psalm 84:10-12).

> *"Once a sinner far from Jesus,*
> *I was perishing with cold,*
> *But the blessed Saviour heard me*
> *when I cried;*
> *Then He threw His robe around me,*
> *And He led me to His fold,*
> *And I'm living on the*
> *hallelujah side!"*

VICTORY THROUGH JOY

Problems will become smaller instead of larger if we laugh at them. We will realize how insignificant they are. We will find ourselves living in a perpetual atmosphere of continuous victory. Our attitude toward our neighbor, brother, or sister will become more Christlike. We will present a picture of Godliness.

People see what they read on our countenance. If they read a frown, no matter how much we talk about the Lord and no matter how close we are to Him, others will not know this. They will know only what they see. We are obligated as Christians to wear a smile of victory that shows more than outward appearance. A smile shows tremendous confidence and faith in God Almighty and His Word. Nothing that comes against us can hinder us; we will come forth with absolute victory; therefore we have every reason to smile.

It is not our problem that troubles us, but our reaction to the problem. The way to overcome our reaction to the problem is to change our attitude. We can do that only with a smile; we cannot do it with a frown. When we smile, we are operating in faith. A smile is a sign of assurance, of victory, that the Lord is with us. When we tend to become irritated, we need to remember: God is only a smile away.

> *"It is joy unspeakable and full of glory,*
> *Full of glory, full of glory;*
> *It is joy unspeakable and full of glory,*
> *Oh, the half has never yet been told."*

QUESTION:

WHY DON'T YOU QUIT ASKING FOR MONEY OVER TELEVISION AND TRUST GOD FOR THE FINANCES? SECOND, DOESN'T GOSPEL TELEVISION WEAKEN AND DRAW MONEY AWAY FROM THE LOCAL CHURCH?

ANSWER:

It has always been somewhat of a mystery to me how so many individuals know the mind of God in respect to a certain subject when God has not called them into that particular work. It seems that if they understood all the complexities involved that they would be doing the work of God themselves. As one man said, "If it were easy, anyone could do it."

THE TELEVISION MINISTRY

I remember when we were on radio only (without the television ministry), we seldom had to ask for any funds whatsoever. However, with the advent of our television ministry, we often find ourselves in the position of having to solicit funds — either personally, over television, or by direct mail. I do not by any means enjoy this, and I solemnly wish we would never have to mention the subject. However, the bills must be paid.

Television exhausts such a tremendous amount of money. (Today our national and international Telecasts cost about $600,000 a week — *that is well over one-half million dollars every week*!) At the same time, they reach an incredible number of people. I am so thankful the Lord has given us one of the largest audiences in the world — about 5 million a week in the United States and Canada alone. When a person considers the vast number of people reached, the cost per household per week becomes low, probably the lowest ever for the presentation of the Gospel. There are only a handful of men in the world who are in this position. If you will notice, most of them find themselves soliciting funds.

FAITH

God spoke to my heart about two years ago and told me if I would stay faithful to Him and walk softly before Him, the anointing of the

Holy Spirit in convicting power would be so strong on the Telecast, it would result in hundreds of thousands of people being saved. We are starting to see that, and we thank God for it.

I am a faith preacher. I am asking God for more things today than I have ever asked in my life (for His work). I am receiving more answers to prayer than ever before, some so monumental it boggles my mind. Due to the worldwide scope of this Ministry, it has to be that way. Now some persons would say, "Just use your faith and never ask for money." Of course, what those people do not realize is that there is no individual in the world (to my knowledge) who can do that. It is unscriptural.

ASKING

Jesus said, *"Ask, and it shall be given you"* (Matthew 7:7). He was addressing a great crowd of followers. Now, would a person be so foolish as to say He was not trusting God because He admonished the people this way? I do not think a person could as much as suggest such a thing.

Jesus also said, *"Give, and it shall be given unto you"* (Luke 6:38). The Apostle Paul, in writing to the church at Corinth, told the people that *"God loveth a cheerful giver,"* and as they would give they should do so *"not grudgingly, or of necessity"* (II Corinthians 9:7). Incidentally, this admonition given by the Holy Spirit was contained in a letter. The Bible is replete with prophets, priests, et cetera asking for financial help. They were not lacking in faith. They were simply going by the admonition, *"Ask, and it shall be given you"* (Luke 11:9). (This was in vogue even in Old Testament times. Compare Genesis 24:43-46; Joshua 14:12; I Samuel 25:8; I Kings 17:10, 11; John 4:7.)

In most church services the pastor receives an offering while encouraging the people to give. Does this mean they are lacking in faith? Certainly not.

CHRISTIAN APPEALS

I admit that many appeals are carried out in bad taste, some even dishonestly. However, that does not mean that an appeal given out of a genuine need, with dignity and repose, shows a lack of faith or is wrong.

In my years of dealing with people, I have noticed this: A Christian community comprises several segments of people. A few people are dedicated and faithful in their giving, but that number is small. If everyone was like that, appeals for funds would never have to be made.

The second group has to have a little prodding. They will give; and then when they are reminded to give again, their answer is, "Oh, I gave just the other day." "The other day" might have been eight months ago. God speaks to these people, but either they are busy or they do not acknowledge the responsibility as theirs. Consequently, the work of God is hindered.

The third group never gives anything unless some tremendous shock approach is used to stir them. It is a shame, but that is the way they are. You see, thousands of people over the years have written me or told me in person they have been blessed immeasurably by this Ministry, and then with a smile they will say, "I am one of the ones, Brother Swaggart, you are talking about. God has spoken to my heart that I should give, but I have never gotten around to doing it."

I seek God hours a day, every day. God, in answer to my prayers, speaks to the people respecting this Ministry. Some people obey Him. Many do not. The sad fact is, some are just not close enough to God to hear and obey Him. Then, the minister has to resort to natural means to stir those people's memory and remind them of their responsibility. If every person obeyed God, every need would be met (with plenty to spare). The work of God would progress, immeasurably so, and the people would be blessed abundantly.

Now, one more thing in respect to the appeal for funds: I have noticed also in my years of ministry that most of the people who complain about a preacher asking for money do so because they themselves do not contribute anything. They feel guilty and would rather not be reminded. Of course, this is not always the case. Sometimes good, responsible, dedicated Christians have honest questions about this; but most of the time it is as I have mentioned.

THE LOCAL CHURCH

Now, to the second part of your question. No, Gospel television does not hinder the local church, nor does it siphon money from the local church.

Our Ministry is one of the strongest advocates of the local church in the world today. We teach and preach that the local church is the foundation of the work of God on earth. As such, it comes before my ministry or any other. That is God's order of events, and we adhere to it strictly. In 25 years of evangelistic work I have never asked over radio, television, or in crusades for individuals' tithes, and I never will. We ask for offerings and we urge people to give. Sometimes we may appeal strongly, but that is the extent of it. However, for me to do anything to hinder the local body would be anathema to everything I stand for.

In the last 10 years the local church (all over the world) has experienced its greatest growth ever. Churches 10 years ago that were averaging 40 to 50 in Sunday School are now averaging several thousand. Of course, there are many reasons for this, and television is one of the reasons. You see, millions of people, due to the outpouring of the Holy Spirit and a general spiritual awakening, are becoming interested in God. They do not attend church, but they will turn on the television set and watch a Gospel program. Oftentimes the Holy Spirit will stir their heart; they will become awakened to their need. Almost without exception these people will seek out a good local church to attend, and television is the cause of it. Only the Lord knows how many people our Telecasts have placed in local churches.

A pastor wrote me the other day and told me of nearly 30 people who had joined his church (good, faithful, dependable supporters, I might add) as a result of our Telecast. That is just one incident. It could be multiplied thousands of times. Of course, this is what we like to see. I call myself a church preacher. I want to link my ministry with good, Spirit-filled churches because no matter how effective I am and how many people I may win to God, if those people are not anchored in a good, Spirit-filled church, then all of my labor has basically been in vain.

One Godly pastor told me he felt the tremendous growth of his church was due partly to Gospel television programming. He was speaking of programming in general. I cannot answer for all Gospel programming, but the principles I have laid down above are what we work toward. Actually the local church bears the end results of our effort.

The local churches are experiencing the greatest growth ever, as I said earlier. Their finances are better than ever. Of course, there will always be a few churches that are not progressing, and some of those would enjoy using television as the scapegoat. Yet the fact is, these have always existed and always will exist until Jesus comes.

QUESTION:

SHOULD A CHRISTIAN EXPECT GOD TO GIVE BACK TO HIM WHEN HE GIVES TO THE LORD?

ANSWER:

Yes, it is proper for a Christian to expect the Lord to give back to him as he gives to God, providing he gives with the right attitude, the right motive, and the right spirit.

GOD'S PROMISES

God's Word is filled with promises that He will give to His children who serve and obey Him and give to His work and cause. Jesus said, *"Give, and it shall be given unto you; good measure, pressed down, and shaken together, and running over, shall men give into your bosom"* (Luke 6:38). God tells us, *"Prove me now herewith, saith the Lord of hosts, if I will not open you the windows of heaven, and pour you out a blessing, that there shall not be room enough to receive it"* (Malachi 3:10). Of course, there are many other suchlike promises in the Word of God. Consequently, if we are led to believe (by our Heavenly Father and our Redeemer) that God will give back to us as we give to Him, we should expect it.

MAN'S MOTIVES

However, you will notice that I mentioned motive. If a Christian gives to God solely for financial rewards, his motives are crass and improper. Some preachers today have so strongly advocated that we are to give to God expecting Him to return certain said amounts of money to us that it has caused a rupture in respect to the sacredness and holiness of many people's giving.

Any individual who gives to God expecting a certain monetary return fosters an improper motive and is not giving in love. Consequently, it is not a gift at all. It is an investment at best and a gamble at worst and will not be honored by the Holy Spirit in that context.

We must remember God does not always pay in the coin of the realm.

Sometimes He returns our gifts in various ways — healthy children, a healthy body, a family that is living for and serving the Lord Jesus Christ. We must remember that God has already paid everything for us through the death and resurrection of His Son, Jesus Christ.

In summation, we may expect God to return to us according to our motives in giving. We should always give from a heart of love, never from a mercenary attitude. We should give to God because we love Him, we love His work, and we want to be a part of it. Knowing that, we can trust His return to us (in whatever way He deems desirable) to be to our advantage.

QUESTION:

IN GIVING MY MONEY TO SPREAD THE GOSPEL ALL OVER THE WORLD, I WANT TO MAKE SURE THAT IT ACCOMPLISHES ITS INTENDED PURPOSE. HOW CAN I BE SURE THAT THIS IS DONE?

ANSWER:

What a person gives to God is precious and consecrated (Deuteronomy 26; Luke 6:38), holy unto Him. Paul said, *"God loveth a cheerful giver"* (II Corinthians 9:7). When people give to God, they are giving of the labor of their hands (Genesis 3:19) or of their mind (II Samuel 24:24).

I will never forget an incident that happened one night in a crusade in Detroit, Michigan. After the service a lady came up and handed me a roll of bills. I have known many people to do this, but I did something that night I had never done before. I asked her what kind of work she did. It was obvious from the roughness of her hands and her inexpensive clothing that her life had been hard. She dropped her head and speaking softly said, "I scrub floors for a living, Brother Swaggart."

I said, "Do you mean literally on your hands and knees?"

Again, softly, she answered yes. The roll of bills was in my hand — $32. When I asked her how much money she made that week, she answered in the same hushed voice, "Thirty-two dollars." She had given all she had for this Ministry.

This was a long time ago, and I have learned a few things since then.

I forget my exact words, but I tried to give the money back. She looked up at me with eyes that flashed (she was quite a number of years older than I) and said, "Young man, I did not give that money to you; I gave it to God. If you don't want it, leave it on the floor; but He told me to do it and I'm obeying Him." Then she walked away.

It is difficult to explain how I felt at that moment. I was weeping. I realized the labor that she had expended to earn it and the great sacrifice of giving it all away. As I walked back over to the corner of the auditorium, the Spirit of the Lord spoke this to my heart: "Son, millions of dollars will pass through your hands for My work. Always remember, whether the amount is great or insignificant, it is sacred to Me. If you ever misuse it, not only will you answer to Me in the Judgment, but you will answer to the people who gave it."

I have never forgotten that, and I would like to believe, before God Almighty, that every dime and dollar we have had come our way, we have used exactly as we felt He wanted it used.

A person's giving is sacred and holy to God, and we should always look at it in this light — never as just a few dollars that we put in the offering plate or send through the mail or whatever.

WE SHOULD EXPECT FRUIT

The Lord spoke of a person's offering multiplying when He said it would bring forth fruit *"some thirtyfold, some sixty, and some an hundred"* (Mark 4:20). In other words, our money is to be used to win souls for the glory of God. Jesus said, *"I am the true vine, and my Father is the husbandman"* (John 15:1). We are the branches that bear the fruit. A branch that does not bear fruit is taken away. *"Every branch that beareth fruit, he purgeth it, that it may bring forth more fruit"* (verse 2).

This speaks of tremendous responsibility. Every single individual should work for God, extensively so. We should do everything within our capability to bring forth fruit. This may mean participating in church visitation programs, teaching Sunday School classes, working on the church facilities, or any number of things. But it also means giving of our finances to bring forth fruit. What makes this so frustrating and difficult for some Christians to understand is that they sacrifice and give, and yet their giving does not bring forth fruit to their account.

Thousands of churches purport to preach the Gospel when they really do not. The majority of pastors standing in pulpits do not even believe the Bible. Consequently, neither the people's money nor their efforts can bring forth fruit. So, by and large, it is wasted. Thank God not all pastors and preachers are that way, and all churches are not that way — but the majority, sad to say, are.

So it is utmostly important that we be careful where and why we give our money and what is done with it, because it is nothing short of an extension of our labor of love. If it is wasted and misused, then as far as God is concerned, we have given nothing.

WHERE SHOULD WE GIVE?

I can address myself only on the subject of evangelism. That was basically the question you asked, and I will confine myself to this particular aspect of giving.

Of course, in the field of evangelism — for the spread of the Gospel all over the world — we should, first of all, be led by the Holy Spirit. He is perfectly capable of speaking to us, and we should be capable of hearing Him. However, even though I have put it simply, we all know it is not quite that easy. God expects us to use common sense and accept responsibility in the matter.

This is the major problem for so many Christians. They pass it off as, "I've done what I'm supposed to do by giving. My responsibility in the matter is over." Nothing could be further from the truth. Even though you might have been totally sincere in the matter, if the recipients wasted and misused that which you gave, then as far as God is concerned, you have accomplished nothing in your giving and might just as well have kept the money for yourself. (At the least, He will hold you accountable for not being more prudent, for not being more responsible in knowing where your money was to go.)

A short time ago a brother called me, almost weeping. Some months back he had mentioned that he had given quite heavily to a particular work. I do not even remember if he told me who he was giving to, but I had cautioned him at that time that much of the money given for missions never gets to its intended destination. That certainly is not true in all cases, but I am concerned it *is* true in many cases.

He said, "Brother Swaggart, I just found out that all the money I gave to [a particular ministry] for [a particular project] was not going for that cause at all."

This brother was so shattered by the experience that it caused him to stumble. I reminded him over the phone that I had mildly warned him that he should be more careful. Then in tears he said, "This money has been virtually wasted. It was not used for the purpose I had given it, and it's hurt me deeply." The sad fact is, this is true in case after case.

In my talking with a missionary sometime ago respecting mission endeavors in his particular country, he told me about a television ministry that had raised possibly hundreds of thousands of dollars for that country. (He had been a missionary there for 15 years.) He said, "Brother Swaggart, even though they talk constantly of our country and the great works they have here and the great amounts of money being given, as far as I know, there is not one single solitary dollar that I have even seen being spent here by them. It is possible they have done something I don't know about, but I doubt it." He went on to say that the country is small, and he probably knows everything that goes on there respecting the work of God. He has been unable to locate any church they have built, any Bible School they have helped . . . or children. He cannot find anything whatsoever even though he travels the length and breadth of that land constantly.

Thousands of people sent money to this particular television ministry thinking they were giving to a worthy project, when, in fact, precious little if any of those funds ever got there. I realize this is a shocking statement that will cause many persons to recoil at the very reading of it and say, "I can't believe this is true." I pondered in my own heart whether I should say it, but I must always tell the truth and say it like it is.

One of the most renowned missionary leaders in the world sat in my office not too long ago. Speaking of another particular television ministry, he said, "You know, Brother Swaggart, they have raised multiple thousands of dollars for a particular project in one mission endeavor in a certain part of the world. And do you know how much money actually made it to that project?"

I looked at him and said, "Well, I have no way of knowing, but I would say probably about 1 or 2 percent."

He said, "You hit it right on the head!" I will never forget that. I was able to answer him because I know something about that ministry, and I knew they could not do what they were trying to do. It simply was not possible. Yet many people, in good faith, gave toward that one particular need. Admittedly, the need was there, but the money never arrived at the destination.

Does this mean that the people presenting the need stole the money? No, it does not mean that at all. It just means that in many fund-raising events the expenses are so high that after all the bills are paid, there is nothing left.

IS OUR MONEY ACCOMPLISHING ITS TASK?

Now, we are getting to the heart of the problem. First of all, are these people involved in preaching the Gospel? Stop a few moments and think about that question. A lot of things look flashy and glamorous; a lot of talk is done when there is no actual Gospel being proclaimed. You asked the question about Christian television talk shows, and I will answer you. They may be good, they may be informative, but they are not preaching or teaching the Gospel. There may be some few times when some teaching is done within the body of the program by the host or guest or whoever, but most of the time that is not the case. For one of these programs to be aired in a foreign country will probably do little good in reaching the heathen with the Gospel of Jesus Christ. God has still chosen *"by the foolishness of preaching to save them that believe"* (I Corinthians 1:21).

I was with another missionary the other day in Mexico. He is a great man of God, having given nearly 20 years of his life to Latin America. We were discussing various television programming and how best to reach the people in his particular country. Various ideas were given respecting music, talk shows, discussions, and so forth. As I left the table to return to my room, he followed me.

When we were alone, he told me, "Brother Swaggart, please whatever you do, don't change the style of your programming. All of the other formats may be glamorous and look good, but they don't get the job done."

He went on to say, "I know what I'm talking about. We've had it all in my country: Christian television talk shows, musical programs, everything you can think of, and old-fashioned preaching of the Gospel exactly as you do it is the *only* thing that will set the captive free, that will reach in through the power of Holy Spirit conviction and bring men to a saving knowledge of Jesus Christ. *Nothing* else will do it."

As I walked away from him that day, I knew what he was saying was true, yet I am concerned that many Americans either do not know it or have forgotten. Regardless of the effort being made, unless the powerful preaching of the Word with the anointing and convicting power of the Holy Spirit accompanies those efforts and reaches the heart of men, by and large little or nothing will be accomplished.

WHAT IS BEING PREACHED?

Even still, although the Gospel (or part of it) may be going forth, we should know what is being preached: What kind of Gospel is it? Is it error? Is it a hindrance?

Two young ladies came to my door the other day. I knew when I opened the door they were Mormons. Even though the Mormon people are sincere, the Gospel they proclaim is not the Gospel of the Word of God in the Lord Jesus Christ and, consequently, it will not do good to anyone. Rather, to adhere to its pernicious teachings will cause a person to lose his soul.

So the question must be asked: What kind of Gospel is being preached (or taught)? Is it the plain, unadulterated Word of God that will set the captive free? Does it lay out God's great plan of salvation with the prime purpose of its propagation the saving of souls? Does it draw Christians into a closer walk with God? Does it preach a Gospel of power, proclaiming the Word of God as the answer to men's problems? All of these things must be considered. The Lord Jesus Christ warned, *"He that hath ears to hear, let him hear"* (Mark 4:9). In other words, know what is being said, and think about it carefully. Be careful of what you listen to; do not believe everything. Use your ears to *"take heed what ye hear"* (Mark 4:24).

A lady wrote to me the other day: "Brother Swaggart, I'm not certain that my money is being used wisely." She had good reason to be concerned; it was not. Her hard-earned money was being wasted, misused, and misspent — and all the while she believed her offerings were being used to accomplish great things for God. In reality, they were not.

WHAT ARE THE RESULTS?

With today's inflation and ailing economy, we need more than ever to see our money used where it will accrue more results for the kingdom of God. A lot of ministers today *talk* about great works being accomplished all over the world when, in actuality, there is little proof a person can find that anything is being done. This is sad, but I know it to be a fact.

We have every right to question the output of our money. Any preacher (if he so desires) can talk endlessly about great and grandiose works all over the world and make individuals think that so much is being done. But if you will notice, little is ever pinpointed. Even if it is, we have every right to check out all the specifics.

In the body of your question to us, you made some statements about this particular Ministry, and I will endeavor to enlarge upon what you have said and possibly help answer any questions you or anyone else may have.

One, we have always made it a practice to tell our donors exactly what we are doing. By the help and grace of God we have *always* done exactly what we said. For example, when we asked for funds to build a church in Mombasa, Kenya, East Africa, we did just that (actually we built two). If our project is to build a Bible School in India, we build that particular school in that specific country. Then we asked for money to feed 15,000 children in Calcutta, India, on a daily basis, and we can prove we are feeding that many or more every single day. If we say we are building a children's school in a certain country respecting the Children's Fund, we build it! Given time for the building to go up, it is there for anyone to see. Also, we work through reputable missionaries that you can contact any time that you would want to verify one of our projects or inquire of the status.

Since there is always the possibility of funds/projects not matching perfectly, we always tell our people this: "If perchance more funds than are needed for this particular project come in, we will apply those funds to a similar or like project." Rather than cutting project funds short, we fund and support many others that we never mention — either because they are not significant enough to warrant special funding or we just simply do not have the time to solicit the funds because of the urgency of the situation.

For example, when I was in Mexico not too long ago, there was a critical need for $65,000 to build a church. I will not go into all the details, but we promised to supply that money — and we did. The need was urgent, and we felt these funds would, in the building of this church, reach hundreds of souls for Christ in the needy land of Mexico. It had to be done immediately. There was no time to recruit sponsors. This has happened many times.

We have earned the reputation among hundreds of missionaries that if we tell them we will do something, we do it. They can depend on it and plan toward it. They do not have to worry that we will not come through. Of course, we give the glory to God and our thanks to all our wonderful friends and partners who support us.

Two, the Gospel we preach is the Word of God, and because it is the eternal Word of God, I can say without fear of contradiction that our message is getting results. For instance, thousands of our little booklets, *There's a New Name Written Down in Glory,* are sent to people all over the United States, Canada, and other parts of the world who have given their heart and life to the Lord Jesus Christ as a result of the Telecast and request them.

Old-fashioned, Holy-Spirit-conviction preaching reaches out and touches their heart, melting them and bringing them to Jesus Christ. In other words, this old-fashioned Bible preaching is the answer to the world's problems. Here is something we must understand. When the Gospel of Jesus Christ is preached in power and under the anointing, it will reap the same results in any country in the world, in any culture, as it does in the United States. For the Gospel is for all people, of all cultures, of all races, and for all time. It is the same message; it changes not. This is the thing that is thrilling.

Three, our total effort is spent in spreading the Gospel all over the world. We do not have other projects that are paramount to where we dabble in missions just enough to call ourselves an outreach effort. Our very ministry and message — the very heart, soul, and burden of our spirit — is to carry the Gospel of Jesus Christ to every soul on the face of the earth! Television is the major vehicle through which we can carry it more expediently.

CONCLUSION

Our giving in the field of evangelism is crucially important in the eyes of God. Satan is keenly adept at siphoning hundreds of millions of dollars into worthless projects that do little or nothing for the cause of Jesus Christ. Each of us as individuals must accept responsibility for our money, its outlay, its accomplishments, and its results.

Last of all, I pledge to you as I have pledged to God: we will do everything within our power to use every dime and dollar of the money that comes into these offices to reach as many souls as possible in the shortest period of time. I believe that I can say your money will bring forth *"thirtyfold, some sixty, and some an hundred"* (Mark 4:20).

"Say not ye, There are yet four months, and then cometh harvest? behold, I say unto you, Lift up your eyes, and look on the fields; for they are white already to harvest" (John 4:35).

QUESTION:

DO YOU THINK IT IS SCRIPTURALLY PERMISSIBLE FOR A CHRISTIAN TO PARTICIPATE IN STATE LOTTERIES, WHICH ARE SEEMINGLY GAMBLING?

ANSWER:

No, it is not permissible for a child of God to participate in lotteries or in other kinds of gambling. Yes, you are correct in your assumption. The state lotteries are one form of gambling. I will qualify my answer by stating some facts that every Christian ought to know and understand respecting gambling. I will answer your questions in depth: Is it wrong? What is it doing to the United States? Is it the answer to our problems?

When a person thinks of gambling, the mind immediately goes to well-known places like Las Vegas and Reno. Now Atlantic City has become prominent in the business, and other financially troubled cities are viewing (with dollar signs in their eyes) Atlantic City's resurgent economy since the gambling boon hit. Many states are now promoting state lotteries as a means of solving some of their fiscal problems, and most states now allow gambling in some form.

According to *Time* magazine, gambling (both legal and illegal) is one of the biggest and fastest-growing commercial activities in the United States, and more than 80 percent of all Americans regard it as acceptable. Considering the fact that *all* citizens are sick of taxes and feel the system is unfairly harsh, a logical conclusion to state-sponsored gambling could be looked upon as a beautiful solution to an ugly problem. Politicians, including mayors and governors, having scraped the bottom of the barrel trying to raise money to keep their city or state from bankruptcy, are looking upon the state lottery as a painless way of raising revenue.

REDUCTION OF TAXES

It is a fairly obvious assessment that working-class America is being taxed to death. Searching desperately for new sources for funds, many politicians view legalized gambling as a way to solve their state's revenue problems and thus ease their own tax load. Also, lower taxes bring voters to the polls in election year!

All kinds of gimmicks are being used by particular states to get individuals to participate in the lotteries. New York started out their billing with "your chance of a lifetime"; now it is merely "be a player." The beneficiary is, supposedly, education.

Pennsylvania's lottery presumably benefits the elderly and disabled. In fact, we are told when the publicity experts began their "selling" job, they made the citizens feel they were kicking their aged mother if they refused to buy a lottery ticket.

A LONG HISTORY

We are told:
• Lottery proceeds helped fortify Colonial America (believe it or not) against the British.
• A lottery started the University of Pennsylvania.
• Lotteries have been used to repair streets, build docks and flood control, plus other improvements.

Compulsion for gambling infects America to the tune of nearly $100 billion a year, an amount equal to the national defense expenditure. Also, being the kind of "business" it is, it comes as no great surprise that it is controlled largely by organized crime, which nets approximately 20 percent of this income or about $25 billion. About half of this money, sad to say, goes to the police or other governmental officials as payoffs, and the rest goes into such vicious activities as dope peddling, loan sharking, bootlegging, white-slave trading, and slick confidence schemes.

In New York City alone, the numbers racket grosses nearly $1 billion a year. Nearly $30 billion a year is wagered illegally on sports. In the city of Detroit nearly .25 million people a day play the numbers game.

GAMBLING ILLS

In 1957 Gamblers Anonymous was founded. Today it is one of the fastest-growing organizations in the United States, with nearly 500 local chapters. Gamblers Anonymous was founded because of the terrific toll gambling takes upon the family structure, causing untold hardship on the entire family. The average expenditure of families betting on the *lotteries* is between $100 and $150 annually. Gambling is just as addicting as alcohol or drugs.

One compulsive gambler, as related in a *Time* magazine article, told of robbing his children's piggy bank and then selling his own blood so he could have one more fling with the dice. This is not an isolated case. It is happening in multiple hundreds of thousands of lives.

Now the champions of *legalized* gambling (which includes the lotteries, and so forth) claim that their approach will do several things: relieve the tax burden, take the money out of the hands of the crime syndicate (since the people are going to bet anyway), and in effect control gambling, thus providing a stabilizing influence in society.

However, the facts do not support this optimism — quite the contrary when we realize that the Washington Monument (built as a result of lotteries) cost about seven times what it should have. Based on the sheer fiscal inefficiency of this scheme, anti-lottery drives were started; and a number of states, due to this one debacle, wrote anti-lottery laws into their constitution. Nowadays many of these are being rewritten, favoring the lottery as a means to raise easy funds when, in reality, it is already been tried and has failed miserably.

INEFFICIENT FUND-RAISING

Investigators have concluded that to raise $25 million in new revenue, $125 million has to be sold in chances. Government-sponsored betting has been termed a "horrendously inefficient way to raise revenue," and yet it is being promoted today as never before.

State lotteries return about 40 cents on the dollar for the stated purposes of the government. This means at best the public puts out about two and a half times as much money for the lottery tickets as it would have to pay if the government simply used our taxation. (These same individuals will criticize a nonprofit organization for raising funds for the work of the Lord if a few dollars on the hundred are spent to raise these funds!)

Even the well-known Irish Sweepstakes has cleared only about 20 percent of the total sum spent in its 40-year history. That is a horrendous way to raise funds. Besides the sheer inefficiency, these efforts have terrible effects on the economy.

When money is tight, the government encourages people to spend more so that businesses can get back on their feet and the recession will wind up. When citizens spend more money in purchasing goods and services, businesses hire more employees and unemployment drops. Welfare rolls are cut and taxes are reduced. However, lotteries produce just the opposite. The lure of legalized gambling causes expenditures all right, but there is no purchase of goods or services rendered. New employees are not hired, and more people (not fewer) are forced to return to welfare. Consequently, taxes rise higher and higher.

It is a proven fact that when a race track (or some such effort) opens, business in that particular area suffers. The opening of the Santa Anita Race Track outside of Los Angeles each year brings with it a rise in crime, bad checks, and absenteeism from work. This could be said of every other horse racing track in the United States as well.

ORGANIZED CRIME

The pitch to legalize gambling says that the money put into it, instead of going into the pockets of organized crime, will be used for worthwhile projects such as education, the elderly, and so forth. However, the opposite is the case.

Wherever gambling is legalized, the crime rate, it seems, almost doubles the national average. Take, for example, the state of Nevada. Almost completely enslaved by the gambler-gangster forces, we are told, even oversized police forces in Las Vegas and Reno cannot remedy the situation.

Legalized gambling encourages illegal betting. One bookie stated that state-sponsored gambling is a kindergarten. "When the kids graduate," he said, "I'm their finishing school." Also, lotteries and off-track betting have not significantly reduced the total volume of illegal gambling, and hence do not appear to have reduced the corruption of public officials and the like.

According to *Time* magazine, legalized gambling has generally been a boon to bookies. Citizens interested in betting, once hooked, find that illegal wagering offers other advantages like tax-free payoffs and, sometimes, better odds.

Actually, people's morals become degraded when lotteries, or suchlike, go into effect. The state actually becomes a party to the something-for-nothing philosophy, encouraging its citizens to place their faith in blind chance. The pitch to the public is dishonest, catering mostly to the ignorant and those who can ill afford it. The chances of even modest winnings run from 500 to 1, to 1,000 to 1, and even up to 25 million to 1 for the top prizes. Of course, whenever a top prize is won, the news media play it up via television to such an extent that another crop of suckered individuals start to believe and hope that their number will eventually be drawn. The old virtues of hard work, perseverance, and acceptance of one's own personal responsibility for the future, it seems, has gone askance.

GAMBLING AND POVERTY

In 1960 Great Britain enacted a national betting and gaming act, which was supposed to help solve its social ills. Instead, it encouraged multiple hundreds of thousands who had not previously even considered it to take part in gambling. Great Britain's problems are worse today than they have ever been, as multiple millions of its people are caught up in the bondage of so-called legalized gambling.

The late Thomas E. Dewey said, "It is fundamentally immoral to encourage the belief by people as a whole in gambling as a source of revenue." The entire history of legalized gambling in this country and abroad proves nothing but poverty, crime and corruption, demoralization of moral and ethical standards, and ultimately a lower living standard and misery for all people. Yet, politicians, it seems, are bent toward these gambling rocks of destruction.

More than a generation ago, the *New York Times* declared lotteries to be a disguised form of taxation incomparably *more* repressive in its totality simply because it fostered its efforts upon those that could ill afford it — the poor or even the *very* poor. As we have said previously, it is a sad obituary when a state officially sanctions the idea that the underprivileged can improve his position by engaging himself in luck or chance. Actually, it is a sorry brand of economic immorality that undermines the proven success of hard work and thrift.

A short time ago, the *National Observer* reported that "Legalized gambling is, in truth, a monumental cop-out. It can actually work against taxpayers by relieving pressure for tax reform and therefore by helping to perpetuate inequities."

In other words, gambling is the least responsible way of raising public revenue. The fact is that we cannot afford the psychological and moral decay of officially promoted gambling.

THE BIBLE

We believe and teach that clear scriptural principles lie behind the Christian's opposition to gambling.

One, everything we have is given by God and held in trust. Everything we are, everything we have, is God's investment in us. We are told in the Parable of the Talents (Matthew 25) to put God's investment to work by reinvesting our life as well as our possessions to where they will produce honor and gain for the Master. Actually, the only form of risk-taking approved in the Word of God is that of risking our life for the cause of Christ (Acts 15:26).

Two, our life is to be lived in faith. Every child of God should value the goodness and the orderliness of God's creation, realizing first and foremost that life is not a gamble, blind luck, or chance; rather, life is controlled by a loving, Heavenly Father.

The gambler, wanting something for nothing, pursues lady luck. He takes his trust away from God, believing that blind chance will deal him a better hand. Yet every Christian knows that God's plan for life does not fluctuate with the whims of chance.

Three, gambling always violates God's basic laws. The commandments dealing with theft and covetousness are directly related to gambling. It is a something-for-nothing attitude, and even though the victim may enter willingly into this effort of chance, the guilt is not canceled on the part of the beneficiaries.

The Lord told us, in capsuling the Ten Commandments, that we are to love our neighbor as ourselves (Matthew 22:37-40). This means we should not want to win at another's expense. We should not want to risk being even partially to blame for depriving a family of its needs.

Some persons question whether involvement in a state-run lottery or a gambling casino deprives needy people of their livelihood; however, it is even more true there than anywhere else — simply because the state-run lotteries, the big gambling casinos, or whatever cannot survive without a profit. From where does this profit come? Most of the time it comes from those who can least afford it; namely, the underprivileged who enter out of a need, hoping to gain something by blind chance.

Who inevitably wins? The professional gambler! Moreover, when a gambler *wins,* he is actually taking his ill-gotten gain from the poor, gullible person who cannot afford to lose even one dollar.

Actually, the child of God is to place his trust in the Lord to meet his needs. Our security is in Him, not in our possessions or in anything we may get from someone else. We should not look elsewhere for bonanzas. It is true enough, the child of God *can* expect troubles and difficulties. Yet if, during these times, we refuse to violate God's laws, we demonstrate our complete dependence on Him and our commitment to His Word.

Four, God's Word condemns a self-centered attachment to money. Covetousness and greed are condemned in the Word of God: *"The love of money is the root of all evil"* (I Timothy 6:10). The Christian ideal is not taking from others, but giving; for Jesus said, *"It is more blessed to give than to receive"* (Acts 20:35).

This Scripture opens our understanding in that while the Prodigal Son was condemned for squandering his money in riotous living, his father was commended for the lavish way in which he welcomed the repentant boy home (Luke 15:11-32). In the same vein, Jesus praised Mary's expenditure of expensive ointment worth almost a year's wages (of a day laborer) because she acted unselfishly in her love for her Saviour (John 12:1-9). Extravagant giving is praised — *"God loveth a cheerful giver"* (II Corinthians 9:7) — while taking from others is condemned (a reflection of just the opposite of love).

INVESTMENT OPPORTUNITIES

Aren't investments made on Wall Street or any other investment opportunities the same thing as gambling? No, they are not. When an investment is made in stocks, the profits (if any) are derived because the product becomes more valuable. This can be due to supply and demand of the public or to a person's (or corporation's) ability in marketing that product wisely. In the case of profits from business ventures, hard work, thriftiness, and perseverance usually play a role in profit-making. Luck seldom has anything to do with it. (Of course, we would not discount knowledge and ability in the particular business field, but the above proven qualities are critically important.)

It is true that a self-centered attachment to money would apply to investments as well as to gambling. Still, the basic reason people gamble is that they want something for nothing, whereas an investment in a business proposition is made with total confidence that if profits are earned, it will be because of someone's hard work, intelligence, and so forth — in other words, productivity.

There is no productivity in gambling. Gambling takes all and gives nothing. In gambling, everyone loses — the one who bets and the one who wins. For the one who wins, the seed of bondage is planted in thinking that this can become a way of life and hence be the answer to all of his problems, when, in actuality, the bondage of gambling can become just as acute as every other bondage Satan has.

THE CHRISTIAN POSITION

Every Christian should speak out against gambling. Because of the many sociological, psychological, economic, and political factors involved, no true child of God can afford to sit by idly and allow this travesty upon the public. Our voice must be heard loud and clear that whatever the short-term benefit of legalized gambling may be, it can never be in the best long-range interest of the state, the city, or the people.

The child of God should be opposed to state-run lotteries, so-called charitable groups raising money with bingo games or whatever, or any church that tries to raise funds by lotteries or some other suchlike effort. Our love for others should dictate that we take an uncompromising position.

The gambling bandwagon is backing up steam across the United States. It may be too late to turn it around, but at least the Christian's voice should be heard.

[Note: Parts of the information derived for this article were taken from Time *magazine,* The National Observer, *and William Peterson's book* What You Should Know About Gambling.*]*

QUESTION:

POLITICS

■ Is it right for a preacher of the Gospel to expound on certain political candidates running for office?

■ In the last presidential election and even now on a lesser scale, Fundamentalist preachers such as yourself are advocating a certain kind of government for this nation. Many people are afraid of this. Are their fears justified?

QUESTION:

IS IT RIGHT FOR A PREACHER OF THE GOSPEL TO EXPOUND ON CERTAIN POLITICAL CANDIDATES RUNNING FOR OFFICE?

ANSWER:

Christians should first of all pray for everyone in authority. *"I exhort therefore, that, first of all, supplications, prayers, intercessions, and giving of thanks, be made . . . for all that are in authority; that we may lead a quiet and peaceable life in all godliness and honesty"* (I Timothy 2:1, 2).

If God considered this important enough for us to put it above all else in our praying, certainly we should be concerned about the individual who occupies the office. Christians should work for good government. They should become involved and know the candidates who are running for office and support the ones who are stable and have good policies for sound government. It is proper for Christians to involve themselves in this manner.

Ministers of the Gospel should also be involved in earnestly praying for those who occupy high office. At the same time, ministers of the Gospel should certainly approve of, and even work for good moral, stable candidates who will benefit good government. However, by "work for" I mean limited involvement.

First, ministers who are called to preach this great Gospel of Jesus Christ should not condescend to run for political office. Every time this happens the ministry is hindered and wasted.

Second, ministers of the Gospel (even though they may favor a certain candidate) do little good in becoming involved in political campaigning. All of us who love the Lord Jesus Christ desire good government, and we should pray for it. However, the best way a preacher can help our nation and all concerned is to preach the Gospel of Jesus Christ and let that Gospel perform its work in the heart and life of the unregenerate and thereby cause those individuals to become, through the grace of Jesus Christ and salvation, good citizens who conduct themselves uprightly. This will do more to help society, the nation, and good government than all the political efforts made by ministers of the Gospel.

I do not doubt the motives of many preachers who are politically involved. They are probably good men who love God. However, the things I have mentioned do more to help the cause of Christ and good government than anything else.

QUESTION:

IN THE LAST PRESIDENTIAL ELECTION AND EVEN NOW ON A LESSER SCALE, FUNDAMENTALIST PREACHERS SUCH AS YOURSELF ARE ADVOCATING A CERTAIN KIND OF GOVERNMENT FOR THIS NATION. MANY PEOPLE ARE AFRAID OF THIS. ARE THEIR FEARS JUSTIFIED?

ANSWER:

It is true that ministers such as myself (and also the majority of the American people) are advocating a certain kind of government for this country, but, no, no one need have any fear. Frankly, if we are successful, it will give more freedom to more people than anything this country or any nation has ever known. If we are not successful, our freedoms will be eroded and eventually taken away. Let us look at it a little closer.

THE JUDEO-CHRISTIAN PRINCIPLE

True Christianity advocates that everyone has the right to worship God any way he chooses — Protestant, Catholic, Muslim, Jew, or anyone else — or even not at all. This is his prerogative.

However, it must be understood that not to worship God or to worship Him wrongly is to reap the results of such worship (or the lack of same). Still, the individual has the freedom and the right to do what he likes in this respect.

RELIGIOUS FREEDOM

The United States of America was founded in part because of a desire for religious freedom and because of persecution in other countries. The very concept of the principles of this nation is freedom of religion — that man may worship God any way he chooses. That must never be hindered, weakened, or abridged in this nation.

Many newspapers have reported religion as being the cause of curtailment of freedoms, wars, and even bloodshed. And, sad to say, this is true. However, "religion" is what is being reported and not the Judeo-Christian principle.

You see, although it may be referred to in that manner, Christianity is not a religion. Christianity is a relationship with the Lord Jesus Christ. It is the only relationship in the world that guarantees freedom, and America has experienced the greatest prosperity, the greatest amount of freedom of any nation on the face of the earth — because it is based on Judeo-Christian principles that are based on the Word of God (the Bible).

I am going to say some things now that may seem shocking, but they are the truth and they need to be said.

VARIOUS RELIGIONS

To my knowledge, there is not a country in the world that denies the Judeo-Christian principle and yet affords a maximum amount of freedom for its people. In the countries of the world that espouse Islam, for example, the citizen or visitor adheres to that strict philosophy or his activities are seriously curtailed or, even worse, he may be killed. In countries of the world where Catholicism is dominant, there is little religious freedom; and if Catholicism is totally dominant, there is no freedom at all, as a missionary told me the other day.

He said, "Brother Swaggart, before the Communists took control of eastern Europe, Catholicism in most of these countries was totally dominant. Consequently, the Protestants could build few churches, if any, and we were allowed to preach the Gospel little, if at all. Since the Communists have taken power in eastern Europe (naturally they are atheists), they have no regard for any kind of worship. But even though it is extremely repressive, we have more opportunity to preach the Gospel in eastern European nations since the advent of Communism than we did when Catholicism dominated these countries."

That is a startling statement, but you must understand, Catholicism is a religion — not Christianity — as it is simply not based on the Word of God.

TRUE CHRISTIANITY

Wherever true Christianity is espoused and upheld, men have total freedom to worship God any way they desire — Catholic, Protestant, Jew, or anyone else — as long as their worship does not cause physical violence to other people. And that is the way that it should be — a free and open society.

Are the Fundamentalists endeavoring to curtail our freedoms? Quite the opposite is true. No Fundamentalist (and the word simply means a person who holds to a literal interpretation of the Bible) has endeavored to curtail the freedom of anyone. We have addressed the moral issues of the day that we feel must be addressed or the nation will lose its freedoms. Let us look a little closer.

Take abortion, for instance. We believe that it is murder. We believe that 1.5 million little babies are being murdered in their mother's womb every year. Now, some persons may say that the mother has the right to make any choice she desires over her own life. Of course, even that statement is not totally true. If a woman tried to kill herself, no doubt somebody would try to stop her. But you must understand, the baby's body is not the woman's body. The little one may be nourished by her body, but he is another human being altogether. And that mother, or a doctor, or anyone else has the *legal* right to terminate that person's life. We as Fundamentalists are demanding only that the freedoms of the unborn infant be guaranteed as well.

Would you rather someone had killed you in your mother's womb? Do you not appreciate that somebody such as myself (and other ministers of the Gospel) stood up for your right to be born? If that had not been the case, there is a good possibility you would not be reading this article today.

If the rights of the unborn are not protected, the next step will be *infanticide*, which is the killing of unwanted infants after they are born because of physical defects or whatever. Following that will be *euthanasia*, which simply means terminating the life of elderly people, or whomever, for any number of reasons. Hitler called them "useless eaters," and did away with hundreds of thousands of unwanted persons. I hope you can see from this the gradual erosion of our freedoms if we do not protect them all the way from the womb to the time of natural death.

Look at it this way. These same individuals who are demeaning ministers respecting our efforts to bring back traditional values in this nation proclaim that it is perfectly satisfactory for them (the liberals) to demand whatever they want. Yet if we demand certain things, we are "infringing" on the rights of others.

Let us look at prayer in public schools. The ACLU states constantly that there must be a separation of church and state. That is not the real issue; the issue is a separation of God and state, and that is where we get into real trouble. We have advocated a moment of vocal prayer in our public school systems. No, it is not the perfect answer, but it is better than what we have now — which is a moment of silent prayer or no prayer at all; and, to be frank with you, they are one and the same.

Actually, religion is being taught in our public schools every day. It is called secular humanism, and, yes, secular humanism has actually been labeled a "religion" by the federal courts. So what the ACLU and the liberal community are saying is that it is all right for them to teach *their* religion in the public schools, but we cannot teach *ours*. Samuel Blumenfeld said in his book, *NEA* (an expose on the National Education Association), "If traditional values of honesty, character, integrity, and morality are not brought back into our public schools, then America is going to lose a generation which will cause our nation to be lost, which will bring hell on earth to this country." Mr. Blumenfeld is right. We must remember that these traditional values mentioned are based on the Word of God.

You see, the so-called separation of church and state actually means that the government cannot have a state religion such as the Church of England in Great Britain and such as Catholicism in Italy, in Poland, and in other countries of the world. The Pilgrim fathers left their lands and endured tremendous hardship to get away from this state-controlled religion, and thank God they did. But a little child's leading in prayer and saying whatever he desires to say in his own way, whether he is Catholic, Protestant, Jewish, or whatever, is a far cry from a state-controlled religion!

A BIBLICAL FOUNDATION

When it comes to political issues, purely, I will always have my thoughts relative to these areas of discussion, and I also have one vote. When it comes to moral issues such as abortion, atheism, evolution, Communism, liberalism, infanticide, euthanasia, ERA, homosexuality, lesbianism, perversion, et cetera, I will continue to cry out against them. I am a minister called of God; this is, in part, what He has called me to do.

The liberal community that is trying to take our nation away from God and the traditional values that have made us great, based on the great Judeo-Christian concept which has given us the greatest freedoms any nation has ever known, may label these things I have just mentioned as social issues. Naturally, they *do* affect us socially, but, in reality, they are moral issues that God calls sin.

America has afforded its citizens the greatest prosperity, the greatest freedoms of expression the world has ever known in all of its history. Those freedoms are based squarely on the Judeo-Christian principle, which is the Word of God. Tremendous and strong efforts are being made to take that away from us. If these are lost, the freedoms and prosperity that we enjoy will remain for a while, but then they will erode and be lost as surely as you read the words on this paper. Then this nation will become a totalitarian state, which will be no different from the Soviet Union and other Communist countries. You must remember, the individuals who are advocating this liberal direction lean strongly toward socialism and Communism.

The Bible says, *"If the foundations be destroyed, what can the righteous do?"* (Psalm 11:3).

The Bible, the Word of God, is the foundation of all of our freedoms.

PRAYER

■ How can I get my prayers answered?

QUESTION:

HOW CAN I GET MY PRAYERS ANSWERED?

ANSWER:

You have asked a question to which there is no simple answer, but I will give you what I feel the Lord intended us to know. Possibly, you can derive help and strength from what we will say on the matter.

I will give first what the Lord gave concerning prayer itself and the way we should pray; after that I will issue some warnings that will be of benefit to you.

THE DISCIPLES ASKED THE SAME QUESTION

Jesus' disciples asked of Him, *"Lord, teach us to pray"* (Luke 11:1). (Basically, this is the same thing you have asked.) Jesus' disciples wanted to make certain their petitions would be heard and that God would answer — which, it seems, is the bottom-line reason for prayer. Oh, prayer includes many other things such as praise, intercession, travail, and so forth, and we will touch on these areas in the answer that Jesus gave to His disciples; but basically prayer is petition.

First of all, we can settle the matter in our mind that God *does* answer prayer. God so wants His children to come to Him for those things we need and that He has promised. Not only will He answer, but He will grant us those needs for which we have petitioned.

Many Scriptures could be used concerning prayer (such as Jeremiah 33:3; Mark 11:24; John 14:14; 15:7; and others we could name), but the one that best answers your question is the one given by our Lord Himself. His disciples desired to know how to pray. They had witnessed that the Master's prayers were answered, and they wanted to tap into this great reservoir of power. His examples in prayer inspired them; the prayer He gave them was to be their model. Of course, it was not meant to be quoted verbatim every time we go before the Lord; but within the contents of this particular prayer are some answers to seeing our needs met. (Compare Matthew 6:9-13 and Luke 11:2-4.)

OUR FATHER WHICH ART IN HEAVEN, HALLOWED BE THY NAME

First of all, the Lord Jesus Christ addressed the great God of heaven

271

as *our* Father, the pronoun "our" including *us*! Do you see what this means? We can go to God the Father using the same terminology that Jesus used. Jesus said, *"Whatsoever ye shall ask the Father in my name [in the name of Jesus], he will give it you"* (John 16:23). How is this possible that we can go directly to God as *our* Father? Because He *is* our Father — made possible by the death and resurrection of His Son and our Saviour, the Lord Jesus Christ!

In this model prayer, Jesus began the petition with praise, using the phrase, *"hallowed be thy name."* Common sense dictates that a person does not enter into the presence of someone of high position without first recognizing who that person is. The Lord is simply telling us the same thing here. We are not to enter the presence of the Heavenly Father with a barrage of petitions or a bombardment of our difficulties. First, we must acknowledge who *He* is. He is our Father. His name is to be revered, to be glorified, to be worshiped. We are to thank Him for the many things He has done for us; we are to praise Him; hence, the phrase, *"hallowed be thy name."*

Entering into His presence with praise, with thanksgiving, and with gratitude, it is always well for us to spend a little time enumerating our blessings. Thank Him for them. Be respectful, be appreciative, be grateful. One of the great sins of this age is a lack of gratitude in the heart and life of those who have received so much from our Heavenly Father. So, let us thank Him and be lavish in our praise, for He is worthy of all praise and all glory.

THY KINGDOM COME. THY WILL BE DONE IN EARTH, AS IT IS IN HEAVEN

Second, we should tell the Lord we want His will, that we are not interested in our will being accomplished, our desires being granted, our wants and wishes being delivered, but we want God's will. We want what is done in heaven to be done also in earth — and we want this in our own life also. Make this abundantly clear to Him. If you are asking for an automobile, tell Him you want it *if* it is His will. If you are asking Him to heal someone, ask for it according to His wisdom. (Please see my book on *The Word, the Will, and the Wisdom.*)

This is so important in asking anything of God. We hear so much teaching nowadays on rushing into the presence of God and *demanding* all sorts of things. We are led to believe the louder we cry and the more demands we make that God will somehow become a glorified bellhop and just give us whatever we ask.

That is the best way *not* to see our prayers answered. God cannot be all that concerned with our will in matters. Most of the time our will is all confused anyway; but He knows what is best for us. He knows our needs, while we only *think* we know them. (We confuse needs with desires.) He knows the past, the present, and the future. In this light we should go to our Father and tell Him that we want nothing more than His will and that if our petition is contrary to His will, we would rather it not be carried out. This is the basis on which we should approach our Heavenly Father.

GIVE US THIS DAY OUR DAILY BREAD

Now we are asking the Lord to meet our needs. We have already entered into His presence (the way that we are supposed to) with thanksgiving and praise. We have asked that His will be done and not ours. Now we can make our petitions for those things that we need.

We have need of so many things: food for our family, a house for our living, and health for our body, to name a few. We can feel free under the guidelines of His will to ask for all of these things — with the understanding (always) that they be given according to His will.

Jesus went on to say, *"Your Father knoweth what things ye have need of, before ye ask him"* (Matthew 6:8). Certainly He does, but He wants us to ask Him. Yet, we do not have to repeat it over and over again (Matthew 6:7). We merely make the petition in faith, confident that He hears us, and with full assurance because He already knows what we need before we ask it. So, we do not have to go in fear and trembling, but with the assurance that He loves us and will give us our daily sustenance.

However, there is a second meaning to the passage, *"Give us this day our daily bread."* Jesus is the Bread of Life (John 6:48). When we ask for our daily provisions, no matter how great or small they may be, we must remember they come through Jesus; and if we eat and partake of Him, all of these other things will be added unto us. While we ask for daily provisions, we should remember *daily* to feast upon the Bread of Life, which is the Word of God and which is Jesus Christ.

AND FORGIVE US OUR DEBTS, AS
WE FORGIVE OUR DEBTORS

Following our petitions in prayer, we must not forget to ask forgiveness for any wrongdoing on our part. Jesus also admonished that if we have had difficulties and problems with other people, we should forgive them (even if our forgiveness is not sought). (Read Matthew 5:23, 24; 6:14, 15.) This clears the spiritual cobwebs out of our Christian life, opening the door for a constant, uninterrupted communion with God.

Here we have the matter of our asking Christ's forgiveness and our act of forgiving others. If we do not forgive others, how can we expect Christ to forgive us? Many Christians fail to see their prayers answered simply because of these problems. They harbor grudges. A husband will not forgive his wife, or vice versa. Children will not forgive their parents, or parents will not forgive their children. The list goes on. We must forgive all our debtors before we can ask God for our needs or to forgive us our wrongs.

AND LEAD US NOT INTO TEMPTATION,
BUT DELIVER US FROM EVIL

On first reading, this portion taken from the King James Version may be misleading, for it seems to say that God Himself may lead us into temptation. Of course, God never does this. It is totally out of character for Him. In studying this in the original Greek text, we find it means this: Do not permit us to be overcome by evil, but deliver us from the evil one. Now the statement takes on a whole new meaning. We are always to remember that we are *in* the world but not *of* the world (John 17:11-16). As we live for God, Satan will do everything within his power to see us overcome with evil; but we have the assurance of God that if we hold to His unchanging hand, He will not permit us to be overcome by the evil one (I John 2:13, 14; 4:4). Whenever Satan devises his attacks against us — as he most assuredly will — we have the promise (praise the Lord!) that our Heavenly Father will deliver us. *"No weapon that is formed against thee shall prosper"* (Isaiah 54:17).

FOR THINE IS THE KINGDOM, AND THE POWER, AND THE GLORY, FOR EVER. AMEN

As we close our petition and our prayer to the Lord, we should always remember this: whatever good is accomplished is due to God, our Father. Anything that we may realize — in the realm of salvation or whatever (good) — we have simply because God in His grace and mercy has given it to us. We have earned none of it. Salvation is *"not of works, lest any man should boast"* (Ephesians 2:9). The kingdom is always His, the power is always His, and the glory is always His. We are undeserving, unworthy creatures in desperate need of a redeemer. We *never* receive blessings because we are good, or great, or worthy, or deserving. Every single Christian that ever lived has deserved hell; but because of His grace, His mercy, and His love, we have been redeemed. We must never forget this. We must always remember that the prayer answers we receive are strictly, once again, due to His mercy and His grace.

A MODEL PRAYER

The Lord's Prayer, as we have come to know it, is a model prayer. The Lord addressed Himself in the way He did, not because we should parrot these words every time we go before God in prayer, but as the laying down of a foundation instructing us in the principles of prayer. If we will learn and practice these principles, we will be well on our way to having our prayers and petitions answered.

Basically, I have covered those things that we must *do,* but at the same time I should possibly enumerate some things we must *guard against* in our praying. Many Christians have been led to believe that humility before God is not necessary anymore. As Dave Wilkerson said sometime ago, "The church used to confess her *sins*; now she is confessing her *rights,*" and I may add, in a brash, bold, bossy manner that is unpleasing to our Heavenly Father. It is nothing more than a blatant display of childishness and lack of maturity constantly to ask the Lord for all kinds of *things* because of our "rights." We should be careful of what we ask. For instance, it is always God's will to save people — anytime, anyplace — but just about anything else that we might ask would fall into categories of wisdom and will, God's timing, and our readiness and maturity to receive the blessing.

We may be wise to close our ears to a lot of things we are hearing and carefully screen our reading material nowadays as preachers are bombarding the Christian media on means of acquiring Cadillacs and all kinds of gadgets and gimmicks — calling it answers to prayer.

A WORD OF CAUTION

Be careful of individuals who are always talking about great answers to prayer. There has been a rash of this in the last days also. Some Christians, it seems, forget that God *"maketh his sun to rise on the evil and on the good, and sendeth rain on the just and on the unjust"* (Matthew 5:45). In other words, a great deal of Christians, when something good happens, automatically start beating their chest and heralding the thing as their having great power with God, that God has given them special favor. This could possibly be the case, but it is also possible that it was happenstance or general providence — when we look around us, we realize some of the same things are happening to those who are unsaved as well.

To be sure, *"every good gift and every perfect gift is from above"* (James 1:17), but that does not necessarily mean God personally intervened in the matter (special providence). God does not need false glory; His works do not need exaggeration.

What have I been saying here? Simply this: Do not believe everything you hear. If you have not seen all kinds of things great and grandiose coming your way, with fantastic answers to prayer every day of your life — and if you are possibly thinking that you have been left out — remember this truth: just maybe the facts are being stretched somewhat between the receiving and the reporting by the individuals in the limelight. They are possibly having no more prayers answered than you are.

God does answer prayer, but we do harm to the kingdom of God whenever we trumpet some supposed miracle for our own glory. Too many Christians today are taking the credit for alleged answers to prayer, giving the impression that they have some special "in" with God over anyone else. It is a case of one-upmanship. In other words, the next person has to tell a bigger story than the last person. Let us be careful of rivalry.

CONCLUSION

The other day I received a letter saying, "Brother Swaggart, for two years I have walked around confessing everything from 'A' to 'Z.' I confessed it loudly, repetitiously, for all to hear. I was told that if I did this long enough, I would get whatever I was asking for simply because these were my 'rights' in Jesus Christ. I attempted all kinds of things that I should not have attempted, not even seeking the will of God, because I had been taught that anything I wanted *was* the will of God, and I should just believe God and think big, ask big, and receive big."

"To be honest with you," the lady continued, "in spite of all my confessing and saying things that were not there and that did not actually exist, when people would ask me how things were, I would confess the grandest things in the world — simply because I was told this was the way to get answers to prayer."

She went on to say, "Brother Swaggart, I received no answer to prayer. As I look back now, I realize that God had to teach this young Christian one more lesson. I realize, first of all, this teaching is wrong. I realize, second, that God's name is to be hallowed and not to be used, which is exactly what I was trying to do according to the teaching of the hyper-faith people (faith in word people). Now I am going before God in weeping and humility, asking Him to give me what He wants me to have and what He thinks I am able to take care of."

She closed her letter by saying, "Brother Swaggart, I have received more answers to prayer in the past few months than I did the other years of my so-called great faith and great confession all put together."

This sister learned the key. She began to follow inadvertently the principle and the method of the Lord's Prayer even though she possibly did not know this was what she was doing. She had to learn her lesson the hard way. People can use all kinds of *"vain repetitions"* (Matthew 6:7), and confession, plus heralding their "rights" before God and the world in some bold, brash way. The Scripture says, *"They have their reward"* (Matthew 6:2). In other words, they are not going to get anything.

I suppose my entire answer can be summed up in two thoughts: humility and the will of God. Remember this: God answers prayer; He answers prayer *today*. He is a prayer-answering God; but be careful of what you ask, and be thankful for what you receive.

QUESTION:

SALVATION

■ What is meant by the term "saved by grace"?

■ What is meant by the term "justification"?

■ Is unconditional eternal security scriptural?

■ Please explain I John 3:9 which says, "Whosoever is born of God doth not commit sin; for his seed remaineth in him: and he cannot sin, because he is born of God." Does this mean that it is impossible for a born again Christian to sin?

QUESTION:

WHAT IS MEANT BY THE TERM "SAVED BY GRACE"?

ANSWER:

This is a common term, yet one that is commonly misunderstood. "Saved by grace," "salvation by grace," and "saved by faith" mean basically the same thing. And, really, it is upon this term "saved by grace" that our very salvation is hinged. Consequently, we will do our best to explain it and prayerfully believe that you will have a greater conception of your salvation and what it means.

The term "saved by grace" falls into two categories; therefore, to understand the meaning of the entire term, it is necessary to examine these two categories: salvation and grace. The first word — "saved" — would fall under the topic of salvation.

SALVATION

To be saved, to be moved from sin unto salvation, is what anybody desires who believes anything at all about the Word of God. If there is a hell (and we know there is), we want to miss it. If there is a heaven (and we know there is), we want to go there. We want to accrue to ourselves all the benefits of salvation. We want the bondage of darkness to be broken and our life to be changed. We want our heart to be softened. In other words, we want to accept Jesus Christ as our own personal Saviour and know that this constitutes salvation for our soul.

GRACE

First of all, the question must be asked that was asked by the Philippian jailer: *"What must I do to be saved?"* Paul and Silas answered him, saying, *"Believe on the Lord Jesus Christ, and thou shalt be saved, and thy house"* (Acts 16:30, 31). Paul later wrote: *"If thou shalt confess with thy mouth the Lord Jesus, and shalt believe in thine heart that God hath raised him from the dead, thou shalt be saved. For with the heart man believeth unto righteousness; and with the mouth confession is made unto salvation . . . . For whosoever shall call upon the name of the Lord shall be saved"* (Romans 10:9-13). *"By grace are ye saved through faith; and that not of yourselves:*

it is the gift of God: Not of works, lest any man should boast" (Ephesians 2:8, 9).

WORKS

The first general council of the early church was conducted in Jerusalem. At that council *"there rose up certain of the sect of the Pharisees which believed [in other words, they were Christians], saying, That it was needful to circumcise them [the Gentile converts], and to command them to keep the law of Moses"* (Acts 15:5).

You see, the great law-grace controversy arose even then. We may even say that the works-grace controversy originated there. The Pharisees who believed in salvation also believed that a person had to keep the law of Moses, et cetera. This is what the dispute was all about. Peter rose up and explained how the Gentiles had heard the Gospel by his preaching and how they had been given the Holy Spirit, even as the apostles and Jews (verse 7). Then he said, *"But we believe that through the grace of the Lord Jesus Christ we shall be saved, even as they"* (verse 11).

Notice the terminology. Peter was saying that they were saved by grace and that no work entered into it. The Gentiles did not keep any of the law of Moses. They were saved by grace; that is, by faith. In other words, they trusted Jesus Christ totally and completely for their salvation and not works of the law, church membership, shaking the preacher's hand, confessing to a priest, et cetera.

CHRIST PLUS WORKS

Now, this question must be asked, "Can a person trust Jesus Christ 50 percent and works 50 percent?"

We could even ask further, "Can a person trust Jesus Christ 99 percent and works 1 percent?"

Of course, I must hasten to say that God looks on the heart, and He alone can judge a person. However, in interpreting the Word of God, I must strongly advocate the belief that it is not possible to trust Jesus Christ partly for salvation, and then works partly. Paul plainly said, *"Stand fast therefore in the liberty wherewith Christ hath made us free, and be not entangled again with the yoke of bondage"*

(Galatians 5:1). He continued, *"Christ is become of no effect unto you, whosoever of you are justified by the law; ye are fallen from grace"* (verse 4). In other words, a person cannot mix law and grace; he cannot mix works and grace.

So what happens to the person who says, "Yes, I trust Jesus Christ as my Saviour"; but in trusting Him as Saviour (that is, in his assumption) he is also trusting in his church membership? Is this person saved? If he is thinking that church membership constitutes some part of his salvation, *no*, he is not saved.

What about the Catholic who says, "Yes, I trust Jesus Christ to save my soul"; but he is also depending on his confession to the priest, his association with the Catholic church, his partaking of the Eucharist, et cetera? Is this person saved? No, he is not saved. A person cannot depend on works *and* grace.

ALL OR NONE

You see, most of the church world today does not know what it means to trust Christ solely and totally for salvation. Oh, yes, they believe in Jesus Christ, and they regard and even revere Him; but they are still trusting in good works, in being good, in providing a living, et cetera. Some persons even think that because they live in America, and because America is a so-called Christian nation, that makes them a Christian. Other persons say, "Yes, I believe," and by their saying it, they think they are a Christian, not realizing what the word "believe" actually entails. (It means repenting and placing all trust in some person or thing, pledging to him one's obedience and allegiance.)

How many of you reading this feel that if you were turned out of your church, you would lose your salvation? Of course, many of you would say, "Brother Swaggart, I would be sorry, but my salvation has nothing to do with the membership in my church. I love my church, but I am saved because I have trusted Jesus Christ as my Saviour." You would be absolutely correct. Yet there are many people who feel their soul would be lost if they were turned out of their church.

For instance, how would many of our Catholic friends react if their priest said, "I will no longer receive confession from you and will see to it that no other priest receives confession from you, and you are going to be excommunicated from the Catholic church"? How would they feel? Most Catholics, of course, would feel they had lost their soul, simply because they believe that the Catholic church is the instrument of their salvation.

But stop and think a moment.

ONE WAY: JESUS

If you will stop and consider the matter, you will realize that the Bible is the Word of God: *it does not change*. The Catholic church changes, other churches change, but the Word of God never changes. So a little common sense and a little thinking would cause us to realize that we should adhere strictly to the *Scriptures* instead of some man-made dogma, theory, or religion.

It was Jesus, and Jesus alone, who paid the price for our salvation. It was not some other man, and it was not a religious system. It was *Jesus* who hung on that Cross and not some church. We must understand that it is His atoning sacrifice we must accept. *"I am the way, the truth, and the life: no man cometh unto the Father, but by me"* (John 14:6).

Our Lord does not need any help. He paid the price in full when He said, *"It is finished"* (John 19:30). There is nothing else that can, or needs to, be added to His redemptive work.

SUMMARY

Let me repeat, in summation, that salvation has absolutely nothing to do with a church, a denomination, or good works. It has absolutely nothing to do with the number of schools Jimmy Swaggart builds or how many good works Mother Theresa performs. However, let me quickly add: works may play a big part in our spiritual development. Still again, they have *nothing* to do with our salvation. The old song simply says:

> *"Jesus paid it all,*
> *All to Him I owe;*
> *Sin had left a crimson stain,*
> *He washed it white as snow."*

So that is what "saved by grace" (or by faith) means. It simply means we are trusting 100 percent in Jesus (in what He did at Calvary and in His resurrection) for our salvation. Being "saved by grace" necessarily means that we do not trust in any man-made works, that even though we may engage ourselves in them and may even profit from them, we understand that not *one iota* can be added to our salvation through them.

All anyone has to do to be saved is accept Jesus Christ as his own personal Saviour and believe with all his heart that Jesus died for him at Calvary. He may not understand it all, but the important thing is that he accepts it and vows within his heart to follow Christ the best he can.

If you are reading this and are not saved, just realize you are a lost sinner deserving to go to hell, but because of Christ's mercy and grace, He has given you the opportunity to be saved. If you will trust in His redeeming work on Calvary, with a trust that comes from the heart (Romans 10:9, 10), then no matter where you are — at this very moment — *you will be saved!*

You do not have to join a church or shake a preacher's hand. You do not have to become associated with a particular religious denomination. You do not have to give one dime or dollar or perform any good works. You do not have to keep the law of Moses. You simply trust Jesus Christ as your own personal Saviour, and you are "saved by grace."

QUESTION:

WHAT IS MEANT BY THE TERM "JUSTIFICATION"?

ANSWER:

This is probably one of the singlemost important questions that could ever be asked. Justification — even though the word is hardly known, much less understood, in most Christian circles today — is utmostly important in the great plan of redemption afforded us by our Lord.

The word "justification" comes from the Greek word *dikaiosis*, which means the act of God that declares men free from guilt and acceptable unto Himself, thus accounting righteousness unto them.

Since sanctification is often confused with justification, we will need, first of all, to define the differences in these two works of grace.

God cannot declare a person "not guilty" until he is cleansed from all sin and made pure and holy by the blood of Christ. At the time of confession and accepting Christ's forgiveness, sanctification *makes* a person not guilty. Justification, at the time of salvation, *declares* the forgiven person not guilty.

FORGIVENESS AND JUSTIFICATION

When a person accepts Jesus as his Saviour, he is cleansed from all his old sin and made holy by the blood of Christ. Sanctification means, quite simply, freed from sin, purified. Consequently, the person that seeks, and receives, God's forgiveness is, at the same time he is forgiven, sanctified. It is one and the same thing.

Since the Fall in the Garden of Eden, mankind commits sin (enters willfully into the act of disobedience and rebellion against God), but God (because of His mercy and grace) forgives the sin and sanctifies (frees) the sinner.

But then God goes a step further: He justifies the individual and declares him not guilty.

We, as human beings, can understand forgiveness, because forgiveness is something of which we ourselves are capable. If someone does something against us, for example, we forgive him. However, what that person did does not just evaporate or vanish away — it is still there — but it is forgiven. We cannot erase the act against us, although we may wish it had never happened.

God does not stop with forgiving us; He justifies us. In other words, God wipes the slate clean, and it is as though we had never sinned. Because of our human, finite mind, this is hard for us to comprehend. But we must remember that God is not limited. He can and does erase the whole thing! That is justification; that is God declaring us not guilty.

Sanctification cleanses — justification erases the whole ugly picture and starts us out with a clean slate. A human being cannot do that, nor can the state, or the church. But God can, and He does.

A husband and wife can have an argument, with many harsh

words exchanged between them, and then they forgive each other. But the argument still happened; they cannot erase it. Forgiveness is as far as they can go. However, say the argument is a sin against God (and any sin *is* against God, actually), and the individuals ask Him to forgive them. What happens? God not only forgives, but wipes the record of the argument from the books, and it is as though it never happened. Then when Satan, the accuser, brings it up (Revelation 12:10), God can show him the books, open to the date in question when the argument (or whatever) occurred, and there is no record in glory of this foul deed of sin (whatever it might have been) ever having been committed. That is justification.

JUSTIFICATION BY FAITH

How can a person receive this act of grace? Let us go to the Word of God for the answer. *"Being justified freely by his grace through the redemption that is in Christ Jesus: Whom God hath set forth to be a propitiation through faith in his blood, to declare his righteousness for the remission of sins that are past, through the forbearance of God; To declare, I say, at this time his righteousness: that he might be just, and the justifier of him which believeth in Jesus. Therefore we conclude that a man is justified by faith without the deeds of the law"* (Romans 3:24-26, 28).

Simply put, Paul was saying that works cannot enter into a person's justification. Jesus paid the price for our justification at Calvary, and all we have to do to receive it is to accept Him as our Lord and Saviour. He gives it freely, as He gave His life freely for our forgiveness (sanctification).

The sinner who comes to Jesus with a spiritual hunger and a desire to be born again will be instantly forgiven of his sin (John 3:16). At that time, also instantly, he is sanctified by the grace and power of God (I Corinthians 6:11). Then he is justified. Salvation, sanctification, and justification are all performed in the same work of grace; and the sinner does nothing except believe on the Lord Jesus Christ and resolve to follow Him to the best of his ability.

For the Christian who fails, who falters, and is repentant, these same acts of grace are available. He simply goes to the Lord according to I John 1:9 and confesses his sin. Again, instantly, the Lord cleanses him, sanctifies him, and justifies him. And again, as far as God is concerned, the sin was never committed; the slate is wiped clean.

We must remember, however, these acts of grace cannot be earned through good works or anything that we can do. This is the reason that we stated at the very outset that justification is one of the singlemost important words respecting the redemptive process of the child of God.

BEFORE CHRIST

Now, of course, the question must be asked: Were men justified before the finished work of Christ on the cross?

Yes, they were.

Their justification was made possible by looking forward to the coming Messiah. They did this, actually, by obeying the law as required in the Old Testament. Consequently, the lambs they offered up were a type of the coming anti-type — Christ Jesus. (Today we are justified by looking back to Calvary.) It sounds simple — they would offer up a lamb and be justified of their sins — and it was. But a problem developed, a problem brought about, actually, by the comfortable position the law provided for salvation.

You see, little by little the Jewish people started trusting so completely in the law to save them that they forgot what the system represented. They forgot that it was only a type, or a shadow, of what was to come and could serve only as a *"schoolmaster to bring us unto Christ . . . after that faith is come, we are no longer under a schoolmaster"* (Galatians 3:24, 25). (They trusted so much in the law that when Christ came, they did not accept Him. They rejected and denied Him.) Once they took their eyes off what the lambs were a type, or shadow, of, they could not be saved, they could not be justified, no matter how many lambs they offered up. They could only be saved as they looked *forward* by faith to the coming of Christ, even as today we can only be saved, justified, as we look *backward* to what Christ has already accomplished at Calvary.

It was this blind trust in the law and lack of faith in the coming Messiah that ultimately caused the Jewish people to crucify Jesus Christ. And today we have literally hundreds of millions of people committing the same sin, the same terrible infraction of God's laws.

Hundreds of millions of people in the Catholic church trust in a system of laws — the sacraments, the church — to save them. Like the Jews, they are sincere, they are sticklers for the law, but they forget what the law represents. Like the Jews who died without God because there was no salvation in their law, millions of people who are trusting in man-made laws will be eternally lost.

THE END RESULT

However, the Catholics are not the only ones that are doing this. Many Protestants are doing the same thing. They are trusting in their church membership, their good works, their religion to save them. It is all the same. The end result for anyone who does not trust in the atoning death of Christ on Calvary's cross will be damnation, eternal separation from Christ. There is no redemption, no forgiveness, no sanctification, and no justification, simply because it must be all of Christ or none of Christ.

"For if Abraham were justified by works, he hath whereof to glory; but not before God. For what saith the scripture? Abraham believed God, and it was counted unto him for righteousness" (Romans 4:2, 3).

Justification is God's greatest gift to mankind through His Son, Jesus Christ, but it can be obtained by faith and faith alone.

QUESTION:

IS UNCONDITIONAL ETERNAL SECURITY SCRIPTURAL?

ANSWER:

Some years ago I sat in a certain church and heard a preacher deliver a funeral message over a young man who had been killed in an accident. I looked at the church full of people and listened as the so-called preacher preached the deceased into heaven. I knew the young man had made no pretense of being saved. He seldom, if ever, went to church. The only time he mentioned God's name was in profanity, and yet he was preached into heaven. The preacher stated that even though the deceased had been out of fellowship with God, he had once been saved and he could not lose his salvation; consequently, he was now in heaven.

Now, it made no difference to the deceased what was preached; however, the hundreds of people who sat there and listened to the preacher were led to believe they could live any way they wanted to and still go to heaven.

Millions of people believe the doctrine of unconditional eternal security and will die and go to hell because they make no pretense of living for God.

I heard two sermons not too long ago that asked respectively, "Can a Christian ever be lost?" "Can a born again believer ever be lost?" Of course, the speakers were promoting the doctrine of "once in grace, always in grace," et cetera. No, a Christian cannot be lost; neither can a born again believer be lost. However, a Christian can cease to be a Christian through an act of his own will, and a believer can cease to believe; then that person can be lost.

AUTHORITY OF THE WORD

"It is impossible for those who were once enlightened, and have tasted of the heavenly gift, and were made partakers of the Holy Ghost, And have tasted the good word of God, and the powers of the world to come, If they shall fall away, to renew them again unto repentance; seeing they crucify to themselves the Son of God afresh, and put him to an open shame" (Hebrews 6:4-6). This Scripture is abundantly clear, and to try to explain it away as meaning a sinner under conviction is ignorance of the highest degree. The Apostle Paul said that Demas who was once saved *"hath forsaken me [and the work of the Lord], having loved this present world"* (II Timothy 4:10; see I John 2:15-17).

Jesus said, *"If ye continue in my word, then are ye my disciples indeed"* (John 8:31). Paul said you could fall from grace (Galatians 5:4). He also said, *"Some shall depart from the faith"* (I Timothy 4:1). How can you depart from something you have never experienced? Peter gave a graphic example of a person once being saved and then being lost. He said, *"If after they have escaped the pollutions of the world through the knowledge of the Lord and Saviour Jesus Christ, they are again entangled therein, and overcome, the latter end is worse with them than the beginning. For it had been better for them not to have known the way*

of righteousness, than, after they have known it, to turn [away] . . . .
*But it is happened unto them according to the true proverb, The dog is
turned to his own vomit again; and the sow that was washed to her
wallowing in the mire"* (II Peter 2:20-22). Actually, we could give
hundreds of other Scriptures, but we will not take the space to do it. The
Bible states clearly that a person can lose his salvation through neglect
and disobedience.

TWISTING OF SCRIPTURES

We read concerning Christ's sheep, *"I give unto them eternal
life; and they shall never perish"* (John 10:28). The proponents
of eternal security use this passage erroneously to try and further
their cause. Christ's sheep are those who hear His voice and
follow Him, not otherwise (verse 27). Therefore, as long as we hear
His voice and follow Him, we are safe and secure. There is no promise
here for those who cease to hear and follow. Proponents of eternal
security contend that a sheep is always a sheep and cannot be anything
else. The Bible teaches that if we stray from God's fold, we are *lost*
sheep (Luke 15:6).

Another theory used is that no matter how bad a child may become,
he is always a child of his father. Consequently, those who were once
children of God must remain His children no matter how deep in sin they
may become involved. Spiritual birth is compared to natural birth, but
without basis. Jesus was the Only Begotten Son of God; He could not
become anything else. We are adopted sons (Romans 8:15 through 9:4;
Galatians 4:5; Ephesians 1:5). Consequently, Christians can fall back
into sin and lose their sonship. Adam, once a son of God, lost his
sonship. Another argument used is that a Christian has eternal life, so
consequently it is forever. It is true that life is eternal, but a person does
not necessarily eternally hold onto it.

CONDITIONAL PROMISES

"If ye continue in my word, then are ye my disciples indeed"
(John 8:31).

Scripture plainly teaches if anyone desires to be saved, no matter
how weak and stumbling that Christian may be, he will not be lost

(John 3:15, 16; 10:27-29; Romans 8:35-39; 14:4; Ephesians 1:13). However, if that person wants to turn his back on God, he has the right to do so; and if he does, according to the Word of God, he will be lost. The Gospel, as taught by the Word (as I have given in this chapter), gives the greatest assurance of all. I never worry about my salvation because I know He is able to keep me (Jude 24), and I am going to live for Him (with His help).

SATANIC DOCTRINE

I read an article sometime ago by one of the chief proponents of this doctrine. He said, and I quote, "When the rapture takes place, millions of Christians will leave out of nightclubs, road houses, saloons, gambling dens, even in the act of committing adultery, et cetera, and will be transformed and immediately go to be with Jesus Christ." This doctrine is satanic! I know even as I write this that quite a number of people will grow angry with me, the reason being, of course, that many desire to continue in their sin. It makes them angry for someone to upset their little theory and tell them if they continue as they are, they will be eternally lost. Instead of making their life right with God, they will persist in believing error.

BASIS OF OBEDIENCE

"Being saved makes you secure, so what difference does it make?" some persons would ask. If that is as far as it goes, it would not make any difference. The sad fact is that millions are living in open sin, making no effort at all to live for God, thinking they are going to heaven. Of course, if they do not change, they will die and be eternally lost in hell. Many other true Christians who believe this doctrine do not concern themselves too much with sinful loved ones, even though they may be living a vile life. They think, "Well, they have once been saved, and even though they are out of fellowship with God, they will go to heaven when they die." Little effort is made to get them right with God. Eternal security is taught in Scripture *on the basis of obedience to God.* If men truly want security, they must meet God's terms. No man is obligated to sin. God has made full provision *"to keep [men] . . . and present [them] faultless"* (Jude 24) in heaven if they will cooperate. No provision except hell is made for rebels. All hope of assurance while living in rebellion is a fool's hope.

Any teaching of security that encourages sin is false and satanic.

[Note: For a more in-depth look at this subject you may order our booklet, Is Unconditional Eternal Security Scriptural?*]*

QUESTION:

PLEASE EXPLAIN I JOHN 3:9 WHICH SAYS, "WHOSOEVER IS BORN OF GOD DOTH NOT COMMIT SIN; FOR HIS SEED REMAINETH IN HIM: AND HE CANNOT SIN, BECAUSE HE IS BORN OF GOD." DOES THIS MEAN THAT IT IS IMPOSSIBLE FOR A BORN AGAIN CHRISTIAN TO SIN?

ANSWER:

To say that this means a Christian is automatically sinlessly perfect once he accepts Christ as his Saviour or that it is impossible for a Christian ever again to commit sin is answering a question that is different in context than that of the scriptural statement referred to, and I will try to explain.

THE PRACTICE OF SIN

First of all, the word "commit" (verse 9) in the Greek is *poieo,* meaning "to practice." So I John 3:9 could read, "Whosoever is born of God doth not practice sin." This means that a Christian does not habitually engage himself in sins or in a particular sin. But it does not mean that a person could not at times fall into, or even commit, a sin. However, a child of God does not make a practice of sinning.

There is a difference in an individual who, through heavy temptation, yields to some specific sin (as bad as that is) and a person who habitually does things of this nature all of the time. For instance, a child of God (such as David in the Word of God) may commit adultery. There is no question that it is terrible, it is evil, it is wicked, and it brings forth all kinds of difficulties and problems. But bad as this is, it is still different from a person engaging in adultery (or fornication) continuously; that is, practicing promiscuity. You can see this, I am sure.

SEVERAL ERRORS

There are several errors based on I John 3:9 that I would like to point out to you. The first one is that a born again individual cannot sin. We know, of course, this is not true because the Bible is full of examples of Christians who committed wrongdoings, or even gross sins. And who among us today can say that he has never sinned since he was born again? I am afraid none of us could make that statement, truthfully.

Another teaching says that even though Christians may commit so-called sins, they are not actual sins, as such. Of course, that remark needs no explanation whatever; that it is error is fairly obvious.

And there is still another teaching that God automatically forgives each sin that we commit without our even acknowledging or confessing it. That too is error. The Christian, according to I John 1:9, must come to the Lord and confess each and every sin committed and ask forgiveness of that sin.

A fourth teaching states that God does not actually see our (the Christian's) sins. Instead, He sees the blood of Jesus, in which we are trusting. Naturally, God does see the blood of Jesus Christ, but that does not in any way change the fact that He also sees the sins that we commit. For that reason we must go to Him and confess those sins that we commit (consciously or inadvertently) and turn away from them.

A fifth teaching is that even though we commit sins, they are not imputed unto us. In other words, God takes no cognizance of these sins and in fact does not even recognize them as sins.

Others say that all of the Christian's sins (past, present, and future) are already forgiven. Of course, both these statements are untrue.

HIS SEED

Let us look at a couple of words in the scriptural phrase, *"for his seed remaineth in him: and he cannot sin, because he is born of God."* The word "in" here means "in harmony with" or "in union with." Next, we look at the word "seed," which pertains to the Word of God. The simple meaning, then, is this: as long as a person remains "in union with" or "in harmony with" the seed, which is the Word of God, he cannot sin. A person who conscientiously obeys the Word of God and refuses to break the commandments of God *will not* sin, and therefore *cannot* sin; for sin is the transgression of the seed.

The scriptural reason given here for the Christian not being able to sin is that "His" (God's) seed (the Word of God) remains (or abides) in him; that is, the one born again willfully refuses to transgress the commandment of God and cannot sin. As long as this consecration remains, he will be unable to sin simply because he refuses the advances of Satan that would cause the commitment of sin.

If a Christian allows himself to grow cold in his love for God and ceases to pray and seek God's face and study the Word and is slack in keeping up his spiritual life as he ought to, then that child of God can again be overcome and sin, by transgressing the Word of God (the seed).

A TWOFOLD WORK

So actually, a twofold work takes place here: God's redemptive work in our heart and our cooperation in that work. This does not mean that salvation automatically takes place in a person's life, thus making sin impossible. It does mean that if we as Christians cooperate with God and His Word, and it is allowed to remain supreme in our life (through that continued cooperation) we will be able to repel the onslaughts of Satan and actually not sin.

We will have no desire to sin; Satan cannot make us sin; and certainly God, through His Holy Spirit, will do everything He can (without violating our free will) to prevent our sinning. Consequently, we stay free and pure in Him, but only by that continued cooperation.

SATAN

■ Who is Satan?

■ How much latitude does Satan have in respect to temptation?

■ Can Satan read your mind?

■ What is God's purpose in allowing Satan to continue?

QUESTION:

WHO IS SATAN?

ANSWER:

First, let us see who Satan is not. He is not an evil principle, an object of the mortal mind, an influence, an abstract power, a diseased germ, or some kind of being with hoofs, horns, holding a pitch fork, and so forth.

THE ORIGIN OF SATAN

He was created in the beginning by God, along with other beings, principalities, powers, and angels — a sinless, perfect, beautiful, and righteous being. However, there came a time when this beautiful created being formed a revolution against God and fell from his lofty position. The Bible tells us about his fall in Ezekiel 28:11-19. Even though the Bible mentions the individual Tyrus, we actually know from the following references, this could not possibly apply to an earthly man, but rather to Lucifer. The Bible tells us that Lucifer (his heavenly name before he fell) *"seal[ed] up the sum"* (verse 12). In other words, there was nothing else good that could be said about him. He was *"full of wisdom, and perfect in beauty"* (verse 12). (You must understand that this is referring to him before his fall.) He was created by God, *"perfect . . . till iniquity was found in [him]"* (verse 15).

HIS FALL

Of course, we do not know many of the reasons why Lucifer fell. However, we do know that God created (in the beginning) angels without number, Lucifer being one of those angels. From the way the Bible describes him, he was probably the most powerful one created. There was no angel as wise as he, none as perfect and none as beautiful. The first hint of his fall is found in Ezekiel 28:17, where *"[his] heart was lifted up [in pride] because of [his] beauty, [and it] corrupted [his] wisdom."* We know that when he fell, he determined in his heart to destroy all that pertained to God. For he said, *"I will ascend into heaven, I will exalt my throne above the stars of God: I will sit also upon the mount of the congregation, in the sides of the north: I will ascend above the heights of the clouds; I will be like the most High"* (Isaiah 14:12-14).

Pride was his major sin. He desired to be God. The Word does tell us that he is *"the god of this world"* (II Corinthians 4:4) and the cause of all war, sickness, pain, sin, suffering, and heartache (John 10:10). Thank God, one day he will be *"brought down to hell, to the sides of the pit"* (Isaiah 14:15; Revelation 20:10).

HIS WORKS

We know from Revelation 12:4 that there was a great war in heaven. A third part of the angels joined with Lucifer in his rebellion against God. Satan was dethroned by God from his lofty position and lost his place in God's kingdom. His desire then became to destroy all that pertained to God.

God easily could have destroyed Satan in the beginning. He knew Satan would be the cause of much heartache. Many persons may ask, "Why did God not stop him?" Actually, the truth is that God legally could not do so. He is always righteous and always just. Likewise today, all evil men who cause so many problems on the earth could easily be destroyed by God. God does not do it because He has never operated, does not now operate, and never will operate in the realm of murder, destruction, lying, and killing. He is a God of love. God also knows that the evil these individuals (plus Satan) indulge in will eventually destroy them. *"The wages of sin is death"* (Romans 6:23). He also knows righteousness will overcome. When Satan has run his course and there is not one accusing finger he can point at God and all men will have had their opportunity, then Satan will be locked away forever. God did not kill him because God is not a killer; He is a life-giver. Of course, there are many other reasons that I do not have time to go into as to why Satan is being allowed to continue his deadly deeds.

We know Satan has access to this earth and actually roams the earth (Job 1:7; I Peter 5:8). We also know he has access to heaven (Job 1:6) and to God and probably spends much time there. Above all, he is *"the accuser of [the] brethren"* (Revelation 12:10). In other words, he stands before God and accuses Christians day and night. However, during the Tribulation Period he will be expelled from heaven (Revelation 12:9). The Bible tells us, *"Woe to the inhabiters of the earth and of the sea! for the devil is come down unto you"* (Revelation 12:12). Satan has caused much trouble through the ages. He will come down to this earth with a special vengeance when he is finally denied all access to heaven.

OUR VICTORY

Every Christian can have total victory over the powers of Satan, for *"Greater is he that is in you, than he that is in the world"* (I John 4:4). We need not fear him (II Timothy 1:7). We can resist him, and he will flee from us (James 4:7; I Peter 5:9). Jesus Christ totally defeated him at Calvary (Colossians 2:15). We look forward to that day when the angel will *"come down from heaven"* and lay *"hold on the dragon, that old serpent, which is the Devil,"* and *"cast him into the bottomless pit, and shut him up."* He will be *"cast into the lake of fire and brimstone"* to *"be tormented day and night for ever and ever"* (Revelation 20:1-3, 10).

QUESTION:

HOW MUCH LATITUDE DOES SATAN HAVE IN RESPECT TO TEMPTATION?

ANSWER:

One of Satan's biggest weapons is *bluff*. He consistently leads the Christian to believe he is able to do all manner of things that he cannot do. The Scripture says he will come *"as a roaring lion"* (I Peter 5:8), but he is not a roaring lion. He has been successful in causing most Christians to think he is. Jesus Christ is *"the Lion"* (Revelation 5:5). Satan can do no more than the Christian will allow him to do (through ignorance or otherwise).

SATAN IS LIMITED

Satan was created perfect. He was Lucifer, one of the noted archangels. How long he reigned in this sinless, perfect state as one of God's great archangels, we do not know. However, I am persuaded that during this time his knowledge became great to the point that it was (possibly) limitless. No doubt he still retains much of this vast knowledge. In his dealings with man, and the temptation of man, however, God has put great limitations upon Satan that he is not able to use this vast knowledge in his temptations. He can use only what is relative to the human race. If God had not placed these limitations on Satan, he would be able to force man to do almost anything. Thank God, we have the heavenly promise that Satan cannot go beyond that which is common to man: *"There hath no temptation taken you but such as is common to man: but God is faithful, who will not suffer you to be tempted above that ye are able; but will with the temptation also make a way to escape, that ye may be able to bear it"* (I Corinthians 10:13).

Satan would have the Christian believe he can do anything and that the Christian is helpless in his presence. He wants us to become apprehensive and fearful, living in dread and anxiety with little or no joy. Many Christians live in mortal fear of Satan. "What will he do?" they moan. As a child of God, we need not fear Satan. Now, I respect him, but I do not fear him. I know this vast knowledge he must have, if allowed full reign, could create havoc; but thank God, it can never be used. Satan is extremely limited. The sooner the Christian realizes this, the more stable his foundation.

WE ARE NOT LIMITED

"For though we walk in the flesh, we do not war after the flesh: (For the weapons of our warfare are not carnal, but mighty through God to the pulling down of strongholds;) Casting down imaginations, and every high thing that exalteth itself against the knowledge of God, and bringing into captivity every thought to the obedience of Christ" (II Corinthians 10:3-5).

Here is a revelation telling us in no uncertain terms that even though Satan is limited, we, through Christ, are not limited; yet most Christians do not know this. This actually makes us stronger than Satan in every respect; whereas he has boundaries placed upon him, we have none. The Scripture says the weapons of our warfare are not carnal, but mighty through God.

This is the last thing the evil one wants the child of God to know. How it must irritate him to realize that through Jesus Christ every single Christian is stronger than he is! This means, as a child of God, I do not have to live in fear; I can enjoy victory. I do not have to live in sickness;

I can enjoy health. I do not have to live in worry; I can stand on the promises of my Father who loves and cares for me.

Look at the weapons at our disposal:

• We have the sword of the Word of God (Matthew 4:4; Ephesians 6:10-18).

• We have the authority of the name of Jesus (Mark 16:17; Philippians 2:5-11).

• We have the power of the Holy Spirit (Acts 1:8).

There is no excuse for defeat. Defeat should not be in the Christian's vocabulary.

A lady wrote to me and asked how did I think I could command Satan to do anything, when even Michael the archangel did not dare bring a railing accusation against Satan (Jude 9)? Of course, what the lady did not stop to realize is that when a person becomes saved, he becomes a new creature in Christ Jesus. Actually, he becomes a son of God by adoption (Romans 8:14-17). Naturally, Michael did not bring a railing accusation because both he and Lucifer were angels. Admittedly, Satan was a fallen angel, but, as an angel he still retained his original rank. Legally speaking, he outranked Michael. As a son of God, born of the Spirit and a joint heir with Christ, the Christian is even greater than the angels. Why? Because a son is a member of the family. Therefore, as a child of God, we have the right to command Satan in anything! In the name of Jesus, Satan must obey. As a child of God, let us always realize, we are stronger than Satan (I John 4:4). Let us use the authority God has given us through Jesus Christ.

[Note: For a more in-depth look at this subject you may order our booklet, What Satan Can and Cannot Do.*]*

QUESTION:

CAN SATAN READ YOUR MIND?

ANSWER:

Satan is not *omnipotent* ("all-powerful"), *omniscient* ("all-knowing"), or *omnipresent* ("everywhere"). Satan has for thousands of years tried to make people believe he was all of these things. He said, *"I will ascend above the heights of the clouds; I will be like the most High"*

(Isaiah 14:14). His chief ambition is to be God. He is called *"the god of this world"* (II Corinthians 4:4).

That is different, indeed, from being God as our Heavenly Father is. Satan has to have his demon spirits and fallen angels to help him in his work. Through the medium of their powers *it seems* that he knows all things and is everywhere present, but he is not. He is *ubiquitous* ("seemingly everywhere, constantly encountered, widespread"), whereas God is *omnipresent* ("everywhere present").

Satan is far weaker than most Christians realize. Naturally he has much sway over the unsaved person, but when it comes to God-fearing people, the only power he has is what the Christian allows him to have. Sad to say, most Christians allow him to have almost all he wants and he causes much damage in their life. But his authority is *pseudoauthority* ("false authority"). It is borrowed from the child of God because of ignorance or lack of knowledge of the Word and he takes full advantage of this.

Many Christians think Satan can read their mind, but he cannot. Satan did everything he could, through King Herod, to find the Baby Jesus and kill Him (Matthew 2:13-18). If he had been able to read the mind of individuals, there would have been no problem in finding Jesus. Baby Moses was able to be kept from the sword of Pharaoh (Exodus 1; 2); David was able to flee from the demon-possessed King Saul (I Samuel 20 through 22); Elijah was able to hide from the wicked Queen Jezebel (I Kings 19 through 21). There are many such stories in the Bible of God's people escaping the hands of their enemy showing that the devil is strangely circumscribed or limited. Satan does not have nearly the power that many people, including Christians, attribute to him.

TEMPTATION

"There hath no temptation taken you but such as is common to man: but God is faithful, who will not suffer you to be tempted above that ye are able" (I Corinthians 10:13).

There is a possibility that Satan could do many things if he were allowed by God to do so. He has access to the spirit world (see Job 1), consequently he does know some things that we do not know. But if he were able to read our mind, that would be something above *"such as is common to man."* It is not common for anyone to read our mind. Only

God can do such a thing. If Satan had this ability, he could cause us more problems than we dare realize. In many areas we would practically be defenseless before him.

GATEWAY TO THE SPIRIT

The soul is the seat of passions and the five senses. The spirit is the seat of the intellect, which is the will and knowledge. In other words, the soul feels and the spirit knows. Consequently, the mind (the intellect) is akin to the spirit of man. We know the body will someday die and return to dust to await the resurrection of life or damnation, but the soul and spirit will never die. They are created immortal. The mind is the gateway to the spirit, which Satan uses to further his efforts toward gaining inroads into a person's life.

SUGGESTIONS

This is what confuses many Christians. Wrong thoughts (evil, obscene, wicked) come to their mind. Some persons confuse this as Satan being able to read their mind, but it has nothing to do with mind reading. He is making a suggestion, trying to get the individual to do a certain thing by planting a thought or seed into the mind. Whether or not the individual carries out the suggestion is strictly up to him. Satan cannot force or coerce any Christian to do anything. He can only make his suggestions, then they must be carried out under the auspices of I Corinthians 10:13; namely, *"such as is common to man."*

This is the reason why an impure or unholy thought that crosses a person's mind is not a sin. It comes in the form of a temptation, and it is merely a suggestion made by Satan. If the Christian resists the devil and puts the thought out of his mind, then there is nothing else that Satan can do. He must leave. *"Submit yourselves therefore to God. Resist the devil, and he will flee from you"* (James 4:7).

However, if the Christian harbors that thought and begins to think upon it, then Satan can gain a beachhead or foothold, and he will suggest other things. He will literally torment the mind by implanting more and more thoughts, compelling a person to do whatever the suggestion implies. If the individual does not resist, the devil will see to it that something happens to that person to make it possible for him to put those thoughts into action.

This is where sin comes in. *"Let no man say when he is tempted, I am tempted of God: for God cannot be tempted with evil, neither tempteth he any man: But every man is tempted, when he is drawn away of his own lust, and enticed"* (James 1:13, 14). Satan is not reading a person's mind, he is simply implanting suggestions there. This is as far as he can go if he does not have the individual's cooperation.

SPEECH

We are told, *"Only let your conversation be as it becometh the gospel of Christ"* (Philippians 1:27). "Conversation" here in the Greek (*toliteuo*) actually means "to exercise citizenship or to behave like citizens." In other words, we are to conduct ourselves wisely and to speak and act like children of God according to the Word of God; our manner of life or life-style should be one of victory, power, glory, and honor.

Many times Christians have limited physical ailments. When we begin to voice these particular problems aloud to someone, talking about how bad we feel, how much we hurt, we are getting worse, or whatever the case may be, Satan's minions of darkness, namely demon spirits, take advantage of this and cause the child of God even more problems. Satan feeds on unbelief and doubt. When a Christian starts to talk unbelief and conducts himself in the manner of defeat with lack of victory, he is in the territory in which Satan operates. He can cause the Christian many problems.

Now some persons may say, "Well, if you ask someone to pray for you and you mention the ailment or problem, doesn't he hear you then?" Yes, he does. However, when you start to speak words of victory and power according to the Word of God, even though he hears you and knows there is a problem, you are walking in faith and there is little he can do. Satan does not have to read our mind to know many things that take place. Our conversation is overheard when we speak words of unbelief and doubt; all of this is noted. He also knows many things as a result of the spirit world in which he operates. As far as reading our mind, knowing every solitary thought, what we are going to do, and knowing the future, he does not know these things. He is not God, he has never been God, he never will be God!

SATAN'S DEVICES

Someone once said to a Christian, "You had better not speak that way. You are going to make Satan angry." Of course, the answer is that Satan is already angry. He has been angry all these years. He is angry now and he will continue to be angry. He cannot do the things he wants us to believe he can do. If he could, there would not be a single Christian alive in this world today — he would destroy us all! He cannot do these things simply because he does not have the authority. He will try to intimidate us. He will bluster and blow and go about as a roaring lion, but let us remember he is not a roaring lion. Jesus is *"the Lion"* (Revelation 5:5). Satan is just a deceiver. The child of God can withstand him with the Word of God, putting on the whole armor of God, resisting him with the power and authority of Jesus' name.

"Be strong in the Lord, and in the power of his might. Put on the whole armour of God, that ye may be able to stand against the wiles of the devil. For we wrestle not against flesh and blood, but against principalities, against powers, against the rulers of the darkness of this world, against spiritual wickedness in high places. Wherefore take unto you the whole armour of God, that ye may be able to withstand in the evil day, and having done all, to stand. Stand therefore, having your loins girt about with truth, and having on the breastplate of righteousness; And your feet shod with the preparation of the gospel of peace; Above all, taking the shield of faith, wherewith ye shall be able to quench all the fiery darts of the wicked. And take the helmet of salvation, and the sword of the Spirit, which is the word of God: Praying always with all prayer and supplication in the Spirit, and watching thereunto with all perseverance and supplication" (Ephesians 6:10-18). *"Lest Satan should get an advantage of us: for we are not ignorant of his devices"* (II Corinthians 2:11).

As a child of God we need not fear the devil. We should keep our mind stayed on the Lord Jesus Christ *"by the renewing of [our] mind, that [we] may prove what is that good, and acceptable, and perfect"* (Romans 12:2). *"Whatsoever things are true, whatsoever things are honest, whatsoever things are just, whatsoever things are pure, whatsoever things are lovely, whatsoever things are of good report; if there be any virtue, and if there be any praise, [let us] think on these things"* (Philippians 4:8).

Never forget: *"Greater is he that is in you, than he that is in the world"* (I John 4:4).

QUESTION:

*WHAT IS GOD'S PURPOSE IN ALLOWING
SATAN TO CONTINUE?*

ANSWER:

When a person considers that all the heartache, chaos, sickness, suffering, sorrow, death, war, and disease in the world today are caused by Satan; that the earth has been soaked with human blood for the past 6,000 years because of Satan; that most of the people who have lived and died and then gone to hell have done so because of Satan, he has to question: Why does God allow Satan to continue? Why does He not stop him?

When I was a little boy in Sunday School, I asked that same question. Millions of people have asked it. In the ages past, when Satan led the revolution against God, it seems God's purpose would have been better served if God had locked Satan away, thereby dispelling the harm that Satan would forever do. However, of course, we know that God never makes a mistake. Everything He does is perfect. God has a purpose in allowing Satan to continue. Let us look at it.

CREATION OF LUCIFER

Christ, in the dateless past, created Lucifer (who would become Satan); for *"all things were made by him [Christ]; and without him was not any thing made that was made"* (John 1:3).

God created Lucifer perfect. *"Thou wast perfect in thy ways from the day that thou wast created"* (Ezekiel 28:15). So, all the ways of Lucifer (his comings, his goings, his works, his labors, his ruling prowess) were perfect until iniquity was found in him.

Just when this occurred we do not know. The Bible tells us that *"[his] heart was lifted up because of [his] beauty"* and that *"[his] wisdom [was corrupted] by reason of [his] brightness"* (Ezekiel 28:17). In other words, he got his eyes off God and on himself. At that moment, in the dateless past, he organized and led a revolution against God.

It seems that Lucifer was the most powerful angel created (Ezekiel 28:12). It seems that he ruled, submissive to God, on this planet earth. In other words, he was the supreme ruler of this earth in the dateless past. (This was before Adam and Eve, during the Genesis 1:1 period.) The account in Genesis 1:2 was the result of his fall: *"And the earth was without form, and void; and darkness was upon the face of the deep."*

There is no hint in the Word of God that Christ created the earth in its original state *"without form, and void."* He has never created anything less than perfect.

LUCIFER'S REVOLUTION

The earth became *"without form, and void"* after Lucifer led the revolution against God. From what we can understand in the Word of God, one-third of the angels threw in their lot with Lucifer (Revelation 12:4) and are now helping him govern his kingdom of darkness. It seems that the inhabitants of the earth at that time (before Adam and Eve) also threw in their lot with Satan. It is the feeling of some Bible scholars that demon spirits originated with the death of those who inhabited the earth during Lucifer's rule in the original days of righteousness and purity. Then Lucifer (Satan) led the revolution against God and fell; and, consequently, the creation existing at that time fell as well.

THE ANGELS

Some persons mistakenly have thought that the third of the angels who fell with Lucifer are the demon spirits prevalent in the world today. That simply could not be. Angelic bodies cannot be destroyed; consequently they cannot inhabit anyone. There is no record in the Word of God of an angel's ever having inhabited anybody. Angels have a spirit body. Although their body is different from ours, they cannot inhabit a body other than their own.

THE INHABITANTS OF EARTH

It seems the inhabitants of the earth existing with Lucifer in the dateless past of Genesis 1:1 each had a body similar to man's today, as well as having a soul and a spirit. Consequently, their body went back to the dust of the earth, but their spirit is still with us; and it is this group that endeavors to inhabit individuals. It seems that this is where demons originated. If that is not the case, then no one really knows of their origin.

If Lucifer and the many other spirit beings had remained true to God, there would not have been a curse on the earth. There would not have been a need to re-create the atmospheric heavens and the earth or life on the planet earth as recorded in Genesis 1:3 through 2:25. It is thought by some that if this had been the case, man and the present animal kingdom on earth would never have been created.

The word "ways," found in Ezekiel 28:15 (*"Thou wast perfect in thy ways from the day that thou wast created, till iniquity was found in thee"*) implies that God, even then, placed restrictions and perimeters upon His creation (angels). Lucifer, along with one-third of the angels, failed the test, and iniquity was found in them.

GOD'S RE-CREATION

When God brought the earth back to its second perfect state (as recorded in Genesis 1:3), Satan was allowed to use the body of a serpent to tempt Adam and Eve. Now, here is where the great question arises.

God, with all of His infinite wisdom and knowledge (omniscience), certainly knew what would happen in the future, yet He allowed Satan to tempt Adam and Eve, and all creation since, even though it has caused so much heartache. Why? We are given some reasons, even purpose, in the Word of God. I will enumerate them.

FIRST, TO DEVELOP CHARACTER
AND FAITH IN THE BELIEVER

"My brethren, count it all joy when ye fall into divers temptations; Knowing this, that the trying of your faith worketh patience" (James 1:2, 3).

Trials test our salvation and faith, and the man who stands true in his trials proves his salvation sound and his faith genuine. *"Tribulation worketh patience; And patience, experience; and experience, hope"* (Romans 5:3-5). Peter also mentioned *"the trial of [our] faith"* (I Peter 1:7-13). It seems for this reason Satan has been allowed to continue to test man.

SECOND, TO KEEP MAN HUMBLE

Paul said, *"Lest I should be exalted above measure through the abundance of the revelations, there was given to me a thorn in the flesh, the messenger of Satan to buffet me, lest I should be exalted above measure"* (II Corinthians 12:7).

We can see from this Scripture that God allows Satan to prod man (even the Christian man) to a certain extent to keep him mindful of his yet imperfect state, to keep him humble before God.

THIRD, TO PROVIDE CONFLICT THAT SAINTS MAY BE REWARDED THROUGH THEM

John talked about overcoming the wicked one: *"I write unto you, young men, because ye have overcome the wicked one"* (I John 2:13). Attaining victory over Satan is here shown to be a deed worthy of recognition and reward.

Further on, he differentiated between the spirit of truth and the spirit of error: *"We are of God: he that knoweth God heareth us; he that is not of God heareth not us. Hereby know we the spirit of truth, and the spirit of error"* (I John 4:6).

Since the dawn of sin, there has been constant conflict between good and evil. Man has been faced continually with the decision of where to place his allegiance. Those who follow God and who possess His spirit of truth are made known by those with whom they choose to ally themselves upon this earth. Rewards await those who have undergone spiritual struggles and have chosen to serve God.

To the seven churches in Asia Jesus proclaimed, *"To him that overcometh will I give . . . . "* (Revelation 2 and 3).

FOURTH, TO DEMONSTRATE THE POWER OF GOD
OVER THE POWER OF SATAN

Paul mentioned, in speaking of the ages to come, *"[He] hath raised us up together, and made us sit together in heavenly places in Christ Jesus: That in the ages to come he might shew the exceeding riches of his grace in his kindness toward us through Christ Jesus"* (Ephesians 2:6, 7).

Those who know Jesus Christ as their personal Lord and Saviour have been literally given new life; they are spiritually reborn. Though the redeemed are still subject to undergo battles upon this earth, they are able to overcome by the help of God; and in the ages to come, God will further demonstrate His infinite power through His complete defeat of Satan and through the riches He will bestow on the victorious followers of Christ.

He mentioned it again when he said, *"To the intent that now unto the principalities and powers in heavenly places might be known by the church the manifold wisdom of God"* (Ephesians 3:10).

FIFTH, TO USE SATAN IN AFFLICTING PEOPLE
TO BRING THEM TO REPENTANCE

Paul spoke of this when he wrote of *"[delivering] such an one unto Satan for the destruction of the flesh, that the spirit may be saved in the day of the Lord Jesus"* (I Corinthians 5:5).

God often releases men into the hands of Satan that they may, through trials, realize the hopelessness and despair of sinful living and so recommit their life to Jesus. The suffering of today does not seem so great when eternal life is at stake.

SIXTH, TO PURGE MAN OF ALL POSSIBILITY
OF FALLING IN THE ETERNAL FUTURE

John mentioned that *"the nations of them which are saved shall walk in the light of it [the New Jerusalem]"* (Revelation 21:24). We are also told, *"There shall in no wise enter into it any thing that defileth . . . [or] worketh abomination, or maketh a lie"* (verse 27).

It is necessary that conflict exist now upon the earth that those who are truly committed to God may be revealed for the purpose of future separation of the good and the evil. God will not permit anyone who is defiled by sin to enter into the kingdom He has prepared for His children.

These points that I have listed outline fairly well God's purpose in allowing Satan to continue. Man is in a probationary state today. Most men are failing, sad to say, but some will *"shine as the brightness of the firmament"* (Daniel 12:3).

THE DOOM OF SATAN

The defeat of Satan and all rebels (and their eternal confinement in hell) is revealed in Scripture. His defeat and doom are prophetically foretold. God said, *"I will put enmity between thee and the woman, and between thy seed and her seed; it [the Messiah, the seed of the woman] shall bruise thy head, and thou shalt bruise his heel"* (Genesis 3:15).

We are told in Revelation 16 that Satan will fight against Christ at Armageddon where he will be taken bodily and bound with a chain and cast into the abyss for 1,000 years (Revelation 19:11 through 20:3). At the end of 1,000 years he will be loosed out of the abyss, will lead one more rebellion in the kingdom, and then will be cast bodily *"into the lake of fire and brimstone . . . for ever and ever"* (Revelation 20:7-10).

WHAT WE SHOULD DO TO OPPOSE SATAN

Throughout our earthly existence we are subject to Satan-caused trials and temptations, yet God has given each Christian the ability not only to fight back but to obtain victory. Following are things that we can and should do to oppose and overcome Satan:

• We should put on the whole armor of God, which consists of truth, righteousness, faith, salvation, and the mighty sword of God's Word (Ephesians 6:11-18).

• We should know his devices (II Corinthians 2:11).

• We should give him no place (Ephesians 4:27).

• We should resist him and he will flee from us (James 4:7).

• We should be *"sober"* and *"vigilant"* in waging war against him and remain *"stedfast in the faith"* (I Peter 5:8, 9).

• We should overcome him by the Word of God, as did Jesus and many saints that have gone before us (Matthew 4:1-11; I John 2:14).

• We should overcome him by the blood of Christ and by the word of our testimony (Revelation 12:11).

• We should overcome him by using the authority of the name of Jesus (II Corinthians 2:15; Ephesians 1:19-22).

• We should, finally, overcome him by the Holy Spirit (Acts 1:8; Romans 8:1-13; Galatians 5:16-26). Those who walk in the Spirit shall not fulfill the lust of the flesh.

THE DEVIL'S LAST SONG

Long ago I planned in my passing pride,
That to-day I would reign as king;
But where is my kingdom, where is my crown?
Is the bitter song I sing.

What joy have I won through my evil designs?
What peace in my soul-wrecking plan?
I hoped to conquer both heaven and hell,
But have won nothing more than mere man.

I can see above, o'er the bridgeless gulf,
The glorified heaven-lit strand;
My chains make me feel the double disgrace,
As I crouch 'neath the Infinite Hand.

Where are my princes, my legions of dukes,
And the millions of souls I have won?
My pains and my chains are greater by far,
Because of the deeds I have done.

All my plans and my schemes in a thousand ways,
Like bubbles are blown out of sight;
My fancies and hopes like a passing dream,
Are covered by shadows of night.

Come on, all ye dupes, ye millions of men,
Who heeded my wishes like fools;
Take your share for aye of the galling chains,
Under Him who in triumph rules.

You have lived and died for my noble cause,
Your souls are eternally marred;
You shall see no more than glimpses of light,
Of heaven, from which you are barred.

Then fling all your hopes, my friends, to the winds,
As the echo of sadness replies;
You will feel henceforth the deeper degrees,
Of the hell which beneath us lies.

— *Author Unknown*

SCRIPTURE

■ How did our Bible come into being? What is meant by the term "Apocrypha"? Also, is there such a place as purgatory?

QUESTION:

*HOW DID OUR BIBLE COME INTO BEING? WHAT
IS MEANT BY THE TERM "APOCRYPHA"? ALSO,
IS THERE SUCH A PLACE AS PURGATORY?*

ANSWER:

You have asked a detailed question, and to answer it as it should
be answered would require a volume many times the size of these few
pages. However, I will do my best to digest some of the pertinent
facts concerning all of your questions and give the answers in an
abbreviated manner.

THE CANON OF THE BIBLE

At the end of the first Christian century, the Jewish rabbis, at the
Council of Gamnia, closed the canon of Hebrew books (those books
considered authoritative). Their decision resulted from . . .
* The multiplication and popularity of sectarian apocryphal writings.
* The fall of Jerusalem (A. D. 70) which created a threat to the
religious tradition of the Jews.
* The disputes with Christians over their interpretation of the Jewish
Scriptures in preaching and writing.

There was never any doubt about the five books of the law
(Pentateuch), but beyond that various sects of Judaism disagreed. The
prophetic collection was generally agreed upon by 200 B. C., but
the major problem concerned the *other writings*. Four criteria operated
in deciding what books should occupy a place in the authoritative
Old Testament Scriptures:
* The content of each book had to harmonize with the law.
* Since prophetic inspiration was believed to have begun with Moses
(c. 1450 B. C.) and ended with Ezra (c. 450 B. C.), to qualify for the
canon and to be considered inspired a book had to have been written
within that time frame.
* The language of the original manuscript had to be Hebrew.
* The book had to have been written within the geographical
boundaries of Palestine.

On this basis the 39 books of the Old Testament were selected for the
Palestinian canon of Scriptures. Failing these criteria, the rest of the

ancient Jewish writings came to be classified as *Apocrypha* or *pseudepigrapha* (literally, "false writings").

A number of Christian writings, other than those that came to be accepted for the New Testament, appeared early and were considered by some authorities to be worthy of canonical status. The Didache, the Epistle of Barnabas, I and II Clement, the Shepherd of Hermas, the Apocalypse of Peter, and the Acts of Paul were some of the more popular ones. By the beginning of the third century, 22 of the writings of our present New Testament had been widely accepted. Four principles or considerations operated in determining what books should occupy a place in the authoritative New Testament Scriptures:

- Was the book written by an apostle or by someone associated with an apostle?
- Was the book's content of a spiritual nature?
- Was the book widely received by the churches?
- Was there evidence in the book of divine inspiration?

As far as is known, it was the Easter letter of Archbishop Athanasius of Alexandria in A. D. 367 that first listed the 27 books of our New Testament as authoritative. Jerome, by his Latin translation of these same 27 books (A. D. 382), further established this list as canonical for the churches.

This is a brief explanation of how our Bible (39 books in the Old Testament and 27 in the New Testament) came to be established as the Word of God.

THE APOCRYPHA

This group of books, numbering about 14, is believed to be spurious; literally, "false writings." This in no way implies that the books do not contain some good things, nor does it mean they were written by evil men. It simply means they were believed *not* to be inspired; consequently, they were not placed in the canon of Scripture.

Eleven of these Apocryphal books have been accepted by the Catholic church, included in Roman Catholic canon, and placed in the Douay Version of the Bible (Catholic).

Why were these books not considered inspired or canonical (included in the canon or books of the Bible)? Some of the reasons will relate to the Old Testament; some, to the New Testament.

• As far as the Old Testament was concerned, these particular books were not included in the Hebrew canon of Scripture.

• The Master, the Apostle Paul, nor any other writer in the New Testament ever quoted from these spurious writings (or Apocrypha). Yet they quoted frequently in the New Testament from the books that were included in the Hebrew canon of Scripture.

• Josephus, the Hebrew historian, expressly *excluded* these "false writings" or Apocrypha.

• None of the Apocryphal books claim divine inspiration.

• The Apocryphal books have historical, geographical, and chronological errors.

• For the most part, they teach and uphold doctrines that are contrary to the Scriptures (for instance, lying is sanctioned in some cases, magic is advocated and practiced in other cases, et cetera).

• As literature they are considered to be myth and legend.

• Their spiritual (and even moral) stance is generally far below both the Old and New Testaments.

• Respecting the Old Testament, most of these spurious books were written much later than the books that were considered to be authoritative and inspired.

• As we discussed (in the explanation earlier respecting the New Testament writings) to be canonized a book had to have been written by an apostle or someone associated with an apostle. The book had to be spiritual, had to have been widely received by the churches, and had to show evidence of divine inspiration.

Satan has done everything within his power to hinder, destroy, dilute, and outright do away with the Word of Almighty God. But through the power of God, the Bible as we have it today (its 66 books, both Old and New Testaments, from Genesis to Revelation) is the Word of God. Nothing else can be added to it. When any person or any church claims that other writings, other books, other so-called inspirations should be included in the canon of Scripture, this is a work of the evil one himself. Paul put it aptly when he said, *"Though we, or an angel from heaven, preach any other gospel unto you than that which we have preached unto you, let him be accursed. As we said before, so say I now again, If any man preach any other gospel unto you than that ye have received, let him be accursed"* (Galatians 1:8, 9).

PURGATORY

The Catholic church has defined the existence of purgatory in the Decree of Union drawn at the Council of Florence in A. D. 1439, and again at the Council of Trent, which says: "The Catholic church, instructed by the Holy Spirit, has from sacred Scriptures and the ancient traditions of the fathers taught in sacred councils and very recently in the ecumenical synod, that there is a purgatory, and that the souls therein detained are helped by the suffrages of the faithful, but principally by the acceptable sacrifice of the altar."

The Catholic church also teaches that Christians can indulge themselves in two kinds of sin: mortal sins (which will damn the soul) and venial sins (which will not damn the soul but will consign them to purgatory). All souls, therefore, who die in venial sins or with the temporal punishment of their sins still unpaid, must atone for them in purgatory.

The church gets some of her beliefs from some of the Apocryphal writings (II Maccabees 12:43-46). Of course, as we have explained, these writings were considered by the Jewish rabbis as unworthy of being included in the Word of God.

The Catholic church went on to say that because she is the infallible teacher of divine revelation in the name of Bible and tradition she has the authority to declare the Apocrypha an article of faith in her creeds (the Apostles, the Nicene, and the Athanasian) and in her councils (namely, the Council of Constantinople and also the Fourth Lateran Council in A. D. 1215).

The Catholic church further believes that the faithful on earth, the saints in heaven, and the souls in purgatory are united together in love and prayer. According to her doctrine, the faithful on earth, still struggling to win the victory of salvation, form the "Church Militant" while the saints in heaven are the "Church Triumphant" and the souls in purgatory, still suffering in order to be perfectly purified from the effects of sin, constitute the "Church Suffering."

To sum it all up, the Catholic church states that purgatory is the state or condition in which those who have died in a state of grace, but with some attachment to sin, suffer for a time before they are admitted to the glory and happiness of heaven. In this state and period of passive suffering, they are purified of repented venial sins, satisfy the demands of divine justice for temporal punishment due for sins, and are thus converted to a state of worthiness of the beatific vision.

THE WORD OF GOD

What does the Word of God say concerning purgatory? *Nothing*. All of these teachings are contradicted by the New Testament. We are told that we "[have] *therefore . . . boldness to enter into the holiest by the blood of Jesus, By a new and living way"* (Hebrews 10:19, 20).

The Apostle Paul (considering that Paul wrote the book of Hebrews, as we believe he did) taught that where sins are remitted, there is no need of an offering for sins any longer. Thus Paul concluded his argument on the priesthood of Christ. Christ's offering is efficacious for all past, present, and future sins, but on the condition of proper confession of sin and meeting the terms of continued grace. Hebrews 10:19, 20 gives the child of God full access to heaven. It is a grand conclusion to the doctrinal argument of the worthiness of every child of God to enter the portals of glory. In other words, all Christians, by accepting the blood sacrifice paid for by our Saviour, have instant citizenship in heaven (when God calls them home to be with Him).

It can be understood how the heathen can teach the doctrine of purgatory as it was taught in Egypt, for example. However, no such excuse can be made for the cardinals, bishops, monsignors, and priests of the Roman Catholic church.

Prayers for the dead go hand in hand with purgatory. In Catholic doctrine prayer cannot be completely efficacious without the priests as intermediaries, and no priestly function can be rendered unless there is *special payment* . Therefore, in every land we find the priesthood of the Catholic church devouring widows' houses (compare Matthew 23:14, 29) and making merchandise of the tender emotions of sorrowing relatives sensitive to the immortal destiny of their beloved dead (compare II Peter 2:3).

One of the oppressions under which people in Roman Catholic countries groan is the periodical nature of special devotions for which they are required to pay when death has invaded a Catholic family. Not only are there funeral services and funeral dues for the repose of the departed at the time of the burial, but the priest pays repeated visits afterward to the family for the same purpose, and this entails seemingly endless heavy expense.

The following is an advertisement that appeared in the August 11, 1946, "Our Sunday Visitor," a popular Catholic weekly newspaper:

"ARE YOU INSURED?"
Write and ask about our plan to offer the Gregorian Masses
after your death. This is real insurance for your soul.

The Gregorian Masses for a soul in purgatory are 30 in number and must be offered consecutively. At that time (1946) the minimum price was $30. It was believed and taught by the Catholics that Christ appeared to St. Gregory and promised He would release souls from purgatory on payment of the money.

I remember years ago in South Louisiana turning on the radio and hearing a particular program hosted by a Catholic priest. He was telling the people to send so much money concerning individuals who had died. He went on to state that all of the body was out of purgatory except an arm, a leg, or some other member. *This is one of the reasons the Roman Catholic church is so rich: the tremendous amount of money pouring into its coffers each day by poor individual Catholics thinking they can retrieve the souls of departed loved ones from a place called purgatory* (that does not even exist).

The Roman Catholic doctrine of purgatory is purely pagan and cannot for a moment stand in the light of Scripture. The Bible tells us that *"the blood of Jesus Christ [God's] Son,"* not some heathenistic doctrine, *"cleanseth us from all sin"* (I John 1:7). On the other hand, for those who die without personal union with Christ and consequently are unwashed, unjustified, and unsaved, there can be no other cleansing. For *"he that hath the Son hath life; and he that hath not the Son of God hath not life"* (I John 5:12).

Thus the whole doctrine of purgatory is a system of purely pagan imposture, dishonoring God and deluding men who live in sin with the hope of atoning for it after death, thus cheating them out of their property *and* their salvation.

QUESTION:

SOUL

■ Is there such a thing as soul travel?

QUESTION:

IS THERE SUCH A THING AS SOUL TRAVEL?

ANSWER:

An explanation of soul travel is in order. King Solomon said, *"There is no new thing under the sun"* (Ecclesiastes 1:9). That would include this particular teaching, which has been going around for a long, long time.

Basically soul travel can be defined in this way: An individual states that while he is in one place, his soul (or soul and spirit) will leave his body and travel to another place to perform a work for God. He contends that while his soul travels, his body remains at the same place doing the same thing he was involved in at the time.

I remember a number of years ago a particular preacher who propagated this doctrine. He had, among other things, moral problems. He claimed that while he was preaching in the pulpit, his soul and spirit traveled to a distant country and preached in some city many thousands of miles away and thousands of people had been saved (and other similar stories). Of course, all this is foolishness.

There is no such thing as soul travel. Individuals who try to propagate such foolishness prey on gullible individuals who are scripturally unlearned and spiritually malnourished. These poor, misguided Christians believe their pseudospirituality and look on them as superspiritual beings sent directly from God. This naturally makes the flawed preacher's inflated ego rise above his problems. Some Scriptures are given by proponents of this doctrine that I will go into a little later, but first I must say this. The situation is not biblical and simply does not exist. I will explain further.

DEATH

When the soul leaves the body, the body dies. Doctors have had great difficulties in trying to ascertain exactly when death occurs in a human body. Oh, I realize this has nothing to do with soul travel, but at the same time the explanation is in order.

There is a reason doctors have this problem. Death is a spiritual matter and not just a physical matter. Although it does involve the physical and causes the cessation of life, it is basically a spiritual problem. *"The body without the spirit is dead"* (James 2:26). So, as long as the soul and spirit are within a person, that person's body is alive; but when the soul and spirit leave the body, death occurs. This is called physical death.

I said all of that to say this. If the soul leaves the body, causing the physical body to die, individuals who teach that their soul leaves their body and does certain things in other places simply do not know what they are talking about.

Although it may seem to have nothing to do with the subject at hand, it may clarify the matter somewhat to mention that there are three kinds of death:

Physical death is the separation of the inner man (soul and spirit) from the body (James 2:26).

Spiritual death is separation from God because of sin (Isaiah 59:2; Matthew 8:22; Colossians 2:13; I Timothy 5:6).

Eternal death is eternal separation from God because man chooses to remain separated from God in sin (Isaiah 66:22-24; Matthew 10:28; Revelation 2:11). This is also called the second death or second separation from God (Revelation 2:11; 20:14; 21:8).

Whenever the soul and spirit leave the body, the body dies and returns to dust (Genesis 3:19; James 2:26). The soul and spirit are immortal; at the time of physical death they either are dead in sin or possess eternal life in Christ. In either case they continue in consciousness, whether in heaven or in hell (Luke 12:5; 16:23; I Peter 3:4).

REVELATIONS

Paul said, *"For though I be absent in the flesh, yet am I with you in the spirit, joying and beholding your order, and the stedfastness of your faith in Christ"* (Colossians 2:5). Yet to interpret this Scripture as saying that the Apostle Paul was telling the saints at Colosse that even though he was physically at some other place, his soul and spirit were there with them is utter foolishness. That would be saying he was in two places at one time. Only God can do this.

Paul was using the same phraseology we might use if someone asked us, "Are you going to the crusade in Hawaii?" and we, knowing we would love to but could not, would say, "I cannot go physically, but I will be there in spirit." That is basically what the Apostle Paul was saying:

"I would love to be there and fellowship with you, but I cannot right now. [Paul was imprisoned in Rome at the time, about A. D. 61-63.] I love you, and I have heard of your great love in the spirit. And even though I am absent in the flesh, I will be with you in spirit; and as you rejoice, I will rejoice specifically because of your steadfastness of faith in Christ."

The Apostle Paul gave an account of the tremendous revelation God had given him concerning his being caught up into paradise (II Corinthians 12:1-4). As Paul himself stated, either one of two things happened: he saw a vision or he was taken up physically into heaven. God could have taken him physically to heaven; there is scriptural precedence for an act of this kind. Enoch was taken up into heaven (Genesis 5:24); Elijah was taken up (II Kings 2); no doubt Enoch and Elijah are both still alive in their physical body in the portals of glory today. The Apostle John, it seems, was taken up into heaven physically where he saw the great unveiling of the book of Revelation, which he was later to give to us.

However, the point in all four of these cases must be made, and that is this: Enoch, Elijah, Paul, nor John were in two places at one time. Since Enoch and Elijah were taken, they have not since lived on this earth. The Prophet Elijah did appear on the Mount of Transfiguration with Jesus and Moses for an indeterminately short period of time (Matthew 17:3; Mark 9:4), but he did not live on earth again. He was again taken up into heaven from the mountain.

When the Apostle John was taken from the Isle of Patmos up to the portals of glory (Revelation 4) to receive the revelation, I believe he was taken up bodily and that his body was not on the Isle of Patmos during that time. If the officials had looked for him, they would not have found him. After the revelation was completed, he was again brought down from heaven (again by divine means of transportation); but the thought of John's physical body being on the Isle of Patmos and in heaven at the same time is unscriptural and unreasonable.

John was taken into the wilderness where he saw even more of the great prophetic vision (Revelation 17:3). Whether he was taken physically is not clear. I believe Scripture indicates that he was, and I will explain. In Revelation 18:1, along with other places we could name, John saw more of the great revelation, but he did not say he was taken away to see it. Throughout the great end-time revelation, John saw many things in many places, but he did not see multiple things in multiple places at the same time! John was in one place at one time always.

VISIONS

When it comes to a vision, God can easily give a person a vision of anything. This happens all the time. People see themselves in visions in various situations and in various places. People may also have visions of other people. Say that one of God's children is in dire need of help — be it healing, safety, or whatever — God can give someone a vision of that person to cause him to intercede on the other's behalf. Visions are God-given and happen all the time. But the idea of soul travel is false and erroneous.

In closing, I again emphasize that anytime the soul and spirit leave the body, the body dies. This is the actual moment that physical death takes place.

Second, God definitely can transport a person physically any place He desires, even up to heaven, but the person being transported is only in one place at one time.

Third, from the Scriptures it seems clear that there is no such thing as soul travel. It is simply not scriptural and has no basis for belief.

QUESTION:

SUFFERING

■ What was Paul's thorn in the flesh?

QUESTION:

WHAT WAS PAUL'S THORN IN THE FLESH?

ANSWER:

I remember some years ago I was in a meeting before a group of people where a forum was being held on questions and answers. I had been teaching on divine healing. One brother asked, "Why didn't God heal Paul if it is always God's will to heal the sick?" My answer to him was this: God did not heal Paul because he was not sick. There is no record in the Word of God where the Apostle Paul was ever sick or had any kind of physical disease. He had many troubles, afflictions, and problems; but this great man, through believing God, enjoyed divine health until the day he gave up his life for Jesus Christ. Of course, what the brother had in mind was Paul's "thorn in the flesh."

WHAT WAS THIS THORN?

The Apostle Paul explained, *"Lest I should be exalted above measure through the abundance of the revelations, there was given to me a thorn in the flesh, the messenger of Satan to buffet me, lest I should be exalted above measure"* (II Corinthians 12:7). The Scripture tells us in no uncertain terms the nature of this thorn — it was a messenger of Satan. (In the Greek the word "messenger" is *aggelos* or "angel.") It is never translated disease or physical infirmity. An angel of Satan (spirit being) actually followed Paul around and caused him much trouble.

WHY DID GOD ALLOW IT?

Paul himself told why the thorn was allowed (II Corinthians 12:1-6); he had been given an abundance of revelations (he wrote almost half of the New Testament) and, when *"caught up into paradise . . . heard unspeakable words, which it is not lawful for a man to utter"* (verse 4). He said in verse 7 (twice), *"Lest I should be exalted above measure . . . there was given to me a thorn in the flesh."*

Paul was human, and it is difficult for any man to receive great honor and favor from God and maintain his equilibrium. There has to be a reminder — many great men have had their life and ministry wrecked because they were exalted above measure. Few men can stand it.

333

This is the reason that God allowed this messenger of Satan to cause Paul these problems. (You can find those problems listed in II Corinthians 11:23-28.) God could have stopped this messenger of Satan, but in His divine wisdom He chose simply to tell Paul: *"My grace is sufficient"* (II Corinthians 12:9).

WHAT IS TAUGHT ABOUT IT?

Many persons today do not believe God heals the sick, do not believe in miracles, and blame God for all the misfortunes befalling the Christian. Paul's "thorn in the flesh" is a good example, many people saying it was a sickness, and most probably an eye disease. Two particular Scriptures are used — Galatians 4:15 where Paul spoke to the Galatians and said, *"Ye would have plucked out your own eyes, and have given them to me,"* and also Galatians 6:11 where he said, *"Ye see how large a letter I have written unto you with mine own hand."* Somebody even wrote that Paul had big sores on his eyes that caused facial disfigurements and made his eyes to be almost blind. Of course, this is ridiculous.

In Galatians 4:15 Paul was simply using an idiom such as we would use today, "I would cut off my arm for you," or something of that nature. In Galatians 6:11 he meant simply that he wrote the letter himself where he heretofore (in larger epistles) had dictated them to a scribe. To say that he was nearly blind because this verse refers to the large characters of the alphabet he used in the epistles is not supported by any manuscript or any fact in Scripture. In Paul's day all writing was done in uncial (like the capital letters we use today) only they were about an inch high. So this verse did not have any reference to sickness, blindness, or eye trouble.

THE BIBLE IS VERY PLAIN

Thousands of so-called preachers have led Christians into unbelief by trying to use Paul as an example of their doctrine of sickness: surely if it is always God's will to heal the sick, Paul would have been healed. So, if Paul was not healed, that means it is God's will for His children to be sick sometimes and even suffer loathesome diseases. They twist the Scripture, distorting the truth and causing thousands to live a life of defeat because of their pernicious doctrine.

The Word of God is clear as to the nature of the thorn and why it was allowed. The Apostle Paul was one of the greatest men of God who ever lived, and one of the greatest exponents of divine healing. He believed in the great power of God. When this man prayed for the sick, they were healed — great miracles were performed. Jesus Christ said, *"Ye shall know the truth, and the truth shall make you free"* (John 8:32). Let us not use, any longer, Paul's thorn to keep us from God's healing or anything else.

SUICIDE

■ Do suicides die lost and go to hell, or is it possible that some could be saved?

QUESTION:

DO SUICIDES DIE LOST AND GO TO HELL, OR IS IT POSSIBLE THAT SOME COULD BE SAVED?

ANSWER:

Every minute in the United States and Canada someone attempts suicide. Mental anguish, suffering, pain, and consternation are only a few of the many reasons for this startling statistic. Not only is suicide personal, but it also affects entire families, causing untold grief and sorrow.

There are four suicides mentioned in the Word of God:
- Saul (I Samuel 31:4, 5)
- Ahithophel (II Samuel 17:23)
- Zimri (I Kings 16:18)
- Judas (Matthew 27:5)

Some people would classify Samson as a suicide; however, I do not think so. I feel he died combating forces of evil and gave his life in the work of God. He probably knew that his actions would mean certain death, yet he gave his life. His purpose was to destroy the enemies of God's people and thereby perform a tremendous service. It was not suicide.

As far as we know, all the people we have mentioned died lost. There is no record that any of these people called out to God in their last minutes. Without exception, each of these suicides followed a long series of disobediences to God that climaxed in this deadly deed.

SATAN'S BUSINESS

It is Satan's business to destroy a person (John 10:10). He steals, kills, and destroys. This is his ultimate goal — to drive a person to the place where he would take his own life. Therefore, Satan is the one behind this terrible act.

Consequently, I feel from my study of the Word of God that all suicides die lost, with one exception. I will explain that in a moment.

A suicide actually breaks many commandments. The sixth commandment says, *"Thou shalt not kill"* (Exodus 20:13). The suicide kills, committing his own murder, consequently with no way to ask

God's forgiveness. There is no second chance in eternity. First, second, third, and fourth opportunities are on this side of the grave.

That brings up the question that I basically touched on earlier. Can a person ask God for forgiveness, then commit suicide and the deed be forgiven by God? No, that cannot happen. Jesus said, *"Thou shalt not tempt the Lord thy God"* (Matthew 4:7). Paul said, *"Shall we continue in sin, that grace may abound?"* (Romans 6:1). This is a fallacy that some people have been led to believe. An act of this nature cannot be perpetrated by premeditating the deed and asking for forgiveness before it is done. That is frustrating the grace of God, and it automatically negates itself.

CHRISTIAN SUICIDES

There is an area where I believe some suicides are saved and not lost. It is a terrible thing for a person to be driven to this point of despair, but it is worse for a Christian. A Christian should cast all of his cares and anxieties on the Lord. Jesus came that we *"might have life, and . . . have it more abundantly"* (John 10:10). There are problems, but God gives us victory over those problems if we walk in obedience to the Word of God and rely on Him. The sad fact is this: In spite of the great teaching of the Word of God and the victory afforded by Jesus Christ, some Christians find themselves in perilous straits. If a Christian became mentally disturbed and, due to temporary or total insanity, committed suicide, I believe that person would not be held responsible by God and would die in a saved condition, simply because the individual was not responsible for this action.

Now some person may say, "Aren't all suicides either insane or at least temporarily so?" Even though a would-be suicide may be under great stress, I certainly do not agree they are all insane or even temporarily insane. We come back to the final conclusion. When it comes to a Christian, no one can answer that but God. No one knows the state of that individual's mind but God. We have this infallible promise: *"Shall not the Judge of all the earth do right?"* (Genesis 18:25).

QUESTION:

VIRGIN MARY

■ Did Jesus have brothers and sisters, or was He the only child of Mary, with "his brethren" meaning His cousins?

QUESTION:

*DID JESUS HAVE BROTHERS AND SISTERS, OR
WAS HE THE ONLY CHILD OF MARY, WITH
"HIS BRETHREN" MEANING HIS COUSINS?*

ANSWER:

To answer your question: yes, Jesus had brothers and sisters.
They were his half-brothers and half-sisters since Joseph was not Jesus'
biological father. Of course, it goes without saying that Jesus had no
earthly father; He was begotten of God. Now I will qualify my
answer from Scripture.

First of all, the Word of God says, *"Is not this the carpenter's son?
is not his mother called Mary? and his brethren, James, and Joses,
and Simon, and Judas? And his sisters, are they not all with us?"*
(Matthew 13:55, 56; Mark 6:3). In reply Jesus Himself referred to them
as *"his own house"* and *"his own kin"* (Matthew 13:57; Mark 6:4).

Second, the Lord is called Mary's *"firstborn"* (Matthew 1:25;
Luke 2:7). The natural inference here, of course, is that she did have other
children. The Greek word *prototokos* is used in these two Scriptures, as
well as in Romans 8:29; Colossians 1:15, 18; Hebrews 1:6; 11:28; 12:23;
Revelation 1:5, meaning "the first of many others."

If Jesus had been her only son, the word would have been
monogenes, which occurs in Luke 7:12; 8:42; 9:38; et cetera (referring to
human parentage of an *"only son," "only daughter,"* or *"only child"*)
and in John 1:14; I John 4:9; et cetera (referring to the Lord Jesus as *"the
only begotten of the Father"* . . . *"his only begotten Son"*).

Thus we see clearly that Jesus was the Only Begotten Son of God
(*monogenes*), but the firstborn son of Mary (*prototokos*).

FURTHER PROOF

Third, it was predicted through the psalmist that Mary would have
other children and that the Messiah would have brothers: *"I am become a
stranger unto my brethren, and an alien unto my mother's children"*
(Psalm 69:8).

Fourth, *"his mother and his brethren"* are mentioned as following
Him to Capernaum and seeking to hinder His work (Matthew 12:46-50;
Mark 3:31-35; Luke 8:19-21; John 2:12). The English "brethren" in these

passages is the Greek *adelphos*, meaning "brother"; technically, "one of the same womb." "Cousins" may have gone along, certainly, but people who knew them (as the writers of Holy Scripture knew Jesus and Mary) would not have referred to them as brothers. Jesus' brothers, along with His mother, were following Him on His way to Capernaum. The Bible is clear on the subject, and we can be too.

Fifth, *"his brethren"* are mentioned as not believing on Him until after the resurrection. John 7:3-10 records the account of their unbelief; note, in particular, *"For neither did his brethren believe in him"* (verse 5).

Sixth, Acts 1:14 records their presence in the upper room, along with Jesus' disciples, awaiting the advent of the Holy Spirit — *"These all continued with one accord in prayer and supplication, with the women, and Mary the mother of Jesus, and with his brethren."*

Seventh, James, the leader of the early church, is called *"the Lord's brother"* (Galatians 1:19).

PAGAN CORRUPTION

This question would never have been raised except that the Catholic church became steeped in pagan corruption and began to take portions of Scripture and use them to suit their own peculiar "revelations." This particular phrase came into dispute when they sought to raise Mary from just a *"handmaid of the Lord"* (Luke 1:38) to the mother of God — thus investing her with divine power as a goddess. By raising Mary to this status (which, incidentally, is not scriptural) the way was cleared to identify her with other goddesses of paganism. These goddesses were supposedly mothers of divine sons and yet virgins. Such a goddess is known in Egypt as Isis, the mother of Horus; in India as Isi; in Asia as Cybele; in Rome as Fortuna; in Greece as Ceres; in China as Shing Moo; and in other lands by different names, but always with a son in arms.

AND FINALLY

So it is said that Mary had no other children and that Jesus' brethren were cousins by another Mary and her husband, Cleophas (John 19:25). It is also said that Joseph was too old to have children of Mary, or that he had children by a former marriage. None of this is true, naturally. If it were, Scripture or history (or both) would bear it out.

If Joseph did have children before Jesus was born, then Jesus could not be the legal heir to David's throne, which by law went to the firstborn.

So, in summing up, let me say again: yes, Jesus was Mary's firstborn, and not her only-born. Joseph was His foster father. Jesus *did* have half-brothers and half-sisters, as is plainly stated in the Scriptures, the written Word of God.

[Note: Portions of the source material were derived from Dake's Annotated Reference Bible.*]*

WAR

■ Is it wrong for a Christian to fight, and even kill, during times of war? Also, should the United States totally disarm to prove to the world that we desire peace?

QUESTION:

IS IT WRONG FOR A CHRISTIAN TO FIGHT, AND EVEN KILL, DURING TIMES OF WAR? ALSO, SHOULD THE UNITED STATES TOTALLY DISARM TO PROVE TO THE WORLD THAT WE DESIRE PEACE?

ANSWER:

Some Christians think that the sixth commandment, which states, *"Thou shalt not kill"* (Exodus 20:13) means that it is wrong for a Christian to serve in the Armed Forces; but if for some reason he must serve, he should not engage himself in battle; and if that happens, he should not kill, and so forth. I do not think this is valid reasoning and I will give the reasons why.

ETHICAL CONSIDERATIONS

First of all, God ordained human government to help Him enforce moral laws. Even though governments are appointed by God, this can in no way mean He is responsible, or accountable, for their actions. Of course if they get out of line, God will judge them as He will anyone or anything else.

Second, to murder is always to kill, but to kill is not always to murder. There are scores of times in the Bible when God ordered particular nations, peoples, or individuals to be destroyed (or killed). Why would God do this? He did it because of their great wickedness (Deuteronomy 7:2).

Numbers 35:9-34 speaks of killing a man unawares; that is, by error, or unwittingly. Even in our governmental system in modern-day United States, we recognize degrees of guilt. For example, people can be tried and/or convicted for first-, second-, or third-degree murder, manslaughter, and so forth.

An individual could even kill intentionally and yet it would not be murder. We are told that if a thief, in breaking into a house, be smitten so that he die, there shall no blood be shed for him (Exodus 22:2, 3). In other words, the man defending his home and property would not be punished for that killing. It would not be murder. The Bible recognizes an individual's right to defend his person, his property, his dear ones, and his *country.*

If a Christian in the United States is drafted into the army during a time of war — or a war breaks out while he is serving — and that Christian is placed on the front lines of battle (or any place of this nature), he should defend himself and his country to whatever extent is necessary. If this means having to take the life of the enemy, he should do this. No one, and this would also include those serving our country, should conduct himself in an attitude of wanting to kill (to boost his own ego or any other such foolishness); but where there is no choice or alternative in the matter, a soldier (or policeman or other law-enforcing citizen) can certainly discharge such duties with a clean conscience, and God would not hold him accountable for murder or for any lesser crime of that nature. In other words, he would not (if his actions and motives were right) be guilty of breaking any kind of law, anywhere, either moral or scriptural.

WORLD WAR II

Let us look at World War II. Germany and Japan, I think most people would agree, were the aggressors in that conflict (along with some others). Germany, under the leadership of Adolf Hitler, murdered some 6 million Jews in the horrible Holocaust. He would have enslaved the world except for the intervention of this great United States of America. Admittedly, other nations also contributed greatly to his defeat, but it was the might and the power of the United States that ultimately brought him to his knees and to destruction.

What kind of world would we have now if Hitler had been allowed to follow his course to completion? I think the answer is fairly obvious. So, any moral government is required by God to put down bandit nations that would endeavor to exert their dictatorial authority and enslave millions of people.

VIETNAM

This, in the beginning, was our motive in Vietnam. However, we did not conduct ourselves as we should have, and any nation that involves itself in a conflict must count the cost, for when the decision is made, there is no turning back.

You see, America played at war in Vietnam. Although we had all the good and proper intentions and motives, a satisfactory conclusion could not be reached because of our conduct. Even then, young men who had to face the enemy and were forced to kill, I feel, were held totally guiltless before God Almighty. I would also say this: I feel the shameful way in which the United States has conducted herself toward the veterans of the Vietnam conflict is a stain on our moral character.

However, I hasten to add that any individual (even in a war that is rightly conducted by a moral government) who kills just for the sake of killing is guilty of murder in the eyes of God Almighty. In respect to the horrible conflict of Vietnam, just because our motives were right and our intentions correct, our men were not given the right to murder innocent men, women, and children. You see, *"man looketh on the outward appearance, but the Lord looketh on the heart"* (I Samuel 16:7).

THE OPPOSING SIDE

I suppose the question must be asked, "What about the individuals fighting on the other side?" Once again, even though a nation as a whole may be wrong (such as Germany was in World War II), I am persuaded that some of the German soldiers were possibly Christians. No doubt, there may have been few, but possibly there was a goodly number who loved God, and they had no choice in this conflict. They did not have the means or the power to extricate themselves. Once again, even if these individuals were forced to kill, if their heart was right before God and they were doing it in self-defense and trying their best to conduct themselves morally and responsibly, I feel that God would look at them exactly as He would any Christian.

You see, oftentimes soldiers in a conflict (even though they may be on the wrong side) know little of what is going on in the hierarchy of command. I suspect that many Germans knew little or nothing about the terrible Holocaust (that we mentioned earlier) where 6 million Jews were slaughtered. Of course, everybody knows about it now because of the proliferation of the news plus the lapse of time. However, many of the atrocities committed, the crimes, and all the other terrible things that were done by people in responsible positions were not known at all by the foot soldiers or individuals of like stature who were placed in the line of warfare. Again we go back to the statement, *"For man looketh on the outward appearance, but the Lord looketh on the heart"* (I Samuel 16:7).

DISARMAMENT

Now we will address ourselves to the second part of your question.

No, I do not think that the United States should throw all of her weapons in the ocean or do away with them in any way to appease Soviet Russia just to show the world that we desire peace, consequently hoping that Soviet Russia will follow suit. Soviet Russia will not follow suit. If this should happen, it would have to be the most foolish thing ever attempted by any government on the face of the globe. The consequence would be that our country and the world would be enslaved by demon-possessed Communist masters in no time at all.

I agree that the drain on our gross national product in the United States is great. The money could be better spent than on weapons that maim and kill, but we are faced with the position of having no choice. Jesus spoke of a strong man entering into a person's house and spoiling his goods. The thief could not do that *"except he first bind the strong man [the man of the house] . . . and then he will spoil his house"* (Matthew 12:29).

In other words, the application may be made that if the United States weakens, then one stronger than us will come in and spoil our house (nation).

The United States is a staunch defender of the free world. If it were not for this country, there would (basically) be no free world. Nations such as Canada, Great Britain, and others we could name have the desire, the want-to, but they do not have the power to resist the evil that is so encompassed in the Soviet Union.

POLAND

We look today at Poland and her struggle for freedom. The problems that have persisted in the last few years have little to do with Poland's feelings or desires. I doubt seriously that even her military leaders had a choice in the matter. She is a pawn in Russia's hands. The Soviets tell the leaders what to do and they do it.

The same is true with all the other satellite countries of the Soviet Union. The Soviets told their puppet leaders of Poland if they did not crack down on Solidarity, Soviet troops would come in. I can only surmise that the puppet leaders reasoned within themselves that it would be better to have

Polish soldiers on the streets than Russian soldiers (although I strongly suspect that some of those soldiers were Russians dressed in Polish uniforms). At any rate, Poland had little say in the matter.

There was a time when the United States, if we had had the will to do so, could have put a stop to this terrible problem. In 1956 when Hungary made her bid for freedom, we could have guaranteed that freedom. Even when Czechoslovakia made her bid for freedom in 1967, we still had the power; but now we do not. The policy our leaders have taken in the past few years has almost guaranteed that America would become weaker and the Soviet Union would become stronger.

AMERICA'S CHOICE

President Reagan has made what I believe to be the only logical, sensible choice to follow. He could have chosen between two ways: the first being (as some persons may suggest) to throw all of our weapons into the ocean. Consequently, in so doing, we would show to the world that we are a peace-loving people and desire no war.

Actually, the actions of the United States of America have reflected that all through the years. In the two decades following World War II, we were supreme militarily as well as economically all over the world. We could have forced our will on anyone at any time, even the Soviet Union, but we never did.

We have not enslaved any peoples, nor have we made satellite nations for ourselves. We have not extended our boundaries one foot for the simple reason that the premise of the United States of America is for any people — irrespective of the nation — to have the right and the freedom to govern themselves after their own desires. That is the basis of our Constitution and our very way of life. In this we have proved to the world a million times over that we are not an aggressive power. We have no desire to enforce our way of life upon those who do not want it.

ANOTHER ALTERNATIVE

The other alternative the President has is to make this nation powerful enough that it will stand as a deterrent against Communist aggression. This is obviously the sensible, logical course to take. It is, I will admit, a bitter pill to swallow. Who would desire to spend over $100 billion a year on weapons and armaments? No one in his right mind! However, due to the posture of the world — a world that we did not make — we have no alternative or choice. This is simply the way things are.

Somebody made the statement the other day that the United States must sit down and come to another SALT agreement with Soviet Russia. (Of course Russia enjoys these SALT agreements!) I am glad that Congress did not ratify SALT II when Jimmy Carter so desperately wanted it. Soviet Russia also wanted SALT II just as she wanted SALT I. Why? Because she knew that we would adhere to its agreements and abide by them to the letter, whereas she had no intention whatsoever of abiding by them. In SALT I we became steadily weaker while Russia became steadily stronger. It will be that way the second time around also.

COMMUNISM

Let us look at Communism. First of all, it is an attack against God; it denies God. Second, it denies Jesus Christ. Actually, it would make Him a disciple of Karl Marx. Third, it is a work of the devil, inspired by Satan. It enslaves people and denies their freedom.

Communism denies that man has a soul. It is materialistic and humanistic. In a democracy such as the United States (and many other nations of the world) the state serves the people. In Communism the people serve the state. Its system is that of total slavery. It brainwashes the mind of man, dedicating him to atheism.

Communism forbids the carrying out of the Great Commission of taking the Gospel of Jesus Christ to the whole world. Any nation that comes under the horror of Communism is automatically shut out from the Gospel. Worse yet, Communism has murdered millions of Christians (and anyone, for that matter, getting in her way). Freedom and Communism are totally incompatible; freedom allows supremacy of choice, while Communism totally dominates.

While Communism, it seems, advocates peaceful coexistence, it is in reality a deceptive peace, making it absolutely impossible for Christianity and Communism to co-exist. Eventually, one will have to give way, surrender.

EL SALVADOR

I get somewhat perturbed at our news media. For a while there every time we turned on the television, we saw Poland. The Polish people have been crying for freedom and yet little can be done to help them. On the other hand, the news media were extolling the virtues of the guerrillas in El Salvador.

Little brainpower is required to know that the guerrillas are backed by the Communists, that they are indeed Communists themselves, and that they will set up a Communistic state if they are successful.

Every media means available has been used to demean President Duarte. While I am confident that the present government in El Salvador is not a model of efficiency, my information does come from missionaries who have been there for some 20 years, and they should know. They say they believe with all their heart that President Duarte is dedicated to the good of El Salvador. He is not some tinhorn dictator ruling at the business end of the gun, not caring for his citizens and lining his pockets with ill-gotten gain.

If you will notice, El Salvador continually gets (nothing but) bad press. What a person must understand is that a guerrilla warfare is a terrible war to fight. Who are the guerrillas? Where do they exist and live? Those are not easy questions to answer. Any government that engages itself in warfare at times will make mistakes. People are killed because they are mistakenly believed to be the enemy, when they really are not. Stern measures have to be taken. It is a bad business, but there is no other way to do it.

In the short time that I was in San Salvador (the capital city of El Salvador) sometime ago, the city's power would be cut off as electric power substations were bombed by the guerrillas. The wife of one of our missionaries there has had her car confiscated six times — at the point of a gun, I might add. The car would be used to carry out guerrilla activities. It would be found some days later parked on a side street somewhere.

NICARAGUA

If El Salvador should be overrun by the guerrilla forces, it will then be exactly as Nicaragua is today. There is no freedom in Nicaragua. For all respects, the Gospel is stopped. It is fast becoming another Cuba, a possibility all of Central and South America is now facing. Communist aggression has to be stopped somewhere.

Yet the media, it seems, thrives on constantly extolling the virtues of the guerrillas and demeaning the government of El Salvador. The American people have become brainwashed. A person almost has to look in wonder and amazement at the deception practiced by those that ought to know better. A person would think that these people desire that Soviet Russia would become the ruling nation of the world!

CHAMPION OF COMMUNISM

Let us take a little look at the champion of Communism, the Soviet Union.

By and large, Soviet Russia is little more than a Third World nation. She is not looked at that way, and she is called a superpower, but she is a superpower only in one accord and that is armaments. Her people are deprived, basically living as slaves. The American people and many other nations of the world fare so much better that there is no comparison. The Soviet people hardly have enough to eat, much less enjoy the conveniences of the labor-saving devices and the advanced technology that we enjoy in this country, Canada, and other Western nations.

Most of the earnings of the Russian people are used to buy weapons. So consequently, Russia has become one of, if not *the,* most powerful nations on the face of the earth. Her leaders have absolutely no concern for their people, and are totally oblivious to their needs or desires. They are allowed only enough to survive. Given the choice, these people would opt for freedom and overthrow their Communist masters. They would choose the life-style that we take for granted.

God will one day bring down Communism. By what method we cannot even chance to guess, but through His infinite ways and means, it will happen. "God's mills grind slow but sure" (Greek Proverb). If America had only conducted herself properly in the Vietnam War, Vietnam, Cambodia, Laos, as well as others, would not now be under the iron yoke of Communism, but would be enjoying freedom. Above all of that, the Gospel of Jesus Christ that would liberate these individuals from the terrible bondage and enslavement of sin could be preached. Sad to say, those doors are basically closed forever — at least forever for much of the people of Southeast Asia.

QUESTION:

WATER BAPTISM

■ Is infant baptism a scriptural doctrine?

QUESTION:

IS INFANT BAPTISM A SCRIPTURAL DOCTRINE?

ANSWER:

No, infant baptism is not a scriptural doctrine; and more probable, infant baptism is responsible for sending more people to hell than perhaps any other doctrine or religious error.

It is a terrible thing when a person has been led to believe that his being baptized as a baby constitutes his salvation, and consequently he is on his way to heaven.

JESUS AND THE CHILDREN

The fact that Jesus loves children very much was made evident when He stated, *"Suffer little children, and forbid them not, to come unto me"* (Matthew 19:14). As we have said so many times, we believe all babies and children below the age of accountability are protected by the Lord respecting their eternal soul. In other words, I do not believe any child below the age of accountability has ever gone to hell. Of course, there is no differentiating between those who were baptized as infants and those who were not.

HISTORY OF INFANT BAPTISM

Infant baptism appeared in church history about the year A. D. 370. It came about as a result of the doctrine of baptismal regeneration — the teaching that baptism is essential to salvation; or if you want to turn it around, that water baptism saves the soul (or at least is a part of a person's salvation). So consequently as the teaching of baptismal regeneration started being propagated, it was natural for those holding to this doctrine to believe that everyone should be baptized as soon as possible. Thus, baptism of infants still in the innocent state (and as yet unaccountable for their actions) came into vogue among many of the churches. Once again I state: these two grievous errors (baptismal regeneration and infant baptism) have probably caused more people to go to hell than any other doctrine.

MORE HISTORY

The professed conversion of Emperor Constantine in A. D. 313 was looked upon by many persons as a great triumph for Christianity. However, it more than likely was the greatest tragedy in church history because it resulted in the union of church and state and the establishment of a hierarchy that ultimately developed into the Roman Catholic system. There is great question that Constantine was ever truly converted. At the time of his *supposed* vision of the sign of the cross, he *promised* to become a Christian. But he was not baptized in water until near death, having postponed the act in the belief that baptism washed away all past sins, and he wanted all his sins to be in the past tense before he was baptized. In other words, he wanted the freedom to sin as much as he wanted; and then when he was too old or too sick to care, he would have them all washed away by the act of baptism.

In A. D. 416 infant baptism was made compulsory throughout the Roman Empire. Naturally this filled the churches with unconverted members who had only been "baptized into favor." So whatever power the church had in the past relative to actual conversions was now null and void. The world consequently was plunged into the gloom of the Dark Ages, which endured for more than 12 centuries, until the Reformation.

During this time God had a remnant who remained faithful to Him; they never consented to the union of church and state, or to baptismal regeneration, or to infant baptism. These people were called by various names, but probably could better be summed up by their generic name, *Anabaptists*, meaning rebaptizers. These people ignored infant baptism and rebaptized those who had been saved through personal faith. They also had a generic name for themselves, *Antipedobaptists*, meaning "against infant baptism."

THE STRANGE THING

The strange thing about these two diabolical doctrines of baptismal regeneration and infant baptism is that the great reformers (Martin Luther, for one) brought with them out of Rome these two dreaded errors: the union of church and state and infant baptism. Strangely enough, in those days not only did the Roman Catholic church persecute those who would not conform to its ways, but after the Lutheran church became the established church of Germany, it persecuted the nonconformists as well — of course, not as stringently so and not in such numbers as those before them.

John Calvin, as well as Cromwell in England and John Knox in Scotland, all stuck to the union of church and state and infant baptism and used their power, when they had power, to seek to force others to conform to their own views.

Unaware to a lot of people, this thing came to the Americas well in the early days of this republic. Before the Massachusetts Bay Colony was 20 years old, it was decreed by statute that "if any person or persons within this jurisdiction shall either openly condemn or oppose the baptizing of infants, or go about secretly to seduce others from the approbation or use thereof, or shall purposely depart from the congregation at the administration of the ordinance — after due time and means of conviction — every such person or persons shall be subject to banishment."

Religious persecution existed even in the early days of the United States of America. Roger Williams and others were banished (when banishment meant to go and live with the Indians) because they would not submit to the doctrine of baptismal regeneration or the baptizing of infants.

However, it was the constitution of the Rhode Island Colony (founded by Roger Williams, John Clark, and others) that established religious liberty by law for the first time in 1,300 years (over the world). Thus it was that Rhode Island, founded by a small group of believers, was the first spot on earth where religious liberty became the law of the land. The settlement was made in 1638, and the colony was legally established in 1663. Virginia followed, to be the second, in 1786.

As you can see, the doctrine of infant baptism has a long and bloody history, and it has been one of Satan's chief weapons to condemn untold millions of people to hell.

FURTHER EXPLANATION

What does the above have to do with us today? A great deal!

You see, the union of church and state continues today in most countries of the world. In these state churches pastors and leaders christen babies, which means they make them "Christians" by baptizing them; thus the person having been christened as a baby believes he is on his way to heaven simply because he was christened (or baptized) in infancy. Having been taught all his life that this saved him, he naturally considers himself saved by the act of infant baptism. The Roman Catholic church teaches baptismal regeneration and practices infant baptism. Its statement of doctrine says, "The sacrament of baptism is administered on adults by the pouring of water and the pronouncement of the proper words, and cleanses from original sin."

The Reformed church says, "Children are baptized as heirs of the kingdom of God and of His covenant."

The Lutheran church teaches that baptism, whether of infants or adults, is a means of regeneration.

Because of the following declaration I believe the Episcopal church teaches that salvation comes through infant baptism. In his confirmation the catechist answers a question about his baptism in infancy by saying: "In my baptism . . . I was made a member of Christ, a child of God, and an inheritor of the kingdom of God." (This is printed in the prayer book and can be read there by anyone interested enough to look for it.)

Most people who practice infant baptism believe the ceremony has something to do with the salvation of the child. These are traditions of men, and we can follow the commandments of God or follow after the traditions of men; it is up to us.

CLEAR BIBLE TEACHING

The Word of God is clear regarding the matter of salvation. Jesus said, *"He that believeth on the Son hath everlasting life: and he that believeth not the Son shall not see life; but the wrath of God abideth on him"* (John 3:36). *"He that believeth on him is not condemned: but he that believeth not is condemned already, because he hath not believed in the name of the only begotten Son of God"* (John 3:18).

Basically there are two groups of people in the world today: those who do believe on the Son and those who do not. Those who believe are not condemned; they have everlasting life (whatever church they may belong to). Those who believe not on the Son are condemned already, and they shall not see life, but the wrath of God abides on them.

This is the clear, unmistakable teaching and language of the Bible.

If you will notice, the Word of God never says simply believe and be saved, but rather believe *on the Lord Jesus Christ* and be saved. The Word of God always identifies the object of faith, which is the Lord Jesus

Christ Himself. *"For God so loved the world, that he gave his only begotten Son, that whosoever believeth in him should not perish, but have everlasting life"* (John 3:16). It is not enough just to believe; a person must believe *"in him."*

When the Philippian jailer asked, *"Sirs, what must I do to be saved?"* Paul answered, *"Believe on the Lord Jesus Christ, and thou shalt be saved"* (Acts 16:30, 31). It was not enough simply to believe; that belief, that trust, that dependence had to be *"in him."*

If a person is trusting in baptism for salvation, he cannot be trusting *"in him."* Christ is not *one* way of salvation; He is the *only* way of salvation (John 14:6; 10:1, 7, 9). There is no promise in the Word of God to those who believe *partially* in Christ. In other words, a person cannot trust the Lord Jesus Christ 90 percent and baptism 10 percent, or Jesus 50 percent and baptism 50 percent, or Jesus 95 percent and some church 5 percent, et cetera. As a matter of fact, there is no such thing as partially trusting Christ. The man who is partially trusting is not trusting at all. Yet the sad fact is that the majority of people in churches in the United States and the world today are not trusting Christ at all — they *believe* they are trusting Him partially.

It is even sadder to realize that more people are going to hell through religious organizations than any other way. That is a shocking, startling statement, but it is true. Jesus said, *"Many will say to me in that day, Lord, Lord, have we not prophesied in thy name? and in thy name have cast out devils? and in thy name done many wonderful works? And then will I profess unto them, I never knew you: depart from me, ye that work iniquity"* (Matthew 7:22, 23).

You see, any works offered to Christ for salvation are called by Jesus Himself, "works of iniquity."

There is an old song that expresses my feelings totally. It says:

> *"My hope is built on nothing less*
> *Than Jesus' blood and righteousness;*
> *I dare not trust the sweetest frame,*
> *But wholly lean on Jesus' name.*
> *On Christ, the solid Rock, I stand;*
> *All other ground is sinking sand,*
> *All other ground is sinking sand."*

[Note: Portions of source material for this article were derived from a message by the late Dr. William Pettingill, entitled "Infant Baptism."]

QUESTION:

WINE

■ Did the Saviour use intoxicating wine in the Lord's Supper?

■ Was the water that Jesus turned into wine in John 2 the kind of wine that will make you drunk?

QUESTION:

*DID THE SAVIOUR USE INTOXICATING WINE IN
THE LORD'S SUPPER?*

ANSWER:

Personally, I do not think that He did, and I will give the reasons why
I believe this.

In the description of the Lord's Supper, the Bible never uses the word
"wine." We are told, *"He took the cup, and gave thanks, and gave it to
them, saying, Drink ye all of it"* (Matthew 26:27). Mark says, *"He took
the cup, and when he had given thanks, he gave it to them"* (14:23).
Luke says, *"He took the cup, and gave thanks, and said, Take this, and
divide it among yourselves"* (22:17). Jesus called the drink this *"fruit of
the vine"* in Matthew 26:29 and also in Mark 14:25 and Luke 22:18.

It seems the Holy Spirit carried this directive right on through even
into the early church. The Apostle Paul said, *"After the same manner
also, he took the cup, when he had supped, saying, This cup is the new
testament in my blood"* (I Corinthians 11:25). Then, following, He
mentioned *"this cup"* and then, later on, *"that cup."*

It becomes clear, when these passages are read consecutively,
that God intended for us to use grape juice. I also think the Holy Spirit
took particular pains not to use any words that could be construed as
referring to any kind of intoxicating beverage. There is not a single
reference in the Word of God that a person should use intoxicating wine
for the Lord's Supper.

THE SYMBOL OF DECAY

The very meaning of fermented wine makes it unsatisfactory to
represent the blood of the Lord Jesus Christ. I do not know a whole lot
about fermentation or the wherefores of making alcoholic beverages, but
I do know that fermented wine is grape juice in which decay (or rot) has
taken place. In other words, the process of fermentation is the breakdown
of large molecules caused by the influence of bacteria or fungi. Wine,
then, results from the degenerative action of germs on pure substances.

Fermented wine used in Communion would actually symbolize
tainted, sinful blood and not the pure and perfect blood of Jesus Christ
that had to be made evident to be a perfect cleansing for our sins. Pure,

367

fresh grape juice tends toward life, but fermented wine tends toward death. Alcohol used for drinking purposes is both a narcotic and a poison. It could hardly be used as a symbol for the blood of the Lord Jesus Christ.

Sometime ago when I was studying the book of Mark and using the finest 'Greek scholars I could find, I found something that was startling.

The Jews were required to use unleavened bread with the Passover Feast, and they were commanded that during that time *"there shall no leavened bread be seen with thee, neither shall there be leaven seen with thee in all thy quarters"* (Exodus 13:7). As early as this, bread which had been tainted with bacteria or yeast was considered unsuitable at the religious events celebrated by the Jews. Jesus also used unleavened bread in initiating the Lord's Supper. (Of course, the New Testament made no special issue of the unleavened bread; and as far as that is concerned, any bread made without yeast today would serve as unleavened bread.) Consistently, then, from Exodus to the Gospels, we are told to use only untainted, pure substances in religious celebrations.

Consequently, the point that I make is this: If the Lord specifically chose bread that had no bacteria, no fungus spores in it, to picture His broken body, do you honestly think He would choose alcoholic wine, fermented wine, which is directly the product of fungi or bacteria, to represent His blood? I hardly think so. The pure blood of Jesus Christ would be best represented by pure grape juice.

THE MORAL STATUTES

Next, even the high priests were commanded, *"Do not drink wine nor strong drink . . . when ye go into the tabernacle of the congregation, lest ye die: it shall be a statute for ever throughout your generations"* (Leviticus 10:9). You must remember, those priests entering into the Tabernacle were types of the Lord Jesus Christ who is our Great High Priest. Now I ask you a question: Would Jesus, the night He was betrayed, drink intoxicating wine before going to the crucifixion and entering into His high priestly work? I think not. It would have been a rejection and a contradiction of His own Word given back in Leviticus.

I close by saying this. We must always remember that the word "wine" in the Bible simply means "the fruit of the vine." It can mean either unfermented grape juice or intoxicating wine. So, when the Word is read, whether it is New Testament or Old Testament, this distinction must always be kept in mind.

No, I do not believe the wine that Jesus used at the Lord's Supper was intoxicating wine, nor do I believe it is proper and permissible for us to use intoxicating wine in the Lord's Supper today. I think it is a travesty of His Word and a perversion of His intent.

QUESTION:

WAS THE WATER THAT JESUS TURNED INTO WINE IN JOHN 2 THE KIND OF WINE THAT WILL MAKE YOU DRUNK?

ANSWER:

No, and I will attempt to explain why.

One, if the wine is understood to be intoxicating wine, our Lord is automatically placed in the position of providing men who had already *"well drunk"* (John 2:10) with more wine. If it was real wine, the Lord then would have been breaking His own law against temperance. The total amount of water turned to wine was about 150 gallons. If this had been an intoxicating beverage, it would have served as an invitation to drink and would have placed our Lord in the unsavory position of providing a flood of intoxicants for the men who had already consumed a considerable amount.

GOOD WINE

Two, the word *"good"* was used to describe what the Lord had miraculously brought about. It is the Greek word *kalos* and is defined in *Vine's Expository Dictionary of New Testament Words* as denoting what is intrinsically good. Now the pure, sweet juice of the grape could rightly be denoted as "intrinsically good"; but the rotted, fermented, decayed, spoiled, intoxicating kind of wine could hardly be called good. It is easy to think of the term "good" in describing whatever the Lord makes. For example, in describing the creation, Moses said, *"And God saw every thing that he had made, and, behold, it was very good"* (Genesis 1:31).

It is unthinkable that our Lord would have made corrupted, fermented wine at Cana and called it "good." You see, fermentation is a kind of decomposition, just as are putrefaction and decay. It would be almost blasphemous to call that "good" in connection with our Lord.

Pliny (an ancient Greek scholar) said that "good wine" was a term used to denote the juice destitute of spirit. Albert Barnes says, "The wine referred to here was doubtless such as was commonly drunk in Palestine." That was the pure juice of the grape; it was not brandied nor drugged wine. Nor was it wine compounded of various substances, such as people drink in this land. The common wine of that day, which was drunk in Palestine, was the simple juice of the grape.

Three, it is tantamount to blasphemy, in my opinion, to suppose that the first miracle that Christ performed after being filled with the Holy Spirit (compare Mark 1:9-12; Luke 4:1) was an act of creating intoxicating wine for a crowd of celebrants, the kind of wine that would make them drunk. It is unthinkable!

Four, still another fact from the record in John 2 is this: those men who had already drunk a considerable amount praised the bridegroom for having kept the *"good wine"* until the last. Now, it is a simple fact that alcohol, drunk to any excess, will deaden the taste buds of the drinker. If the wine in Cana of Galilee, that the guests had already been partaking of, was intoxicating wine (and they had already partaken of quite a bit at this point), then when the wine that Jesus had miraculously made was given to them, they could not have detected its taste. Their taste buds would have been deadened. To be honest with you, they would have been drunk by this time, or almost so. Only if they had been drinking the form of the vine's fruit that we know as grape juice and then had been provided some fresh grape juice would the governor of the feast have been able to make the observation he did.

WINE IN BIBLICAL TIMES

There are two words in the Bible (basically) that describe wine. In the New Testament it is the Greek word *oinos,* which can mean either fermented or unfermented wine.

Dr. Ferrar Fenton, a biblical translator (*The Holy Bible in Modern English*), lists six different meanings of the word *oinos*: (1) grapes, as fresh fruit, (2) raisins, (3) thick grape syrup, (4) a thick jam, (5) fresh grape juice, and (6) fermented grape juice. The last type would make you drunk.

Dr. Lyman Abbott said that fermented wine in Bible times was the least common of all wines. Even in the fermented kind, the percentage of alcohol was small.

In the Old Testament, the Hebrew word for wine is *yayin*. That word is found 141 times in the Old Testament, and is used interchangeably, depending on the context.

Five, it is unthinkable that the Master would have broken His own Word. *"Wine is a mocker, strong drink is raging: and whosoever is deceived thereby is not wise . . . . Who hath woe? who hath sorrow? who hath contentions? who hath babbling? who hath wounds without cause? who hath redness of eyes? They that tarry long at the wine; they that go to seek mixed wine. Look not thou upon the wine when it is red, when it giveth his colour in the cup, when it moveth itself aright. At the last it biteth like a serpent, and stingeth like an adder"* (Proverbs 20:1; 23:29-32).

The reasons given above are sufficient proof that Jesus did not change water to the kind of wine that would make you drunk. Instead, it was a sweet, pure grape juice.

Before Prohibition "wine" was considered to be exactly as it was in Bible times. However, when Prohibition was enacted in 1929, the term had to be defined more closely. Consequently, "wine" was designated to mean something that will make you drunk. The other kind of nonintoxicating beverage was called by whatever name desired, grape juice or whatever. Consequently, many people today confuse the simple word "wine" as it was used in the Bible with our understanding of that word, but that is not universally true.

No. Jesus' first miracle was not the making of wine that would make a person drunk. It was pure, sweet, fresh grape juice; and I believe that scripturally, scientifically, and legally we have proof of that.